# The Articulate Executive

## The Harvard Business Review Book Series

# The Articulate Executive

## Orchestrating Effective Communication

With a Preface by
**Fernando Bartolomé**

**A Harvard Business Review Book**

*Editor's Note:* Some articles in this book were written before authors and editors began to take into consideration the role of women in management. We hope the archaic usage representing all managers as male does not detract from the usefulness of the collection.

The *Harvard Business Review* articles in this collection are available as individual reprints. Discounts apply to quantity purchases. For information and ordering contact Operations Department, Harvard Business School Publishing Corporation, Boston, MA 02163. Telephone: (617) 495-6192, 9 A.M. to 5 P.M. Eastern Time, Monday through Friday. Fax: (617) 495-6985, 24 hours a day.

The paper used in this publication meets the requirements of the American National Standard for Permanence of Paper for Printed Library Materials Z39.48-1984

**Library of Congress Cataloging-in-Publication Data**

The Articulate executive : orchestrating effective communication / with a preface by Fernando Bartolomé.
     p.   cm.—(The Harvard business review book series)
  Includes bibliographical references and index.
  ISBN 0-87584-433-2 (acid-free paper)
  1. Communication in management.  2. Interpersonal communication.
I. Series.
HD30.3.A78 1994                           93-23956
658.4'5—dc20                                CIP

# Contents

---

Part II   Learning to Listen

concrete guidelines for improving your interactions
with the press.

Part III   Managing Successful Meetings

Many meetings are unproductive because they are
convened out of habit rather than purpose. This
article shows how meetings may serve many
functions simultaneously, and provides practicable
insights for managing a meeting.

For participants, successful meeting management
results from thoughtful preparation—to define goals
and identify the resources required to achieve them.
The author proposes a four-step procedure designed
to present ideas and proposals in an implementable
manner.

In a spirit of collaboration rather than commandment,
the chairperson encourages the creative exchange of
ideas, ultimately increasing the productivity, impact,
and authority of the entire group.

Part IV   Writing with Confidence

The presentation of ideas has a significant effect on
how they are perceived and acted upon. The author
provides solid advice for mastering the elusive
principles of style.

electronic mail, not only has an enormous impact on the volume and speed of information transmission, but on the social relationships and decision-making mechanisms within organizations. The author considers the challenges and opportunities resulting from the development of electronic networks.

# Preface

## Fernando Bartolomé

This is the age of information. Organizations will live or die, depending on their ability to process raw data, transform the data into information, distribute the information appropriately, and use it speedily to make decisions today and change them tomorrow as new information reaches the organization.

In this age of information, communication, which is basically the process of exchanging information, plays a crucial role. This process is fundamental in organizational life because no individual player generates all the information necessary to make decisions.

The problem, however, is that there are a great number of barriers to the flow of information. These barriers affect both its transmission and reception. When we think about communication we tend to focus more on the problems in sending or transmitting messages than on problems concerning their reception, understanding, and interpretation. Nevertheless, both dimensions of the flow are crucial to effective management.

The purpose of this collection of *Harvard Business Review* articles is to provide managers with conceptual insights and practical advice for improving communication within their organizations. An additional objective is to encourage managers to see themselves as *articulate executives*. The articulate executive is an individual who is able to listen and understand others, analyze and prioritize the wealth of information received, and express, through the written and spoken word, not only an idea or decision, but, even more important, a vision that incorporates the knowledge, wisdom, and values of the entire organization. In this role the articulate executive needs to be able to eliminate barriers to communication, establish a climate that fosters the flow of relevant information, and orchestrate the communication flow in order to make the right decisions today and to change things, if necessary, tomorrow.

The seventeen articles culled from the *Review* offer a comprehensive framework for approaching these challenges. Part I (Analyzing Dysfunctional Communication Dynamics) illustrates how poor communication in organizations is largely a function of deeply ingrained behaviors of social interaction that impede communication flow; at the same time, however, perfectly open and candid communication is not necessarily achievable or even beneficial. Indeed, this collection as a whole argues that an effective communication culture embraces both clarity and ambiguity, consensus and conflict. Part II (Learning to Listen), Part III (Managing Successful Meetings), and Part IV (Writing with Confidence) focus on the mechanics of effective communication, with a particular emphasis on the dynamic, two-way process of communication. Part V (Uncovering the Messages in Hidden Channels) goes beneath the surface to explore the impact and influence of informal and implicit channels of communication. The truly articulate executive must be able to recognize and harness these hidden channels. Finally, in Part VI (Articulating Your Company's Goals and Culture), we come full circle to consider how creating an effective communication culture is closely linked to effective leadership and successful company performance.

## The Sorry State of Affairs

In their classic 1952 article, "Barriers and Gateways to Communication" (Part II) Carl Rogers and F.J. Roethlisberger highlighted some of the most common barriers that impede communication, such as the inclination to judge others, the influence of emotions, and the tendency to assume that others perceive reality as we do. In 1957, Ralph Nichols and Leonard Stevens in "Listening to People" (also in Part II) argued that most managers lack effective listening skills. Their diagnosis still stands. More recently, for example, Fernando Bartolomé has explored many of the obstacles to candid communication that make it difficult for managers to know what is going on in the organizations they are supposed to manage. And in his 1986 article, "Skilled Incompetence" (Part I), Chris Argyris brilliantly described the dysfunctional communication processes that impede effective problem solving in organizations.

Many other academics have made similar points, as have enlightened business leaders who deal with these problems on a daily basis. Listen to Jack Welch (Part VI): "We still don't understand why so many people are incapable of facing reality, of being candid with themselves and others."

Welch sounds naive. But is he? A few paragraphs later he answers his own question. "For a large organization to be simple, its people must have self-confidence and intellectual self-assurance. Insecure managers create complexity." Welch understands the root of the problem: if "we all get the same facts, in most cases, [we] . . . will reach roughly the same conclusion . . . The problem is, we don't get the same information. . . . Business isn't complicated. The complications arise when people are cut off from information they need."

What are the main barriers to effective information flow? The articles in this collection, combined with my own research, suggest several obstacles to a freer flow of information in today's organizations:

Dysfunctional patterns of behavior
Lack of organizational vision and leadership
Structural and geographic barriers
Intercultural barriers
Data overload

## DYSFUNCTIONAL PATTERNS OF BEHAVIOR

For years analysts of communication problems in organizations, like Rosabeth Moss Kanter, Abraham Zaleznik, and Peter Drucker,[1] have basically agreed about the factors, internal and external, that lead to communication failures. They have alerted managers to the dangers of being excessively judgmental, the negative effects of rigidly hierarchical organization, the tendency to make assumptions about other people's intentions or feelings based on our own experience, our lack of skills as listeners, and so forth. With the advent of the organizational development movement—which started conceptually in the 1940s with the work of Kurt Lewin at MIT and exploded in the later 1960s and early 1970s under the influence of people like Warren Bennis, Chris Argyris, and others—the process consultant business flourished.

These men and women tried to help managers become aware of their dysfunctional communication and group work processes, to question the assumptions and deep-seated attitudes that led to those patterns of behavior, and to learn new skills in order to become more productive organizational members. The underlying model of these interventions assumed that if people became aware of the sources of their dysfunctional behavior patterns and were offered more functional options, they would change their behavior. But in most cases this didn't happen or, when it happened, the changes didn't last. Why? Because the prescriptions of the organizational development consultants challenge the dominant culture not only of the organizations where they intervene but also of the larger environment that those organizations inhabit.

Professor Argyris illustrates this point very well. For years this brilliant researcher has analyzed the dysfunctional patterns in organizational communication and group work, and proposed solutions to help organizations overcome their problems. But while clients agree with Argyris' diagnosis and his prescriptions on an intellectual level, they fail to apply them at a practical level, because his model requires an in-depth analysis of human communications, the surfacing of assumptions and motives, and changes in the communication process once the "noise" that endangers the process is dealt with.

The problem is that we are socialized since childhood to interact at a level that is *not* transparent. Children manipulate parents. Parents manipulate children. In families positive emotions are highlighted, negative emotions repressed or disguised. Children gain independence from their families in subtle ways because they know that open rebellion often fails. These games are carried over into the business environment. A job interview, selling a product, and persuading a committee to approve your project proposal are all games that require manipulation and second guessing. Most people in work-related situations involving emotions and potential conflict will resist having their game-playing behaviors exposed.

It is difficult for any organization to develop a culture different from the dominant culture from which it draws its members. In attempting to develop a culture of free-flowing information, many leaders face the prospect of creating, in effect, a counterculture that challenges the mores of the social environment. Some academics argue that today's CEO faces the additional problem of dealing with the negative effects of many a misguided organizational development intervention. Zaleznik, for example, says that many such interventions have led to practices that discourage focusing on real work and encourage focusing on creating processes that, in an attempt to increase cohesion and cooperation, actually destroy healthy aggression and open conflict resolution.[2] In sum, we see that many attempts to improve communication in organizations either fail to address resistance to change or force change that ignores the power and even the value of conflict, ambiguity, and disagreement.

## LACK OF ORGANIZATIONAL VISION AND LEADERSHIP

Only those who have a realistic vision coming from within but informed from without will be able to lead in the creation of more functional organizational cultures. A balance, however, is necessary between inner conviction and self-confidence on the one hand and a realistic view of people and the business environment on the other hand. Leaders with this balance are scarce at the top and often even more so in middle management. As we will see (particularly in Part V), the job of creating an effective communication culture that extends to the entire firm or even to a single department requires a high level of creativity and determination.

## STRUCTURAL AND ORGANIZATIONAL BARRIERS

These are the most obvious barriers to effective communication within organizations. We know these obstacles well: rigid hierarchies make the upward flow of information difficult; multiple layers of hierarchy slow down the communication flow and distort information as it traverses them; specialization, departmentalization, and other forms of organizational differentiation tend to isolate people and impede communication, and it is difficult to establish effective integrative systems; the knowledge explosion has led to a parallel explosion in the need for specialists, which in many cases has outrun our skill in creating mechanisms to enable them to cooperate with each other. We also know that most companies now operate in a global market and that physical distance is a natural barrier to communication. Despite the enormous advances in communication technology—including videoconferencing and TV phones—there will never be a complete electronic substitute for face-to-face interaction. While communication technology gives us the false impression of an easier communication flow, the underlying reality suggests not a reduction, but an *increase*, in communication barriers.

## INTERCULTURAL BARRIERS

The importance of learning to manage a diverse workforce has become a challenge to most managers. In our global village we have to learn to operate across the barriers of national culture and language; meanwhile, we are constantly creating new subcultures in our society and within our organizations—subcultures of engineers, computer programmers, researchers, political analysts, and so forth, who each have their own jargon, rituals, distinctive values, and ideals.

Interestingly, I might note that efforts to promote an understanding and appreciation of diversity in the workplace may actually serve to *decrease* candor—at least initially. As people are made more aware of their prejudices and biases, they may eventually improve their relationships with others. But the first effect of uncovering these often unconscious processes is likely to increase people's defensiveness. For example, many a man today will be wary of expressing disagreement with a female colleague for fear of being accused of sexism. And the same may happen when the issue involves disagreeing with people of a different race, religion, culture, or sexual orientation.

## DATA OVERLOAD

The electronic village is inundated by data. With the creation of worldwide electronic networks, we are constantly bombarded by far more information than we can effectively process. The risk is data overload—not being able to discriminate between useful and useless information, between what is crucial and what is peripheral. Every day this skill becomes more important to managers intent on making good decisions.

## Any Solutions?

So far I have identified several major barriers to effective communication flow in organizations and emphasized the close relationship between communication and decision making. This book is an attempt to facilitate the diagnosis of communication problems by the practicing manager and suggest potential approaches to overcoming these problems—not only to improve one's own communication skills but to promote a culture of communication throughout the organization. From the classic "Management Communication and the Grapevine" by Keith Davis to Gerard Langeler's "The Vision Trap," this collection illuminates the wide range of skills managers must possess in order to become truly articulate executives, and in so doing enhance their own leadership as well as the effectiveness of the organization.

Part I (Analyzing Dysfunctional Communication Dynamics) focuses on understanding and dealing with dysfunctional communication and information-processing activities. Both articles in this section point out that defensive behaviors designed to avoid conflict become institutionalized beneath the surface and serve to perpetuate feelings of distrust. In "Nobody Trusts the Boss Completely—Now What?" I suggest that there are natural barriers to candor resulting from the hierarchical nature of organizations and the tendency of people to protect themselves (especially in order to avoid communicating bad news), and propose ways to help the individual manager detect sources of trouble. My approach is based on the premise that it is very difficult to eliminate organizational game playing or to substantially increase candor in organizations; therefore, managers are better served if they learn to operate under conditions of limited candor and to understand the meaning of those pervasive games.

Chris Argyris, in "Skilled Incompetence," identifies similar communication problems (in which efforts to avoid conflict actually increase tension, distrust, and ambiguity), but is more optimistic than I am that managers may unlearn their "skilled incompetence" and develop new attitudes and more constructive communication skills. For him the most crucial attitudes in order to improve the current situation seem to be curiosity and a willingness to understand—and challenge—the defensive routines that managers develop in order to protect themselves from criticism or blame. Argyris points out that it takes a great deal of courage and patience to shed such routines and experiment with new communication behaviors, but the result is better decision making.

In Parts II, III, and IV we move from the analysis of systemic communication problems to practical applications of effective communication—listening, running successful meetings, and writing. Taken together, the articles in these three sections argue that effective communication (i.e., communication that leads to its intended results) is largely a function of understanding the complex and multilayered relationships among people in the organization.

Receiving and transmitting information are the yin and yang of the communication process. Both are essential; neither alone is sufficient for communication to take place. In today's environment of specialization no one can lead who does not know how to listen to clear and ambiguous, brutal and subtle people, and learn from them. In this regard, the articles in Part II (Learning to Listen) focus on the barriers to effective listening and suggest approaches to improve listening skills.

In "Barriers and Gateways to Communication," Carl Rogers and F.J. Roethlisberger explore what makes communication difficult, with a particular emphasis on barriers to listening. Indeed, Roethlisberger argues that the biggest block between two people is their inability to listen to each other intelligently, understandingly, and skillfully. Together, the authors offer a framework for improving listening skills that forces people to reevaluate their perceptions about how communication works: don't assume that you understand the other person, make an effort to put yourself in their shoes, develop the courage to be influenced by their point of view, and accept that learning to listen well requires practice, patience, and hard work.

The next three articles in Part II focus on how to improve listening skills. Another classic, Ralph Nichols' and Leonard Stevens' "Listening to People," offers guidelines for capturing "the unused potential" of listening. Like Rogers and Roethlisberger, the authors argue that most people do not know how to listen well, and as a consequence, do not understand or remember much of what they hear. And while today's managers may appreciate the importance of listening to a greater degree than the executives of the 1950s, they are not necessarily more adept at listening effectively.

"ABCs of Job Interviewing," by James Jenks and Brian Zevnik and "How to Meet the Press," by Chester Burger are meant to prepare executives for these difficult activities. Both articles highlight the crucial connection between listening and communicating. Jenks and Zevnik argue that interviewers will not do their jobs well unless they learn to listen to the candidates and explore the meanings behind their words. Similarly, Chester Burger suggests that the key to a successful interview with the press is to learn the "rules of the reporter's 'game'"—see the world from the reporter's point of view, discard destructive assumptions and stereotypes about the press, and understand how your comments may be interpreted. Whether conducting an interview or being interviewed, careful listening and careful preparation will help increase the possibility that your messages have their intended effect.

"Meetings, meetings, those damned useless meetings." Those words have resounded through organizational corridors for years. In fact, meetings seem to have proliferated—meetings spawn meetings and task forces generate task forces! Many managers seem to consider them a necessary evil—while group interaction is essential for making decisions and planning their implementation, meetings can often be unproductive, inefficient, and antagonistic. The articles in Part III (Managing Successful Meetings) offer enlightening ideas for making meetings more dynamic and constructive.

Antony Jay's bestselling "How to Run a Meeting" argues that many meetings go awry because they have been convened out of habit rather than purpose. Jay suggests that meetings serve important functions in addition to sharing information and making decisions, such as affirming individual status and group identity and reinforcing mutual goals. In this context, Jay provides the chairperson with useful insights for managing a meeting, keeping in mind each participant's role in relation to the meeting's objectives. In this sense, the chairperson serves more as servant than master, facilitating the discussion to achieve productive results.

In Paul Lovett's "Meetings That Work: Plans Bosses Can Approve," the focus shifts from the chairperson to the presenter trying to exercise influence upward. Like Jay, Lovett argues that the key to successfully managing meetings is careful preparation—to define goals and identify the resources required to achieve them. The next article, "Creative Meetings through Power Sharing," by George Prince suggests that the manager who overcomes excessively judgmental attitudes will be better able to increase candor and organizational effectiveness. He argues that in a spirit of cooperation rather than commandment, the boss can actually increase the impact and authority of the entire group.

Managing group decision-making dynamics has become increasingly challenging in organizations that include a large number of highly educated specialists who may be more technically competent than their bosses. For instance, my own research in the aerospace and pharmaceutical industries indicates that the qualities needed for managing technical specialists include an ability to trust, a high tolerance for uncertainty and risk, and a sense of one's own role as a facilitator rather than as a boss. Indeed, Peter Drucker has suggested that the most pressing managerial problem today is to learn how to manage groups of specialists, or, metaphorically, how to become a conductor in an orchestra that creates its musical score as it goes along.[3]

In Part IV (Writing with Confidence) the focus shifts to the problem of how to use writing as a managerial instrument. Most managers do not like to write and, consequently, most of them are not particularly good at it. Nevertheless, written communication is extremely important, particularly for those concerned with persuading others. The chances of getting your project approved or your bid accepted are increased when your ideas and their supporting materials are presented clearly. Similarly, the dangers of sending the wrong message or offending others are increased when presentation is sloppy. Many organizations, such as consulting firms, that have recognized the critical investment in written communication, employ specialists to ensure that both the content and format of their presentations are as perfect as possible—their livelihoods depend on it.

For the managers who lack such staff, the three articles in this section offer valuable hands-on advice for improving their written communication skills. John Fielden's "What Do You Mean You Don't Like My Style?" takes on the challenge of defining and illuminating the elusive principles of "style," providing many examples to illustrate the effect of different writing styles. In "Clear Writing Means Clear Thinking Means . . ." Marvin Swift takes the reader step-by-step through the revision of a memo, with particular attention to language, tone, and intent, making a direct link between effective writing and sharp, careful thinking. The final article, "How to Write a Winning Business Plan," by Stanley Rich and David Gumpert, takes the specific situation of entrepreneurs preparing business plans for investors' approval to illustrate the importance of careful preparation, evaluation, and packaging of your ideas. All three articles reinforce the key principle of looking outward to anticipate how your written messages will be perceived by their recipients.

To this point, we have considered only the dynamics of explicit communication, whether spoken or written. In Part V (Uncovering the Messages in Hidden Channels), we focus on recognizing and understanding the messages transmitted through implicit, often nonverbal channels. Knapp reports that some researchers believe that about 65% of the social meaning of most human communication is carried by nonverbal cues.[4] But we still cling to the belief that words are the most important instruments of communication and that their meaning is fixed and determined by the dictionary. Many years ago semanticists taught us that words have both an extensional or descriptive meaning and an intentional, subjective personal meaning. But we still tend to ignore their lessons, and often assume that we understand what others mean without checking that we actually do.

To most managers, the idea that objective reality does not exist in the world of human interaction, that we operate only with the approximations that are our perceptions, is very unsettling. And the idea that most communication is subtle, indirect, nonobvious is equally difficult to deal with. But the smarter managers know that they do not live in a nonambiguous world of perfect candor, but in the imperfect world of ambiguous, fleeting messages.

The three articles in Part V will help managers become adept at recognizing and deciphering hidden, subtle messages. Keith Davis' "Management Communication and the Grapevine" helps us understand how messages are transmitted through informal conversation and gossip. Concluding that the grapevine cannot be eliminated, Davis suggests that by analyzing its characteristics managers can influence it to their—and the company's—advantage. In "The Hidden Messages Managers Send" Michael McCaskey explores the messages transmitted through images and metaphors, space, objects, and body language. "As with other languages," he says, "a manager can increase skill in sending nonverbal messages through intelligent practice." And Sara Kiesler, in "The Hidden Messages in Computer Networks," complements Davis and McCaskey by considering the social effects of communications technology.

By analyzing the use of electronic mail Kiesler alerts us to the impact—both positive and negative—of communication technology on the social relationships and decision-making mechanisms within organizations. Because the parameters of communicating electronically are different from other media (for instance, lack of face-to-face interaction, fewer context cues, increased speed of transmission), Kiesler finds that the computer, by "increasing the pool of information and at the same time integrating the effects of status could contribute to organizational strength. It may also contribute to organizational instability." Her observations will help executives consider how they can most effectively harness electronic networks to enhance organizational strength.

Finally, Part VI (Articulating Your Company's Goals and Culture), illustrates the ways in which the leaders of an organization can create cultures that either foster or damage the communication flow.

Jack Welch of General Electric (in Noel Tichy and Ram Charan's

"Speed, Simplicity, Self-Confidence: An Interview with Jack Welch")
is clearly a leader who has spent a lot of time thinking about the
culture he wants to create. One is struck by his combination of ideal-
ism and realism; he can in the same breath say, "People are not lousy,
period" and "Many people are incapable of facing reality, of being
candid with themselves and others." He is a patient optimist who is
aware of the immense difficulty of changing an organizational culture
but believes that "if we all get the same facts, we will reach roughly
the same conclusion."

He reminds me of Whitman's maxim, "I'm big. I contain contradictions." Certainly, Welch is no poet, but like the poet, the business
leader looks for the essence of things; both have a deep intuition of
what matters, and to succeed both need to express their vision in ways
that resonate in their audiences.

Leadership is essentially a process of simplification. In "Barriers and
Gateways," Roethlisberger noted that in order to be effective, managers need to learn to operate in a world characterized by uncertainty,
ambiguity, and imperfection. Welch's method of leadership is to seek
speed, simplicity, and self-confidence. The leader imposes order on a
stubborn reality. Welch maintains that things are simple and only
anxious people make them complex. But it would be more accurate
to say that the environment is complex and good leaders realistically
reduce it to a level of pragmatic simplicity that allows for action.

At GE Welch has tried to create an information-flow culture by
modeling it. The company's value statement serves both as a model
for the simplicity and clarity he espouses and a reflection of his commitment to promoting candor and self-confidence throughout the organization. While the top executive can and should play a crucial role
in creating an information and communication culture, there are some
limits to his or her power, especially in large, complex organizations
like GE, where the more distant and diverse organizational units may
find it difficult to adopt change imposed from the center.

Indeed, the trick to creating a candid culture is not so much to have
it strongly modeled and rewarded by top management as to pay more
attention to the personnel selection process, which, as we see in such
articles as "ABCs of Job Interviewing," depends largely on an executive's ability to exercise strong communications skills. Jack Welch got
it right when he identified self-confidence as the basic ingredient for
candid relationships at work. The more skillful the organization is at
attracting and keeping self-confident people, the easier it will be for

top management to create and maintain a culture of candor, which in turn, helps promote self-confidence.

The final article in this collection provides us with a poetic caveat. In "The Vision Trap," Gerard Langeler vividly illustrates the dangers of a vision gone ballistic. His subtitle could be "how visions can kill common sense" or "the perpetual balancing act between Don Quixote and Sancho Panza."

Langeler, in effect, talks to us about the danger of the executive trying to become a poet and falling in love with the beauty of his or her own words and ideas. He is not really describing the danger of becoming a good poet but a bad one who does not have the connection with the truth on which good poetry is built. The simple idea on which his company based its original success ("beat the competition") was truly more poetic than the clever mission statements that Langeler concocted later on, after the company's original goals were achieved.

Perhaps the most important message of these last two articles is that a communication culture starts with the ability to establish an inner dialogue between the real and the ideal. Only then can we attempt to integrate and project images that are inspiring *and* believable. Regardless of organizational complexity, clear messages from top executives who understand the people they lead and can formulate and project realistic aspirations can help build more transparent, candid, and fluid organizations.

## Conclusion

Our world is full of imperfections and, therefore, full of opportunities. Perhaps the biggest opportunities for today's manager are not dependent on finding new information—important as that is—but using available information and knowledge. One is struck by how much that we know we do not apply. We constantly search for new ideas and new wisdom and fail to utilize established, well-proven knowledge. Rogers' and Roethlisberger's wisdom is as valid today as it was forty years ago. In "Barriers and Gateways" Rogers observed that the social sciences were not being utilized to their greatest potential— if a way is found of facilitating communication and mutual understanding in small groups, there is no guarantee that the finding will be more broadly utilized. He suggested that it may be a generation or more before social science research would be applied to understanding and improving organizational communication. He was too optimistic. So far it has taken more than two generations. Why?

First, because the first place to apply the findings of social science should be in the family and the school. Only when those principles are taught and internalized at home and the necessary attitudes and skills learned at an early age is there a chance that they will be applied naturally by business organizations. Second, to introduce countercultural practices in organizations leaders need to combine insight, power, and a forceful personality which, paradoxically, can facilitate other people's growth instead of dominating and suppressing them.

Changing an organizational culture is a slow process. It requires, first, understanding what you want to change and the barriers to achieving change. It also requires defining as clearly as possible the desirable attitudes and behaviors. Examining the articles in this collection one is impressed by the universal agreement about the attitudes and behaviors that would improve the flow of relevant and productive information in organizations.

When the desirable direction of change is clear the business leader has a great advantage over the political leader: business organizations are not democracies and those leading them can be selective in choosing their "citizens." This is an essential element of leadership—the most important tool a leader has to create an organization with the best communication flow is the selection process.

But there is a necessary caveat: any selection process that tries to create a completely homogeneous and candid organization will be extremely dangerous. Jack Welch may not say it explicitly, but he probably knows that in his own organization many of its most valuable contributors are not the totally candid, transparent, and self-confident individuals who may seem ideal on the surface. Great organizations thrive on diversity—even with respect to communication—and are led by individuals able to recognize and encourage good ideas no matter what shape they may take or how they may be communicated.

## Notes

1. Rosabeth Moss Kanter, "Power Failure in Management Circuits," *Harvard Business Review*, July–August 1979, pp. 65–75; Abraham Zaleznik, "Executives and Organizations: Real Work," *Harvard Business Review*, January–February 1989, pp. 57, 64; Peter F. Drucker, "The Coming of

the New Organization," *Harvard Business Review*, January–February 1988, pp. 45–53.

2. Zaleznik, "Executives and Organizations."

3. Drucker, "The Coming of the New Organization."

4. Mark L. Knapp, "Non-Verbal Communication: Basic Perspectives," in *Bridges Not Walls*, ed. by John Stewart (New York: McGraw-Hill, 1990), pp. 79–97.

# The
# Articulate
# Executive

# PART

# I

# Analyzing Dysfunctional Communication Dynamics

# 1
# Nobody Trusts the Boss Completely—Now What?

**Fernando Bartolomé**

Managers who can head off serious problems before they blow up in the company's face are two steps ahead of the game. Their employers avoid needless expense or outright disaster, and they themselves get the promotions they deserve for running their departments smoothly and nipping trouble neatly in the bud.

In practice, of course, it's never this easy. Everyone knows that one trick to dealing with problems is to learn about them early. But what's the trick to learning about them early? How do effective managers find out that trouble is brewing? What are their warning systems?

All good managers have their own private information networks, and many develop a kind of sixth sense for the early signs of trouble. But by far the simplest and most common way to find out about problems is to be told, usually by a subordinate.

It is easy to get information when things are going well. People love to give the boss good news. But subordinates are never eager to tell their supervisors that the latest scheme isn't working, to assume ownership of a problem by giving it a name, to look like an informer, or to sound like Chicken Little. A subordinate's reluctance to be frank about problems is also related to risk. While it's fairly easy to tell the boss that the machines sent over by the purchasing department aren't working properly, it's much harder to admit responsibility for the malfunction, and harder still—and perhaps dangerous—to blame it on the boss. Yet it is terribly important to get subordinates to convey unpleasant messages. The sooner a problem is disclosed, diagnosed, and corrected, the better for the company.

Almost any organization would operate more effectively with completely open and forthright employees, but absolute frankness is too much to hope for (and probably too much to bear). Candor depends upon trust, and in hierarchical organizations, trust has strict natural limits.

## The Limits of Trust and Candor

In a hierarchy, it is natural for people with less power to be extremely cautious about disclosing weaknesses, mistakes, and failings—especially when the more powerful party is also in a position to evaluate and punish. Trust flees authority, and, above all, trust flees a judge. Managers are inescapably positioned to judge subordinates. Good managers may be able to confine evaluation to formal occasions, to avoid all trace of judgmental style in other settings, even to communicate criticism in a positive, constructive way. But there is no way to escape completely a subordinate's inclination to see superiors as judges.

So one of the limits on candor is self-protection. For example, people often hide the failures of their own departments and hope they will correct themselves. In one typical case, the development group for a piece of special software fell terribly behind on its schedule, but no one told the manager until the delivery date could no longer be met. Delivery was three months late, and the company had to absorb a financial penalty.

The lack of candor was not self-protective in the long run, of course, because the development group was ultimately held responsible for the delay. But human beings are often shortsighted. At one time or another, most of us have chosen an uncertain future calamity over today's immediate unpleasantness.

A variation on this theme is when subordinates protect their own subordinates in order to protect themselves, as in the following example:

I was vice president of finance for a large manufacturing company and supervised a staff of 27. One new hire was failing on an important assignment. Her supervisor—who had hired her—withheld this information from me until her failure could no longer be corrected without serious disruption. He didn't tell me because he knew I would make him face up to the problem and deal with it, which he knew he would find very difficult to do.

Sometimes a subordinate may try to protect a client. In one case, a salesman withheld the information that one of his largest customers was in financial trouble. The customer went bankrupt, and the company lost $500,000.

We can only guess at the salesman's motives—eagerness to get his commission before the troubled company failed, fear of losing an old customer, reluctance to give official warning of a danger that might be exaggerated. The fact remains that he failed to communicate the problem, his boss saw no sign of danger, and the company lost half a million dollars.

Often the motive for silence is at least superficially praiseworthy: people keep quiet about a developing problem while trying to solve it. Most believe solving problems on their own is what they're paid to do, and in many cases, they're right. Subordinates are not paid to run to their bosses with every glitch and hiccup. As problems grow more serious, however, managers need to know about them.

The difficulty here lies in the bewildering territory between minor snags and major disasters. Handled promptly and decisively, the problems in this gray area sometimes turn out to be insignificant, but self-confident supervisors, particularly inexperienced ones, are perhaps too eager to prove they can cope on their own. This case is typical:

I am head of medical research in a pharmaceutical company. My job is part of R&D and is on the critical path to marketing any new product. One of my managers saw that we weren't receiving data critical to the timely generation of a licensing package for worldwide registration of a new drug. He spent four months trying to get the data on his own, or proceed without it, and didn't inform me of the problem. We suffered an eight-month delay in applying for a license to sell. That represents 10% of the patent life of the product, which has estimated peak worldwide sales of $120 million a year.

Politics is another common obstacle to candor. Organizations are political systems, and employees are often involved in political struggles. There is no guarantee your subordinates will be on your side.

A U.S. engineering-products company manufactured a successful product on license from a Swedish company, but the American CEO heartily disliked his Swedish counterpart and came to the private conclusion that the licensing fees were out of line. Knowing that his senior staff would object, he began confidential acquisition talks with one of the Swedish corporation's competitors, a much smaller and technically less sophisticated company. Because the negotiations were too complex for him to handle alone, he circumvented the vice presidents who would have opposed the move and secretly enlisted the help of their subordinates. By the time the negotiations became public, it was too late for the senior staff to stop the deal. The Swedish company canceled its license, and the U.S. company has not sold a single piece of new technology since the acquisition.

This CEO made a grave error in letting his personal feelings interfere with his business judgment, but his incompetence, however great, is not the point. The point is that certain employees concealed information from their immediate superiors. Their motives are easy to guess at and perhaps understandable—after all, they were acting on orders from the CEO. But the fact remains that not one of them spoke up, their superiors suspected nothing, and the consequences for the company were extremely negative.

In these days of mergers and acquisitions, political infighting is often acute after absorption of—or by—another company. Restructuring and consolidation can produce epidemic fear and rupture lines of communication, as this case illustrates:

My electronics corporation acquired a division of another company and merged it with two existing subsidiaries. Many employees were let go in the process of the merger and consolidation. I was named president and CEO of the new company one year after its formation. The new company had its headquarters on the East Coast and its research facilities in the West. The VP for research—whose office was in California—did not tell me that the merger, the layoffs, and the new company policies and procedures had had a terrible impact on employee morale. I was completely unaware of the problem for four months. Then I visited the research facility to announce a new benefits package. After announcing the plan, I asked for questions. All hell broke loose. For the next year and a half I spent about a third of my time and a great deal of other people's time trying to build bridges and establish trust, hoping to lower turnover, improve productivity, and get those Californians to feel like part of the total company.

Why wasn't I told? My guess is that the subordinate who kept me in the dark was afraid for his own job. Or else he felt he had something to gain by undermining my position. I don't know, but it was an expensive failure of communication.

## Building and Destroying Trust

Given the natural obstacles to trust and candor—fear, pride, politics, dislike—managers need to make the most of whatever opportunities they have to increase subordinates' trust. Trust is not easy to build in the best of cases, and the kind of trust that concerns us here has to grow on rocky ground—between people at different levels of authority.

The factors affecting the development of trust and candor fall into six categories: communication, support, respect, fairness, predictability, and competence.

*Communication* is a matter of keeping subordinates informed, providing accurate feedback, explaining decisions and policies, being candid about one's own problems, and resisting the temptation to hoard information for use as a tool or a reward.

For several years, the founder and CEO of a small, South American conglomerate had addressed the needs of each of his six divisions separately. He treated his vice presidents like the CEOs of the divisions, cutting deals with each of them independently and keeping each in the dark about his arrangements with the others. He had always solved problems on this ad hoc basis, and it worked reasonably well. The company had grown swiftly and steadily. But now times were tougher, the company was bigger, and he began getting complaints from his VPs about resource allocation. None of them was satisfied with his own division's share, but none was in a position to consider the needs of the company as a whole.

At this point, the CEO recognized that his way of managing was part of the problem, did an abrupt about-face, and created an executive committee comprising himself and his six VPs. They all took part in setting priorities, allocating resources, and planning company strategy. Conflicts remained, of course, as each vice president fought for resources for his division. But trust increased substantially, and for the first time there was communication between divisions and a willingness and opportunity for the company's leadership to work together as a team.

Another CEO moved the offices of his small company without notice. His staff simply arrived at work one Monday morning to learn that the movers were coming on Tuesday. When asked to explain, the man gave his reasons but clearly didn't feel his employees needed to know. He insulted and belittled the people he depended on for information and support.

It is important to communicate with subordinates not only as a group but also as individuals. This woman's boss may have believed money spoke for itself:

I have been working for my current boss for two years and never had a performance appraisal. I guess I'm doing okay because I get good raises every year. But I have no idea what the future may hold for me in this company.

Middle- to upper-level managers often find it difficult to talk with superiors about their own performance and career prospects. When they feel they aren't getting the feedback they need, they are uncomfortable asking for it. Communication must flow in both directions if it is to flow at all. Information won't surge up where it barely trickles down.

*Support* means showing concern for subordinates as people. It means being available and approachable. It means helping people, coaching them, encouraging their ideas, and defending their positions. It may mean socializing with them. It certainly means taking an interest in their lives and careers. Here are three examples of good and poor support:

During one period of my life, I had some serious personal problems that affected my work. My boss protected me at work and gave me a lot of moral support. Eventually, I was able to solve my problems, thanks in part to her help. That strengthened our professional relationship enormously.

I presented a proposal to the executive committee. Some members were in favor, others against. I was so young and nervous, I didn't see how I could possibly convince them I was right. Then my boss took on the defense of my proposal, argued energetically in favor of it, and we won. When I think back on it now, I realize that few events in my career have pleased me more or given me a more genuine sense of gratitude.

I approved a credit and had been authorized by my boss to waive certain credit warranties. Then some other people started questioning what I had done and throwing doubt on my competence. Instead of supporting me, my boss took the side of my critics.

It is often tempting to abandon an employee who is in trouble, out of favor, or simply unpopular, but the extra effort expended in behalf of such a person can pay big dividends later. When you have to terminate employees, the worst possible method is to let them twist in the wind. Get rid of those you have to get rid of. Support the others for all you're worth. Subordinates trust most deeply the superiors they feel will stand by them when the chips are down.

*Respect* feeds on itself. The most important form of respect is delegation, and the second most important is listening to subordinates and acting on their opinions. In the first two examples below, the boss shows genuine respect for the subordinate's judgment and intelligence. In the third, the relationship actually deteriorates in the course of the meeting.

My boss put me in charge of a project. It involved a big risk for me, but an even bigger risk for her if I failed. I asked her how she wanted me to do it and who else I should contact for clearance. She said, "You have free rein on this. Whatever you do is okay with me."

Six years ago, just after I joined the bank, my boss told me he had decided to buy a company and asked me to look into it and give him my opinion. I did my homework and told him I thought it was a bad idea. So he eliminated me from the team he had put together to manage the acquisition. Somehow I succeeded in persuading him to listen to a fuller presentation of my analysis. He not only took the time, he really listened to my arguments and finally canceled the purchase.

My boss and I agreed that we had to reduce the personnel in my department. I wanted to cut five positions; he wanted to cut eight. I argued my case for an hour. In the end he forced me to cut eight jobs, without even answering my arguments, and I realized he hadn't paid attention to anything I'd said.

In interpersonal relations, the law of reciprocity tends to rule. When supervisors use a lot of fine words about trust and respect but behave disdainfully, subordinates are likely to respond in kind.

*Fairness* means giving credit where it's due, being objective and impartial in performance appraisals, giving praise liberally. The opposite kind of behavior—favoritism, hypocrisy, misappropriating ideas and accomplishments, unethical behavior—is difficult to forgive and hugely destructive of trust. These two examples make the point well:

One of my subordinates had what I thought was a terrific idea, and I told my boss. He agreed and immediately dictated a memo to the division manager outlining the idea and giving full credit where it was due. I learned sometime later that he never sent that memo but substituted another in which he took a good share of the credit for himself—and gave an equal share to me. I not only felt cheated, I felt I had somehow taken part in a plot to cheat the person who had the idea in the first place. It not only destroyed my relationship with that boss, it almost ruined my relationship with my subordinate.

We were involved in a very difficult lawsuit with a former client. The battle lasted four years, and in the end we lost the case before the Supreme Court. When I gave the news to my boss, I was afraid he would take it badly, as a kind of personal failure. But he understood that we lost because of factors completely out of our control, and, instead of criticizing us, he praised our hard work and dedication.

Chronic lack of fairness will dry up trust and candor quickly, but every act of support and fair play will prime the pump.

*Predictability* is a matter of behaving consistently and dependably and of keeping both explicit and implicit promises. A broken promise can do considerable damage, as this example illustrates:

When my boss hired me, she promised me a percentage of the profits on the project I was to manage. My arrival was delayed, so I took over the project as it was winding down—without any profits to speak of. As soon as I cleaned up the loose ends, I took over a new project that was my responsibility from the outset. I managed it well, and profits were substantial. I felt badly cheated when I was told that my percentage deal applied to the first project only, that I had no such agreement on the second. I complained bitterly, and the company made it right. But it left a bad taste in my mouth, and I left shortly afterward.

Another form of predictability is consistency of character, which is, after all, the best proof of authenticity.

*Competence*, finally, means demonstrating technical and professional ability and good business sense. Employees don't want to be subordinate to people they see as incompetent. Trust grows from seeds of decent behavior, but it thrives on the admiration and respect that only a capable leader can command.

## Learning to Recognize Signs of Trouble

Building trust and candor is a gradual process, a long chain of positive experiences: trusting employees with important assignments, publicly defending their positions and supporting their ideas, showing candor and fairness in evaluating their work, and so forth. And because trust takes time to build and has natural limits once achieved, it is easy to destroy. Betraying a confidence, breaking a promise, humiliating an employee in public, lying, withholding information, or excluding subordinates from groups in which they feel they rightly belong—any of these can do instant and irreparable damage to a trust relationship that has taken months or years to develop.

Given these limitations, can managers rely on subordinates to come forward with problems before they become critical?

The obvious answer is no, not entirely. Honest, forthright communication is the best source of information about problems that managers have, and good ones make the most of it. At the same time, they learn to recognize subtle signs of danger, and they develop and refine alternative sources of information to fill in the gaps. My interviews indicate that there are several important warning signs that managers can look for.

*Decline in information flow* is often a first sign of trouble. Streams of information suddenly go dry. Subordinates communicate less, express opinions reluctantly, avoid discussions—even meetings. Reports are late, subordinates are more difficult to reach, and follow-up has to be more thorough and deliberate. In this example, the first warning was a series of glib reassurances that didn't quite jibe with reality:

I was exploration manager for an oil company in Venezuela. I began to notice that when I asked about one particular project, I got very short and superficial answers assuring me that everything was okay. But there were some contradictory signals. For example, labor turnover in the project was quite high. I had a gut feeling that something was seriously wrong. I contacted the area manager, but he couldn't put his finger on any specific problem. I called the field supervisor and still got no clear answers. I went to the field location and spent two days. Nothing. Then I sent a trustworthy young assistant to work with the field crews for a week, and he uncovered the problem. Local labor subcontractors were bribing the workers, increasing turnover, and taking in a lot of money for supplying replacements. We were not only spending more on labor bounties, we were often working with green hands instead of well-trained workers.

*Deterioration of morale* can reveal itself in lack of enthusiasm, reduced cooperation, increased complaints about workload, a tendency to dump more minor problems on the boss's desk. At a more advanced stage, absenteeism starts to rise and aggressive behavior—increased criticism, irritability, finger pointing, and the like—appears.

*Ambiguous verbal messages* come from subordinates who aren't quite comfortable with the information they are passing on. They may be reluctant to blow a potential problem out of proportion, or they may be testing to see if the door is open for a more serious discussion.

In one example, the head of an R&D lab asked the woman in charge of a large research project how a newly hired scientist was working out. The woman said, "He's very bright, but a bit strange. But he's working very hard and is extremely enthusiastic. He's okay." The boss missed the message. "I'm glad everything's okay" was all he said.

In this case, the woman's answer was a typical sign of trouble in sandwich form—positive, negative, positive. The subordinate who answers this way may simply be testing her boss's attention. When he failed to pick up on the "he's a bit strange" remark, she dropped the matter. Her boss never found out that she felt threatened by the scientist's brilliance and that his prima donna behavior made her angry. The friction between them grew, and she eventually took a job with another division.

*Nonverbal signals* can take a wide variety of forms, from body language to social behavior to changes in routines and habits.

The director of the international division of a major U.S. bank noticed that his chief of Asian operations had begun to work with his office door closed during his frequent visits to New York. This was unusual behavior: he was a gregarious soul, always available for lunch or a chat, and a closed door was out of character.

After two or three such visits, the director invited him to lunch to talk business. After a bottle of good wine, the younger man brought up what was really on his mind. He had heard rumors that his name had come up to head the European division—the most prestigious foreign assignment—and that the director had opposed him. The rumors were wrong. In fact, the bank was looking for someone to take the director's job, as he was about to be promoted, and the Asian operations chief was a prime candidate.

Consciously or unconsciously, the man sent a signal by closing his door. The lunch invitation was a nonthreatening way of finding out what the signal meant. At the time this took place, business had not yet begun to suffer, but more serious trouble might have erupted if this man had continued to brood over false rumors. This prompt response to a nonverbal signal kept a small problem from growing into a big one.

Body language, incidentally, is easily misinterpreted. Popular books have encouraged many people to believe they are experts, but interpreting body language is risky business. Distress signals may be triggered by events in a person's private life, for example, and have nothing to do with the office. A more prudent approach is to see body language merely as an indication of a potential problem, without jumping to conclusions about what the problem may be.

*Outside signals,* such as customer complaints and problems spotted by other company divisions, are also clear warnings, but they often come too late. By this time, the trouble has usually reached the stage of impaired results—decreasing productivity, deteriorating quality, dwindling orders, declining numbers. By now the manager has long since failed.

## Turning Hints into Information

When experienced managers see changes in the behavior of the people they supervise, they do their best to amplify hints and gather supplemental information.

As I pointed out at the beginning of this article, by far the easiest way of obtaining information is to get it from a subordinate, in plain English. Managers who have built good relationships with their subordinates often rely on this method. When they see the early warning signs of trouble, they ask questions.

As I have stressed, the answers to their questions will be only as honest as subordinates want to and dare to give. In other words, successful questioning depends partly on the level of trust. However, it also depends partly on a manager's ability to peel away superficial and sometimes misleading symptoms, much like the outside layers of an onion. Effective managers have good clinical sense. This man, for example, had a gut feeling that he had not yet reached the core of the problem:

My department was responsible for trade with the Far East, and I needed a good manager for China. I found what I thought was the perfect man. He not only knew all the traders but also spoke fluent English, French, Chinese, and Japanese. The new position was a promotion for him in terms of title and meant a big salary increase.

For the first year, he worked hard, things went well, and we made a lot of money. At the same time, he started to complain about his salary, arguing that other managers reporting to me and doing the same kind of work were getting 20% more—which was true. I told him he'd already had a 25% increase and that if he continued doing well, he could expect further raises over the next couple of years.

Then I began hearing his complaint from third parties all over the Far East. I discussed the matter with him many times, and eventually his salary rose to within 5% of the other managers. But something was still wrong. Then he suddenly got sick and disappeared from the office for two weeks. When he returned, his opening words were about salary.

Over the next couple of months, however, his health continued to deteriorate, and I began to wonder if salary was the real problem after all. I had several long talks with him and finally learned the truth. His deteriorating health was related to the job and the level of responsibility, which was too great for him to handle. He was so anxious that he couldn't sleep and was having problems with his family. As soon as we both understood the cause of his problem, I promised him a different job with less stress and frustration. He immediately became more relaxed and happier with his salary and his life.

The salary issue was only a symptom—a particularly misleading one, since the man was in fact underpaid by comparison with his colleagues. Notice also the escalation of symptoms from complaints to illness and the fact that it took the narrator several discussions to get at the actual truth. His persistence grew from a gut feeling that salary was not the real problem but rather a masking symptom.

When conflicts arise between superiors and subordinates, the most common method of punishing the boss is to withhold information. So the greater the conflict is, the less effective direct questioning will be. Furthermore, if an honest answer means pointing out some of the boss's own shortcomings, almost anyone will think twice.

One way of circumventing this difficulty is to design anonymous forms of communication—suggestion boxes, questionnaires, and performance appraisals of managers by the people who work for them.

One manager took advantage of an odd condition in his office space to coax anonymous information from his staff. The offices were on the ninth and tenth floors of an office building and had two elevators of their own, which every employee rode several times a day. The boss put a bulletin board in each of them and posted frequent notices, including a weekly newsletter about office activities, personnel changes, and industry developments. He then let it be known informally that the bulletin boards were open to everyone—no approvals required—and when the first employee notices appeared, he made a point of leaving them in place for a full week. There were only two rules. First, no clippings from newspapers and magazines—contributions had to be original. Second, nothing tasteless or abusive—but complaints and bellyaching were okay.

The bulletin boards flourished, partly because most people had at least an occasional chance to ride alone and post their own views in private. For a while, there was even an anonymous weekly newspaper that handed out praise and criticism pretty freely and irreverently. It made some people uncomfortable, but it had no more avid reader than the boss, who learned volumes about the problems and views of his staff and organization.

Criticizing the boss's managerial style and professional competence is probably the hardest thing for employees to do. Remember two critical points: First, top performers are the most likely to feel secure enough to criticize, so ask them first. Second, many of your subordinates have learned the hard way that honest negative feedback can be dangerous. Never ask for it unless you are certain you can handle it.


## Building Information Networks

There are big differences between consuming, disseminating, and creating information. Effective managers seem to have a talent for all three.

Using information well is primarily a matter of not *misusing* it—of being discreet about its sources, of using it not as a weapon but only as a means of solving problems and improving the quality of work life.

Spreading information well means not spreading gossip but also not hoarding the truth. People in organizations want—and have a right to—information that will help them do their jobs better or otherwise affect their lives. In general, they also work better and suffer less stress and fewer complications when they are well informed. At the same time—and more important for this discussion—information attracts information. Managers who are generous with what they know seem to get as much as they give.

Creating information, finally, is a question of assembling scattered facts and interpreting them for others. Shaping data in this way is a skill that needs exercise. It is an act of education and, of course, an act of control.

The final positive outcome for information-rich individuals is that information flows to them as well as away from them. This ability to attract, create, and disseminate information can become an immense managerial asset, a self-perpetuating information network, and a means of creating the trust that the upward flow of candid information depends on.

# 2
# Skilled Incompetence

**Chris Argyris**

The ability to get along with others is always an asset, right? Wrong. By adeptly avoiding conflict with coworkers, some executives eventually wreak organizational havoc. And it's their very adeptness that's the problem. The explanation for this lies in what I call skilled incompetence, whereby managers use practiced routine behavior (skill) to produce what they do not intend (incompetence). We can see this happen when managers talk to each other in ways that are seemingly candid and straightforward. What we don't see so clearly is how managers' skills can become institutionalized and create disastrous side effects in their organizations. Consider this familiar situation:

The entrepreneur-CEO of a fast-growing medium-sized company brought together his bright, dedicated, hardworking top managers to devise a new strategic plan. The company had grown at about 45% per year, but fearing that it was heading into deep administrative trouble, the CEO had started to rethink his strategy. He decided he wanted to restructure his organization along more rational, less ad hoc, lines. As he saw it, the company was split between the sales-oriented people who sell off-the-shelf products and the people producing custom services who are oriented toward professionals. And each group was suspicious of the other. He wanted the whole group to decide what kind of company it was going to run.

His immediate subordinates agreed that they must develop a vision and make some strategic decisions. They held several long meetings to do this. Although the meetings were pleasant enough and no one seemed to be making life difficult for anyone else, they concluded with no agreements or decisions. "We end up compiling lists of issues but not deciding," said one vice president. Another added, "And it gets pretty discouraging when this happens every time we meet." A third worried aloud, "If you think we are discouraged, how do you think the people below us feel who watch us repeatedly fail?"

This is a group of executives who are at the top, who respect each other, who are highly committed, and who agree that developing a vision and strategy is critical. Yet whenever they meet, they fail to create the vision and the strategy they desire. What is going on here? Are the managers really so incompetent? If so, why?

## What Causes Incompetence

At first, the executives in the previous example believed that they couldn't formulate and implement a good strategic plan because they lacked sound financial data. So they asked the financial vice president to reorganize and reissue the data. Everyone agreed he did a superb job.

But the financial executive reported to me, "Our problem is *not* the absence of financial data. I can flood them with data. We lack a vision of what kind of company we want to be and a strategy. Once we produce those, I can supply the necessary data." The other executives reluctantly agreed.

After several more meetings in which nothing got done, a second explanation emerged. It had to do with the personalities of the individuals and the way they work with each other. The CEO explained, "This is a group of lovable guys with very strong egos. They are competitive, bright, candid, and dedicated. But when we meet, we seem to go in circles; we are not prepared to give in a bit and make the necessary compromises."

Is this explanation valid? Should the top managers become less competitive? I'm not sure. Some management groups are not good at problem solving and decision making precisely because the participants have weak egos and are uncomfortable with competition.

If personality were really the problem, the cure would be psychotherapy. And it's simply not true that to be more effective, executives need years on the couch. Besides, pinpointing personality as the issue hides the real culprit.

**THE CULPRIT IS SKILL**

Let's begin by asking whether counterproductive behavior is also natural and routine. Does everyone seem to be acting sincerely? Do things go wrong even though the managers are not being destructively manipulative and political?

For the executive group, the answer to these questions is yes. Their motives were decent, and they were at their personal best. Their actions were spontaneous, automatic, and unrehearsed. They acted in milliseconds; they were skilled communicators.

How can skillful actions be counterproductive? When we're skillful we usually produce what we intend. So, in a sense, did the executives. In this case, the skilled behavior—the spontaneous and automatic responses—was meant to avoid upset and conflict at the meetings. The unintended by-products are what cause trouble. Because the executives don't say what they really mean or test the assumptions they really hold, their skills inhibit a resolution of the important intellectual issues embedded in developing the strategy. Thus the meetings end with only lists and no decisions.

This pattern of failure is not only typical for this group of managers. It happens to people in all kinds of organizations regardless of age, gender, educational background, wealth, or position in the hierarchy. Let me illustrate with another example that involves the entire organizational culture at the upper levels. Here we'll begin to see how people's tendency to avoid conflict, to duck the tough issues, becomes institutionalized and leads to a culture that can't tolerate straight talk.

## Where the Skillful Thrive

The top management of a large, decentralized corporation was having difficulty finding out what some of its division presidents were up to. Time and time again the CEO would send memos to the presidents asking for information, and time and time again they'd send next to nothing in return. But other people at headquarters accepted this situation as normal. When asked why they got so little direct communication from their division heads, they'd respond, "That's the way we do things around here."

Here is an organization that isn't talking to itself. The patterns that managers set up among themselves have become institutionalized, and what were once characteristic personal exchanges have now become organizational defensive routines. Before I go on to describe what these routines look like, let's look at how this situation arose.

Built into decentralization is the age-old tug between autonomy and control: superiors want no surprises, subordinates want to be left alone. The subordinates push for autonomy; they assert that by leaving them alone, top management will show its trust from a distance. The superiors, on the other hand, try to keep control through information systems. The subordinates see the control devices as confirming their suspicions—their superiors don't trust them.

Many executives I have observed handle this tension by pretending that the tension is not there. They act as if everyone were in accord and trust that no one will point out disagreements and thereby rock the boat. At the same time, however, they do feel the tension and can't help but soft-pedal their talk. They send mixed messages. (See "Four Easy Steps to Chaos.")

### Four Easy Steps to Chaos

How does a manager send mixed messages? It takes skill. Here are four rules:

**1**

Design a clearly ambiguous message. For example, "Be innovative and take risks, but be careful" is a message that says in effect, "Go, but go just so far" without specifying how far far is. The ambiguity and imprecision cover the speaker who can't know ahead of time what is too far.

The receiver, on the other hand, clearly understands the ambiguity and imprecision. Moreover, he or she knows that a request for more precision would likely be interpreted as a sign of immaturity or inexperience. And the receivers may also need an out some day and may want to keep the message imprecise and ambiguous. Receivers don't want "far" defined any more clearly than the senders do.

**2**

Ignore any inconsistencies in the message. When people send mixed messages, they usually do it spontaneously and with no sign that the message is mixed. Indeed, if they did appear to hesitate, they would defeat their purpose of maintaining control. Even worse, they might appear weak.

**3**

Make the ambiguity and inconsistency in the message undiscussable. The whole point of sending a mixed message is to avoid dealing with a situation straight on. The sender does not want the message's mixedness exposed. An executive is not about to send a mixed message and then ask, "Do you find my message inconsistent and ambiguous?" The executive also renders the message undiscussable by the very natural way of sending it. To challenge the innocence of the sender is to imply that the sender is duplicitous—not a likely thing for a subordinate to do.

**4**

Make the undiscussability also undiscussable. One of the best ways to do this is to send the mixed message in a setting that is not conducive to open inquiry, such as a large meeting or a group where people of unequal organizational status are present. No one wants to launder linen in public. While they are sending mixed messages during a meeting, people rarely reflect on their actions or talk about how the organizational culture, including the meeting, makes discussing the undiscussable difficult.

The CEO in this example kept saying to his division presidents, "I mean it—you run the show down there." The division presidents, wanting to prove their mettle, believed him until an important issue came up. When it did the CEO, concerned about the situation and forgetting that he wanted his division chiefs to be innovative, would make phone calls and send memos seeking information.

### DEFENSIVE ROUTINES EMERGE

One of the most powerful ways people deal with potential embarrassment is to create "organizational defensive routines." I define these as any action or policy designed to avoid surprise, embarrassment, or threat. But they also prevent learning and thereby prevent organizations from investigating or eliminating the underlying problems.

Defensive routines are systemic in that most people within the company adhere to them. People leave the organization and new ones arrive, yet the defensive routines remain intact.

To see the impact of the defensive routines and the range of their effects, let's return to the division heads who are directed by mixed messages. They feel a lack of trust and are suspicious of their boss's intentions but they must, nonetheless, find ways to live with the mixed messages. So they "explain" the messages to themselves and to their subordinates. These explanations often sound like this:

"Corporate never *really* meant decentralization."
"Corporate is willing to trust divisions when the going is smooth, but not when it's rough."
"Corporate is more concerned about the stock market than about us."

Of course, the managers rarely test their hypotheses about corporate motives with top executives. If discussing mixed messages among themselves would be uncomfortable, then public testing of the validity of these explanations would be embarrassing.

But now the division heads are in a double bind. On the one hand, if they go along unquestioningly, they may lose their autonomy and their subordinates will see them as having little influence with corporate. On the other, if the division executives do not comply with orders from above, headquarters will think they are recalcitrant, and if noncompliance continues, disloyal.

Top management is in a similar predicament. It senses that division managers have suspicions about headquarters' motives and are covering them up. If headquarters makes its impression known, though, the division heads may get upset. If the top does not say anything, the division presidents could infer full agreement when there is none. Usually, in the name of keeping up good relations, the top covers up its predicament.

Soon, people in the divisions learn to live with their binds by generating further explanations. For example, they may eventually conclude that openness is a strategy that top management has devised intentionally to cover up its unwillingness to be influenced.

Since this conclusion is based on the assumption that people at the top are covering up, managers won't test it either. Since neither headquarters nor division executives discuss or resolve the attributions or the frustrations, both may eventually stop communicating regularly and openly. Once in place, the climate of mistrust makes it more likely that the issues become undiscussable.

Now both headquarters and division managers have attitudes, assumptions, and actions that create self-fulfilling and self-sealing processes that each sees the other as creating.

Under these conditions, it is not surprising to find that superiors and subordinates hold both good and bad feelings about each other. For example, they may say about each other: "They are bright and well intentioned but they have a narrow, parochial view"; or "They are interested in the company's financial health but they do not understand how they are harming earnings in the long run"; or "They are interested in people but they pay too little attention to the company's development."

My experience is that people cannot build on their appreciation of others without first overcoming their suspicions. But to overcome what they don't like, people must be able to discuss it. And this requirement violates the undiscussability rule embedded in the organizational defensive routines.

Is there any organization that does not have these hang-ups and problems? Some people suggest that getting back to basics will open lines of communication. But the proffered panacea does not go far enough; it does not deal with the underlying patterns. Problems won't be solved by simply correcting one isolated instance of poor performance.

When CEOs I have observed declared war against organizational barriers to candor and demanded that people get back to basics, most often they implemented the new ideas with the old skills. People changed whatever they could and learned to cover their asses even more skillfully. The freedom to question and to confront is crucial, but it is inadequate. To overcome skilled incompetence, people have to learn new skills—to ask the questions behind the questions.

Defensive routines exist. They are undiscussable. They proliferate and grow underground. And the social pollution is hard to identify until something occurs that blows things open. Often that something is a glaring error whose results cannot be hidden. The recent space shuttle disaster is an example. Only after the accident occurred were the mixed messages and defensive routines used during the decision to launch exposed. The disaster made it legitimate for outsiders to require insiders to discuss the undiscussable. (By the way, writing a tighter set of controls and requiring better communication won't solve the problem. Tighter controls will only enlarge the book of rules that William Rogers, chairman of the president's committee to investigate the *Challenger* disaster, acknowledged can be a cure worse than the illness. He pointed out that in his Navy years, when the players went by the book, things only got worse.)

Managers do not have the choice to ignore the organizational problems that these self-sealing loops create. They may be able to get away with it today, but they're creating a legacy for those who will come after them.

## How to Become Unskilled

The top management group I described at the beginning of this article decided to learn new skills by examining the defenses they created in their own meetings.

First, they arranged a two-day session away from the office for which they wrote a short case beforehand. The purpose of these cases was twofold. First, they allowed the executives to develop a collage of the problems they thought were critical. Not surprisingly, in this particular group at least half wrote on issues related to the product versus custom service conflict. Second, the cases provided a kind of window into the prevailing rules and routines the executives used. The form of the case was as follows:

1. In one paragraph describe a key organizational problem as you see it.
2. In attacking the problem, assume you could talk to whomever you wish. Describe, in a paragraph or so, the strategy you would use in this meeting.
3. Next, split your page into two columns. On the right-hand side, write how you would begin the meeting: what you would actually say. Then write what you believe the other(s) would say. Then write your response to their response. Continue writing this scenario for two or so double-spaced typewritten pages.
4. In the left-hand column write any of your ideas or feelings that you would not communicate for whatever reason.

The executives reported that they became engrossed in writing the cases. Some said that the very writing of their case was an eye-opener. Moreover, once the stories were distributed, the reactions were jocular. They enjoyed them: "Great, Joe does this all the time"; "Oh, there's a familiar one"; "All salespeople and no listeners"; "Oh my God, this is us."

What is the advantage of using the cases? Crafted and written by the executives themselves, they become vivid examples of skilled incompetence. They illustrate the skill with which each executive sought to avoid upsetting the other while trying to change the other's mind. The cases also illustrate their incompetence. By their own analysis, what they did upset the others, created suspicion, and made it less likely that their views would prevail.

The cases are also very important learning devices. During a meeting, it is difficult to slow down behavior produced in milliseconds, to reflect on it, and to change it. For one thing, it's hard to pay attention to interpersonal actions and to substantive issues at the same time.

A collage from several cases appears in Exhibit I. It was written by executives who believed the company should place a greater emphasis on custom service.

The cases written by individuals who supported the product strategy did not differ much. They too were trying to persuade, sell, or cajole their fellow officers. Their left-hand columns were similar.

In analyzing their left-hand columns, the executives found that each side blamed the other for the difficulties, and they used the same reasons. For example, each side said:

> "If you insist on your position, you'll harm the morale I've built."
> "Don't hand me that line. You know what I'm talking about."
> "Why don't you take off your blinders and wear a company hat?"
> "It upsets me when I think of how they think."
> "I'm really trying hard, but I'm beginning to feel this is hopeless."

These cases effectively illustrate the influence of skilled incompetence. In crafting the cases, the executives were trying not to upset the others and at the same time were trying to change their minds. This process requires skill. Yet the skill they used in the cases has the unintended side effects I talked about. In the cases, the others became upset and dug in their heels without changing their minds.

Here's a real problem. These executives and all the others I've studied to date can't prevent the counterproductive consequences until and unless they learn new skills. Nor will it work to bypass the skilled incompetence by focusing on the business problems, such as, in this case, developing a business strategy.

### THE ANSWER IS UNLEARNING

The crucial step is for executives to begin to revise how they'd tackle their case. At their two-day seminar each manager selected an episode he wished to redesign so that it would not have the unhappy result it currently produced.

## *Exhibit I  Case of the Custom-Service Advocate*

| Thoughts and feelings | Actual conversation |
| --- | --- |
| | **I:** |
| He's not going to like this topic, but we have to discuss it. I doubt that he will take a company perspective, but I should be positive. | Hi Bill. I appreciate having the opportunity to talk with you about this custom service versus product problem. I'm sure that both of us want to resolve it in the best interests of the company. |
| | **Bill:** |
| | I'm always glad to talk about it, as you well know. |
| | **I:** |
| I better go slow. Let me ease in. | There are a rising number of situations where our clients are asking for custom service and rejecting the off-the-shelf products. I worry that your salespeople will play an increasingly peripheral role in the future. |
| | **Bill:** |
| | I don't understand. Tell me more. |
| | **I:** |
| Like hell you don't understand. I wish there was a way I could be more gentle. | Bill, I'm sure you are aware of the changes [I explain]. |
| | **Bill:** |
| | No, I don't see it that way. My salespeople are the key to the future. |
| | **I:** |
| There he goes, thinking like a salesman and not like a corporate officer. | Well, let's explore that a bit. |

In rewriting their cases, the managers realized that they would have to slow things down. They could not produce a new conversation in the milliseconds in which they were accustomed to speak. This troubled them a bit because they were impatient to learn. They had to keep reminding themselves that learning new skills meant they had to slow down.

Each manager took a different manager's case and crafted a new conversation to help the writer of the episode. After five minutes or so, they showed their designs to the writer. In the process of discussing these new versions, the writer learned a lot about how to redesign his words. And, as they discovered the bugs in their suggestions and the way they made them, the designers also learned a lot.

The dialogues were constructive, cooperative, and helpful. Typical comments were:

> "If you want to reach me, try it the way Joe just said."
> "I realize your intentions are good, but those words push my button."
> "I understand what you're trying to say, but it doesn't work for me. How about trying it this way?"
> "I'm surprised at how much my new phrases contain the old messages. This will take time."

Practice is important. Most people require as much practice to overcome skilled incompetence as to play a not-so-decent game of tennis. But it doesn't need to happen all at once. Once managers are committed to change, the practice can occur in actual business meetings where executives set aside some time to reflect on their actions and to correct them.

But how does unlearning skilled incompetence lead to fewer organizational snafus? The first step is to make sure executives are aware of defensive routines that surround the organizational problems that they are trying to solve. One way to do this is to observe them in the making. For example, during a meeting of the top line and corporate staff officers in our large decentralized organization, the CEO asked why the line and staff were having problems working effectively. They identified at least four causes:

> The organization's management philosophy and policies are inadequate.
> Corporate staff roles overlap and lead to confusion.

Staff lacks clear-cut authority when dealing with line.
Staff has inadequate contact with top line officers.

The CEO appointed two task forces to come up with solutions. Several months later, the entire group met for a day and hammered out a solution that was acceptable to all.

This story has two features that I would highlight. First, the staff-line problems are typical. Second, the story has a happy ending. The organization got to the root of its problems.

But there is a question that must be answered in order to get at the organizational defensive routines. Why did all the managers—both upper and lower—adhere to, implement, and maintain inadequate policies and confusing roles in the first place?

Why open this can of worms if we have already solved the problem? Because defensive routines prevent executives from making honest decisions. Managers who are skilled communicators may also be good at covering up real problems. If we don't work hard at reducing defensive routines, they will thrive—ready to undermine this solution and cover up other conflicts.

# PART

# II

## Learning to Listen

# 1
# Barriers and Gateways to Communication

Carl R. Rogers and F.J. Roethlisberger

## Part I: Carl R. Rogers

It may seem curious that someone like me, a psychotherapist, should be interested in problems of communication. But, in fact, the whole task of psychotherapy is to deal with a failure in communication. In emotionally maladjusted people, communication within themselves has broken down, and as a result, their communication with others has been damaged. To put it another way, their unconscious, repressed, or denied desires have created distortions in the way they communicate with others. Thus they suffer both within themselves and in their interpersonal relationships.

The goal of psychotherapy is to help an individual achieve, through a special relationship with a therapist, good communication within himself or herself. Once this is achieved, that person can communicate more freely and effectively with others. So we may say that psychotherapy is good communication within and between people. We can turn that statement around and it will still be true. Good communication, or free communication, within or between people is always therapeutic.

Through my experience in counseling and psychotherapy, I've found that there is one main obstacle to communication: people's tendency to *evaluate*. Fortunately, I've also discovered that if people can learn to *listen* with understanding, they can mitigate their evaluative impulses and greatly improve their communication with others.

## BARRIER: THE TENDENCY TO EVALUATE

We all have a natural urge to judge, evaluate, and approve (or disapprove) another person's statement. Suppose someone, commenting on what I've just stated, says, "I didn't like what that man said." How will you respond? Almost invariably your reply will be either approval or disapproval of the attitude expressed. Either you respond, "I didn't either; I thought it was terrible," or else you say, "Oh, I thought it was really good." In other words, your first reaction is to evaluate it from *your* point of view.

Or suppose I say with some feeling, "I think the Democrats are showing a lot of good sound sense these days." What is your first reaction? Most likely, it will be evaluative. You will find yourself agreeing or disagreeing, perhaps making some judgment about me such as, "He must be a liberal," or "He seems solid in his thinking."

Although making evaluations is common in almost all conversation, this reaction is heightened in situations where feelings and emotions are deeply involved. So the stronger the feelings, the less likely it is that there will be a mutual element in the communication. There will be just two ideas, two feelings, or two judgments missing each other in psychological space.

If you've ever been a bystander at a heated discussion—one in which you were not emotionally involved—you've probably gone away thinking, "Well, they actually weren't talking about the same thing." And because it was heated, you were probably right. Each person was making a judgment, an evaluation, from a personal frame of reference. There was nothing that could be called communication in any real sense. And this impulse to evaluate any emotionally meaningful statement from our own viewpoint is what blocks interpersonal communication.

## GATEWAY: LISTENING WITH UNDERSTANDING

We can achieve real communication and avoid this evaluative tendency when we listen with understanding. This means seeing the expressed idea and attitude from the other person's point of view, sensing how it feels to the person, achieving his or her frame of reference about the subject being discussed.

This may sound absurdly simple, but it is not. In fact, it is an extremely potent approach in psychotherapy. It is the most effective way we've found to alter a person's basic personality structure and to improve the person's relationships and communications with others. If I can listen to what a person can tell me and really understand how she hates her father or hates the company or hates conservatives, or if I can catch the essence of her fear of insanity or fear of nuclear bombs, I will be better able to help her alter those hatreds and fears and establish realistic and harmonious relationships with the people and situations that roused such emotions. We know from research that such empathic understanding—understanding *with* a person, not *about* her—is so effective that it can bring about significant changes in personality.

If you think that you listen well and have never seen such results, your listening probably has not been of the type I am describing. Here's one way to test the quality of your understanding. The next time you get into an argument with your spouse, friend, or small group of friends, stop the discussion for a moment and suggest this rule: "Before each person speaks up, he or she must *first* restate the ideas and feelings of the previous speaker accurately and to that speaker's satisfaction."

You see what this would mean. Before presenting your own point of view, you would first have to achieve the other speaker's frame of reference. Sounds simple, doesn't it? But if you try it, you will find it one of the most difficult things you have ever attempted to do. And even when you have been able to do it, your comments will have to be drastically revised. But you will also find that the emotion is dissipating—the differences are reduced, and those that remain are rational and understandable.

Can you imagine what this kind of approach could accomplish in larger arenas? What would happen to a labor-management dispute if labor, without necessarily conceding agreement, could accurately state management's point of view in a way that management could accept; and if management, without approving labor's stand, could state labor's case so that labor agreed it was accurate? It would mean that real communication was established and that some reasonable solution almost surely would be reached.

So why is this "listening" approach not more widely used? There are several reasons.

*Lack of Courage.* Listening with understanding means taking a very real risk. If you really understand another person in this way, if you are willing to enter his private world and see the way life appears to him, without any attempt to make evaluative judgments, you run the risk of being changed yourself. You might see things his way; you might find that he has influenced your attitudes or your personality.

Most of us are afraid to take that risk. So instead we *cannot listen*; we find ourselves compelled to *evaluate* because listening seems too dangerous.

*Heightened Emotions.* In heated discussions, emotions are strongest, so it is especially hard to achieve the frame of reference of another person or group. Yet it is precisely then that good listening is required if communication is to be established.

One solution is to use a third party, who is able to lay aside her own feelings and evaluations, to listen with understanding to each person or group and then clarify the views and attitudes each holds.

This has been effective in small groups in which contradictory or antagonistic attitudes exist. When the parties to a dispute realize they are being understood, that someone sees how the situation seems to them, the statements grow less exaggerated and less defensive, and it is no longer necessary to maintain the attitude, "I am 100% right, and you are 100% wrong."

The influence of such an understanding catalyst in the group permits the members to come closer to seeing the objective truth of the situation. This leads to improved communication, to greater acceptance of each other, and to attitudes that are more positive and more problem solving in nature. There is a decrease in defensiveness, in exaggerated statements, in evaluative and critical behavior. Mutual communication is established, and some type of agreement becomes much more possible.

*Too Large a Group.* Thus far, psychotherapists have been able to observe only small, face-to-face groups that are working to resolve religious, racial, or industrial tensions—or the personal tensions that are present in many therapy groups. What about trying to achieve understanding between larger groups that are geographically remote, for example, or between face-to-face groups that are speaking not for themselves but simply as representatives of others? Frankly, we do not know the answer. Based on our limited knowledge, however, there are some steps that even large groups can take to increase the amount of listening *with* and decrease the amount of evaluation *about*.

To be imaginative for a moment, suppose that a therapeutically oriented international group went to each of two countries involved in a dispute and said, "We want to achieve a genuine understanding of your views and, even more important, of your attitudes and feelings toward X country. We will summarize and resummarize these views and feelings if necessary, until you agree that our description represents the situation as it seems to you."

If they then widely distributed descriptions of these two views, might not the effect be very great? It would not guarantee the type of understanding I have been describing, but it would make it much more possible. We can understand the feelings of people who hate us much more readily when their attitudes are accurately described to us by a neutral third party than we can when they are shaking their fists at us.

Communication through a moderator who listens nonevaluatively and with understanding has proven effective, even when feelings run high. This procedure can be initiated by one party, without waiting for the other to be ready. It can even be initiated by a neutral third person, provided the person can gain a minimum of cooperation from one of the parties. The moderator can deal with the insincerities, the defensive exaggerations, the lies, and the "false fronts" that characterize almost every failure in communication. These defensive distortions drop away with astonishing speed as people find that the person's intention is to understand, not to judge. And when one party begins to drop its defenses, the other usually responds in kind, and together they begin to uncover the facts of a situation.

Gradually, mutual communication grows. It leads to a situation in which I see how the problem appears to you as well as to me, and you see how it appears to me as well as to you. Thus accurately and realistically defined, the problem is almost certain to yield to intelligent attack; or if it is in part insoluble, it will be comfortably accepted as such.

## Part II: F.J. Roethlisberger

When we think about the many barriers to personal communication, particularly those due to differences in background, experience, and motivation, it seems extraordinary that any two people can ever understand each other. The potential for problems seems especially heightened in the context of a boss-subordinate relationship. How is communication possible when people do not see and assume the same things or share the same values?

On this question, there are two schools of thought. One school assumes that communication between A and B has failed when B does not accept what A has to say as being factual, true, or valid; and that the goal of communication is to get B to agree with A's opinions, ideas, facts, or information.

The other school of thought is quite different. It assumes that communication has failed when B does not feel free to express his feelings to A because B fears they will not be accepted by A. Communication is facilitated when A or B or both are willing to express and accept differences.

To illustrate, suppose Bill, an employee, is in his boss's office. The boss says, "I think, Bill, that this is the best way to do your job." And to that, Bill says, "Oh yeah?"

According to the first school of thought, this reply would be a sign of poor communication. Bill does not understand the best way of doing his work. To improve communication, therefore, it is up to the boss to explain to Bill why the boss's, not Bill's, way is the best.

From the second school's point of view, Bill's reply is a sign of neither good nor bad communication; it is indeterminate. But the boss can take the opportunity to find out what Bill means. Let us assume that this is what she chooses to do. So this boss tries to get Bill to talk more about his job.

We'll call the boss representing the first school of thought "Smith" and the boss subscribing to the second school "Jones." Given identical situations, each behaves differently. Smith chooses to *explain*; Jones chooses to *listen*. In my experience, Jones's response works better than Smith's, because Jones is making a more proper evaluation of what is taking place between her and Bill than Smith is.

## "OH YEAH?"

Smith assumes that he understands what Bill means when Bill says, "Oh yeah?" so there is no need to find out. Smith is sure that Bill does not understand why this is the best way to do his job, so Smith has to tell him.

In this process, let us assume Smith is logical, lucid, and clear. He presents his facts and evidence well. But, alas, Bill remains unconvinced. What does Smith do? Operating under the assumption that what is taking place between him and Bill is something essentially logical, Smith can draw only one of two conclusions: either (1) he has not been clear enough or (2) Bill is too stupid to understand. So he has to either "spell out" his case in words of fewer and fewer syllables or give up. Smith is reluctant to give up, so he continues to explain. What happens?

The more Smith cannot get Bill to understand him, the more frustrated and emotional Smith becomes—and the more Smith's ability to reason logically is diminished. Since Smith sees himself as a reasonable, logical chap, this is a difficult thing for him to accept. It is much easier to perceive Bill as uncooperative or stupid. This perception will affect what Smith says and does.

Under these pressures, Smith evaluates Bill more and more in terms of his own values and tends to treat Bill's as unimportant, essentially denying Bill's uniqueness and difference. He treats Bill as if he had little capacity for self-direction.

Let us be clear. Smith does not see that he is doing these things. When he is feverishly scratching hieroglyphics on the back of an envelope, trying to explain to Bill why this is the best way to do his job, Smith is trying to be helpful. He is a man of goodwill, and he wants to set Bill straight. This is the way Smith sees himself and his behavior. But it is for this very reason that Bill's "Oh yeah?" is getting under Smith's skin.

"How dumb can a guy be?" is Smith's attitude, and unfortunately Bill will hear that more than Smith's good intentions. Bill will feel misunderstood. He will not see Smith as a man of goodwill trying to be helpful. Rather he will perceive him as a threat to his self-esteem and personal integrity. Against this threat Bill will feel the need to defend himself at all cost. Not being so logically articulate as Smith, Bill expresses this need by saying, again, "Oh yeah?"

Let us leave this sad scene between Smith and Bill, which I fear is going to end with Bill either leaving in a huff or being kicked out of Smith's office. Let us turn for a moment to Jones and see how she is interacting with Bill.

Jones, remember, does not assume that she knows what Bill means when he says, "Oh yeah?" so she has to find out. Moreover, she assumes that when Bill said this, he had not exhausted his vocabulary or his feelings. Bill may mean not just one thing but several different things. So Jones decides to listen.

In this process, Jones is not under any illusion that what will happen will be a purely logical exchange. Rather she is assuming that what happens will be primarily an interaction of feelings. Therefore, she cannot ignore Bill's feelings, the effect of Bill's feelings on her, or the effect of her feelings on Bill. In other words, she cannot ignore her relationship to Bill; she cannot assume that it will make no difference to what Bill will hear or accept.

Therefore, Jones will be paying strict attention to all of the things Smith has ignored. She will be addressing herself to Bill's feelings, her own feelings, and the interaction between them.

Jones will therefore realize that she has ruffled Bill's feelings with her comment, "I think, Bill, this is the best way to do your job." So instead of trying to get Bill to understand her, she decides to try to understand Bill. She does this by encouraging Bill to speak. Instead of telling Bill how he should feel or think, she asks Bill such questions as, "Is this what you feel?" "Is this what you see?" "Is this what you assume?" Instead of ignoring Bill's evaluations as irrelevant, not valid, inconsequential, or false, she tries to understand Bill's reality as he feels it, perceives it, and assumes it to be. As Bill begins to open up, Jones's curiosity is piqued by this process.

"Bill isn't so dumb; he's quite an interesting guy" becomes Jones's attitude. And that is what Bill hears. Therefore Bill feels understood and accepted as a person. He becomes less defensive. He is in a better frame of mind to explore and reexamine his perceptions, feelings, and assumptions. Bill feels free to express his differences. In this process, he sees Jones as a source of help and feels that Jones respects his capacity for self-direction. These positive feelings toward Jones make Bill more inclined to say, "Well, Jones, I don't quite agree with you that this is the best way to do my job, but I'll tell you what I'll do. I'll try to do it that way for a few days, and then I'll tell you what I think."

I grant that my two orientations do not work in practice quite so neatly as I have worked them out on paper. There are many other ways in which Bill could have responded to Smith in the first place. He might even have said, "OK, boss, I agree that your way of doing my job is better." But Smith still would not have known how Bill felt when he made this statement or whether Bill was actually going to do his job differently. Likewise, Bill could have responded to Jones differently. In spite of Jones's attitude, Bill might still have been reluctant to express himself freely to his boss.

Nevertheless, these examples give me something concrete to point to in making the following generalizations:

1. Smith represents a very common pattern of misunderstanding. The misunderstanding does not arise because Smith is not clear enough in expressing himself. Rather, Smith misevaluates what takes place when two people are talking together.

2. Smith's misunderstanding of the process of personal communication is based on common assumptions: (a) that what is taking place is something logical; (b) that words mean something in and of themselves, apart from the people speaking them; and (c) that the purpose of the interaction is to get Bill to see things from Smith's point of view.

3. These assumptions set off a chain reaction of perceptions and negative feelings, which blocks communication. By ignoring Bill's feelings and rationalizing his own, Smith ignores his relationship to Bill as an important determinant of their communication. As a result, Bill hears Smith's *attitude* more clearly than the logical content of Smith's words. Bill feels that his uniqueness is being denied. Since his personal integrity is at stake, he becomes defensive and belligerent. And this frustrates Smith. He perceives Bill as stupid, so he says and does things that make Bill still more defensive.

4. Jones makes a different set of assumptions: (a) that what is taking place between her and Bill is an interaction of sentiments; (b) that Bill—not his words in themselves—means something; and (c) that the object of the interaction is to give Bill a chance to express himself.

5. Because of these assumptions, there is a psychological chain reaction of reinforcing feelings and perceptions that eases communication between Bill and Jones. When Jones addresses Bill's feelings and perceptions from Bill's point of view, Bill feels understood and accepted as a person; he feels free to express his differences. Bill sees Jones as a source of help; Jones sees Bill as an interesting person. Bill, in turn, becomes more cooperative.

If I have identified correctly these very common patterns of personal communication, then we can infer some interesting hypotheses:

Jones's method works better than Smith's not because of any magic but because Jones has a better map of the process of personal communication.

Jones's method, however, is not merely an intellectual exercise. It depends on Jones's capacity and willingness to see and accept points of view that are different from her own and to practice this orientation in a face-to-face relationship. This is an emotional and intellectual achievement. It depends in part on Jones's awareness of herself, in part on the practice of a skill.

Although universities try to get students to appreciate, at least intellectually, points of view different from their own, little is done to help them learn to apply this intellectual appreciation to simple, face-to-face relationships. Students are trained to be logical and clear—but no one helps them learn to *listen* skillfully. As a result, our educated world contains too many Smiths and too few Joneses.

The biggest block between two people is their inability to listen to each other intelligently, understandingly, and skillfully. This deficiency in the modern world is widespread and appalling. We need to make greater efforts to educate people in effective communication—which means, essentially, teaching people how to listen.

## Retrospective Commentary
## John J. Gabarro

Reading "Barriers and Gateways" today, it is hard to understand the stir the article created when it was first published. But in 1952, Rogers' and Roethlisberger's ideas about the importance of listening were indeed radical. Not only did they stake out new territory that was anathema to the gray flannel ethic—namely, the idea that people's feelings mattered. But they also challenged the sanctity of hierarchical relationships by suggesting that managers take their subordinates' thoughts and feelings seriously.

Today, however, these insights are so basic as to be obvious, which shows how much impact their ideas have had and how far management communication has come. Or has it? Contemporary managers do have a better grasp of how important listening is to good communication. Nonetheless, most still have a hard time putting this lesson into practice. One reason could be their own sophistication: simple lessons can be easily forgotten. Another reason, however, could be that this lesson is not so simple after all, that what the authors told us 40 years ago is more difficult to do than it appears and is really only half the story. The benefit of revisiting R&R, then, is both to remind ourselves of still-relevant, indeed powerful, insights and to find, from the vantage point of 40 years later, what R&R may have overlooked.

What speaks loudest to business today are three insights that in fact transcend institutional and social boundaries: they are the communication barriers and gateways that, as the authors show, can occur between two nations as well as between two individuals. These insights have endured because they are basic truths about human interaction.

*The greatest barrier to effective communication is the tendency to evaluate*

*what another person is saying and therefore to misunderstand or to not really
"hear."* The Bill and Smith scenario, which vividly illustrates this process, rings true today because such communication breakdowns still
happen routinely. In fact, in today's arguably more complex business
environment, they may be more likely to happen.

Greater work force diversity, for example, can complicate communication, as a common language of shared assumptions and experiences becomes harder to establish. Indeed, if in 1952 Roethlisberger
thought it "extraordinary" that any two people could communicate,
given their "differences in background, experience, and motivation,"
he would surely have thought it a miracle today.

*Checking the natural tendency to judge yields a better understanding of the
person with whom you are communicating.* Of course, greater diversity also
makes disciplined listening all the more important—because the potential for misunderstanding is greater. This gateway, then, is more
vital than ever. By suspending assumptions and judgments, a manager
can get to the heart of an employee's feelings, a better signpost to what
the employee is saying than his or her words alone.

*A better understanding of the other person's point of view in turn helps you
communicate better.* Effective communication is equal parts listening and
expression; the clarity of one depends on the clarity of another. A
manager with a clearer picture of whom he's talking to is able to
express himself more accurately..

These insights have been the impetus behind a number of progres-
sive practices—corporate efforts to empower employees, for example.
When a manager shows a willingness to listen to an employee, she is
more likely to engender trust and thus honesty. And by encouraging
the employee to talk straight, without fear of reprisal, she boosts his
self-confidence because he sees that the organization values his input.
What's more, the manager stays tapped into a vital information
source—the front lines.

Or consider the technique of "active listening," developed in the
1970s and still widely used in many management- and sales-training
programs. A salesperson applying active listening, for example, reacts
nonjudgmentally to what a prospect is saying, rephrasing it to make
sure he truly understands the customer's point of view. The benefits
are twofold. First, this process minimizes the likelihood that the salesperson is laying his biases on the customer's needs. Second, the prospect feels listened to and understood.

Ultimately, though, R&R may have had too much faith in nonevaluative listening. Researchers doing work in this field, and, for that

matter, managers trying to apply these lessons, now realize how overly optimistic the authors were. First, a fundamental but unarticulated premise is that understanding equals resolution, but this is not the case. While understanding can improve the negotiation process—as various research, from Richard Walton's work in labor relations to Roger Fisher's in international negotiations, has shown—it cannot by itself resolve conflict.

Second, the process of establishing trust is not as one-dimensional as R&R imply. Jones would probably not be able to secure Bill's trust merely by showing a commitment to nonevaluative listening. Bill will assess many other aspects of Jones's behavior and character in deciding whether to talk openly with her: her motives, her discretion, the consistency of her behavior, even her managerial competence. Only if this assessment is positive will Bill respond candidly to Jones's overtures. Thus, as a rule, a minimum baseline of confidence is needed to evoke the kind of trust that honest communication requires. This is especially true where there is a power imbalance, which tends to foster greater initial distrust. (This dynamic works both ways: an employee may distrust her manager for fear of reprisal; but a manager may distrust his employee for fear that she'll say only what he wants to hear.)

Finally, managers today come up against a few more communication barriers than R&R envisioned. One is the pressure of time. Listening carefully takes time, and managers have little of that to spare. In today's business culture especially, with its emphasis on speed (overnight mail, faster computers, time-based competition), already pressed managers may give short shrift to the slower art of one-on-one communication.

Another barrier in this era of mergers, acquisitions, and delayering is insecurity and the fear that it breeds. When downsizing and layoffs loom, both the Bills and the Joneses of this world have good reason for not opening up, especially when people believe that their true feelings or beliefs may get them fired.

Even so, these limitations don't entirely explain why, some 40 years later, a salesperson can win over clients with active listening but a manager fails to have the slightest idea what makes his employees tick. This is because managers face still another, more significant, barrier, one I call the managerial paradox: while it is crucial that managers be able to listen nonjudgmentally (to understand other points of view and get valid information), the essence of management is to do just the opposite—to make judgments. Managers are called on daily to evaluate product lines, markets, numbers, and, of course, people. And in turn, they are evaluated on how well they do this. The danger, then, is that this bias for judging will subvert a manager's inclination to listen carefully and, in doing so, sabotage his or her ability to make accurate business and people judgments.

Managers may be tempted to resolve this paradox as an either/or. And for good reason: rarely in their training have the two mind-sets been reconciled. Business schools, for the most part, still reinforce evaluative listening; they teach students to defend their own positions while scoring points against others'. And those behavioral experts who do focus on nonevaluative listening tend to focus almost exclusively on the importance of empathy. But if one thing has made itself clear in the past 40 years, it is that managers must have the capacity to do both. They must recognize that to make judgments, you must suspend judgment.

# 2
# Listening to People

## Ralph G. Nichols and Leonard A. Stevens

Recently the top executives of a major manufacturing plant in the Chicago area were asked to survey the role that listening plays in their work. Later, an executive seminar on listening was held. Here are three typical comments made by participants:

"Frankly, I had never thought of listening as an important subject by itself. But now that I am aware of it, I think that perhaps 80% of my work depends on my listening to someone, or on someone else listening to me."

"I've been thinking back about things that have gone wrong over the past couple of years, and I suddenly realized that many of the troubles have resulted from someone not hearing something, or getting it in a distorted way."

"It's interesting to me that we have considered so many facets of communication in the company, but have inadvertently overlooked listening. I've about decided that it's the most important link in the company's communications, and it's obviously also the weakest one."

These comments reflect part of an awakening that is taking place in a number of management circles. Business is tied together by its systems of communication. This communication, businessmen are discovering, depends more on the spoken word than it does on the written word; and the effectiveness of the spoken word hinges not so much on how people talk as on how they listen.

## The Unused Potential

It can be stated, with practically no qualifications, that people in general do not know how to listen. They have ears that hear very well, but seldom have they acquired the necessary aural skills which would allow those ears to be used effectively for what is called *listening*.

For several years we have been testing the ability of people to understand and remember what they hear. At the University of Minnesota we examined the listening ability of several thousand students and of hundreds of business and professional people. In each case the person tested listened to short talks by faculty members and was examined for his grasp of the content.

These extensive tests led us to this general conclusion: immediately after the average person has listened to someone talk, he remembers only about half of what he has heard—no matter how carefully he thought he was listening.

What happens as time passes? Our own testing shows—and it has been substantiated by reports of research at Florida State University and Michigan State University[1]—that two months after listening to a talk, the average listener will remember only about 25% of what was said. In fact, after we have barely learned something, we tend to forget from one-half to one-third of it *within eight hours*; it is startling to realize that frequently we forget more in this first short interval than we do in the next six months.

### GAP IN TRAINING

Behind this widespread inability to listen lies, in our opinion, a major oversight in our system of classroom instruction. We have focused attention on reading, considering it the primary medium by which we learn, and we have practically forgotten the art of listening. About six years are devoted to formal reading instruction in our school systems. Little emphasis is placed on speaking, and almost no attention has been given to the skill of listening, strange as this may be in view of the fact that so much lecturing is done in college. Listening training—if it could be called training—has often consisted merely of a series of admonitions extending from the first grade through college: "Pay attention!" "Now get this!" "Open your ears!" "Listen!"

Certainly our teachers feel the need for good listening. Why then have so many years passed without educators developing formal methods of teaching students to listen? We have been faced with several false assumptions which have blocked the teaching of listening. For example:

1. We have assumed that listening ability depends largely on intelligence, that "bright" people listen well, and "dull" ones poorly. There is no denying that low intelligence has something to do with inability to listen, but we have greatly exaggerated its importance. A poor listener is not necessarily an unintelligent person. To be good listeners we must apply certain skills that are acquired through either experience or training. If a person has not acquired these listening skills, his ability to understand and retain what he hears will be low. This can happen to people with both high and low levels of intelligence.

2. We have assumed that learning to read will automatically teach one to listen. While some of the skills attained through reading apply to listening, the assumption is far from completely valid. Listening is a different activity from reading and requires different skills. Research has shown that reading and listening skills do not improve at the same rate when only reading is taught.

This means that in our schools, where little attention is paid to the aural element of communication, reading ability is continually upgraded while listening ability, left to falter along on its own, actually degenerates. As a fair reader and a bad listener, the typical student is graduated into a society where the chances are high that he will have to listen about three times as much as he reads.

The barriers to listening training that have been built up by such false assumptions are coming down. Educators are realizing that listening is a skill that can be taught. In Nashville, for example, the public school system has started training in listening from elementary grades through high school. Listening is also taught in the Phoenix school system, in Cincinnati, and throughout the state of North Dakota. About two dozen major universities and colleges in the country now provide courses in listening.

At the University of Minnesota we have been presenting a course in listening to a large segment of the freshman class. Each group of students that has taken listening training has improved at least 25% in ability to understand the spoken word. Some of the groups have improved as much as 40%. We have also given a course in listening for adult education classes made up mostly of business and professional people. These people have made some of the highest gains in listening ability of any that we have seen. During one period, 60 men and women nearly doubled their listening test scores after working together on this skill one night a week for 17 weeks.

## Ways to Improvement

Any course or any effort that will lead to listening improvement should do two things:

1. Build awareness to factors that affect listening ability.
2. Build the kind of aural experience that can produce good listening habits.

At least a start on the first of these two educational elements can be made by readers of this article; a certain degree of awareness is developed by merely discussing factors that affect listening ability. Later we shall discuss some steps that might be taken in order to work at the second element.

### TRACKS AND SIDETRACKS

In general, people feel that concentration while listening is a greater problem than concentration during any other form of personal communication. Actually, listening concentration *is* more difficult. When we listen, concentration must be achieved despite a factor that is peculiar to aural communication, one of which few people are aware.

Basically, the problem is caused by the fact that we think much faster than we talk. The average rate of speech for most Americans is around 125 words per minute. This rate is slow going for the human brain, which is made up of more than 13 billion cells and operates in such a complicated but efficient manner that it makes the great, modern digital computers seem slow-witted. People who study the brain are not in complete agreement on how it functions when we think, but most psychologists believe that the basic medium of thought is language. Certainly words play a large part in our thinking processes, and the words race through our brains at speeds much higher than 125 words per minute. This means that, when we listen, we ask our brain to receive words at an extremely slow pace compared with its capabilities.

It might seem logical to slow down our thinking when we listen so as to coincide with the 125-word-per-minute speech rate, but slowing down thought processes seems to be a very difficult thing to do. When we listen, therefore, we continue thinking at high speed while the spoken words arrive at low speed. In the act of listening, the differential between thinking and speaking rates means that our brain works with hundreds of words in addition to those that we hear, assembling thoughts other than those spoken to us. To phrase it another way, we can listen and still have some spare time for thinking.

The use, or misuse, of this spare thinking time holds the answer to how well a person can concentrate on the spoken word.

*Case of the Disenchanted Listener.* In our studies at the University of Minnesota, we find most people do not use their spare thinking time wisely as they listen. Let us illustrate how this happens by describing a familiar experience:

A, the boss, is talking to B, the subordinate, about a new program that the firm is planning to launch. B is a poor listener. In this instance, he tries to listen well, but he has difficulty concentrating on what A has to say.

A starts talking and B launches into the listening process, grasping every word and phrase that comes into his ears. But right away B finds that, because of A's slow rate of speech, he has time to think of things other than the spoken line of thought. Subconsciously, B decides to sandwich a few thoughts of his own into the aural ones that are arriving so slowly. So B quickly dashes out onto a mental sidetrack and thinks something like this: "Oh, yes, before I leave I want to tell A about the big success of the meeting I called yesterday." Then B comes back to A's spoken line of thought and listens for a few more words.

There is plenty of time for B to do just what he has done, dash away from what he hears and then return quickly, and he continues taking sidetracks to his own private thoughts. Indeed, he can hardly avoid doing this because over the years the process has become a strong aural habit of his.

But, sooner or later, on one of the mental sidetracks, B is almost sure to stay away too long. When he returns, A is moving along ahead of him. At this point it becomes harder for B to understand A, simply because B has missed part of the oral message. The private mental sidetracks become more inviting than ever, and B slides off onto several of them. Slowly he misses more and more of what A has to say.

When A is through talking, it is safe to say that B will have received and understood less than half of what was spoken to him.

## RULES FOR GOOD RECEPTION

A major task in helping people to listen better is teaching them to use their spare thinking time efficiently as they listen. What does "efficiently" mean? To answer this question, we made an extensive study of people's listening habits, especially trying to discover what happens when people listen well.

We found that good listeners regularly engage in four mental activities, each geared to the oral discourse and taking place concurrently with that oral discourse. All four of these mental activities are neatly coordinated when listening works at its best. They tend to direct a maximum amount of thought to the message being received, leaving a minimum amount of time for mental excursions on sidetracks leading away from the talker's thought. Here are the four processes:

1. The listener thinks ahead of the talker, trying to anticipate what the oral discourse is leading to and what conclusions will be drawn from the words spoken at the moment.
2. The listener weighs the evidence used by the talker to support the points that he makes. "Is this evidence valid?" the listener asks himself. "Is it the complete evidence?"
3. Periodically the listener reviews and mentally summarizes the points of the talk completed thus far.
4. Throughout the talk, the listener "listens between the lines" in search of meaning that is not necessarily put into words. He pays attention to nonverbal communication (facial expressions, gestures, tone of voice) to see if it adds meaning to the spoken words. He asks himself, "Is the talker purposely skirting some area of the subject? Why is he doing so?"

The speed at which we think compared to that at which people talk allows plenty of time to accomplish these four mental tasks when we listen; however, they do require practice before they can become part of the mental agility that makes for good listening. In our training courses we have devised aural exercises designed to give people this practice and thereby build up good habits of aural concentration.

## LISTENING FOR IDEAS

Another factor that affects listening ability concerns the reconstruction of orally communicated thoughts once they have been received by the listener. To illustrate:

The newspapers reported not too long ago that a church was torn down in Europe and shipped stone by stone to America, where it was reassembled in its original form. The moving of the church is analogous to what happens when a person speaks and is understood by a listener. The talker has a thought. To transmit his thought, he takes it apart by putting it into words. The words, sent through the air to the listener, must then be mentally reassembled into the original thought if they are to be thoroughly understood. But most people do not know what to listen *for*, and so cannot reconstruct the thought.

For some reason many people take great pride in being able to say that above all they try to "get the facts" when they listen. It seems logical enough to do so. If a person gets all the facts, he should certainly understand what is said to him. Therefore, many people try to memorize every single fact that is spoken. With such practice at "getting the facts," the listener, we can safely assume, will develop a serious bad listening habit.

Memorizing facts is, to begin with, a virtual impossibility for most people in the listening situation. As one fact is being memorized, the whole, or part, of the next fact is almost certain to be missed. When he is doing his very best, the listener is likely to catch only a few facts, garble many others, and completely miss the remainder. Even in the case of people who *can* aurally assimilate all the facts that they hear, one at a time as they hear them, listening is still likely to be at a low level; they are concerned with the pieces of what they hear and tend to miss the broad areas of the spoken communication.

When people talk, they want listeners to understand their *ideas*. The facts are useful chiefly for constructing the ideas. Grasping ideas, we have found, is the skill on which the good listener concentrates. He remembers facts only long enough to understand the ideas that are built from them. But then, almost miraculously, grasping an idea will help the listener to remember the supporting facts more effectively than does the person who goes after facts alone. This listening skill is one which definitely can be taught, one in which people can build experience leading toward improved aural communication.

## EMOTIONAL FILTERS

In different degrees and in many different ways, listening ability is affected by our emotions.[2] Figuratively we reach up and mentally turn off what we do not want to hear. Or, on the other hand, when someone says what we especially want to hear, we open our ears wide, accepting everything—truths, half-truths, or fiction. We might say, then, that our emotions act as aural filters. At times they in effect cause deafness, and at other times they make listening altogether too easy.

If we hear something that opposes our most deeply rooted prejudices, notions, convictions, mores, or complexes, our brains may become overstimulated, and not in a direction that leads to good listening. We mentally plan a rebuttal to what we hear, formulate a question designed to embarrass the talker, or perhaps simply turn to thoughts that support our own feelings on the subject at hand. For example:

The firm's accountant goes to the general manager and says: "I have just heard from the Bureau of Internal Revenue, and . . ." The general manager suddenly breathes harder as he thinks, "That blasted bureau! Can't they leave me alone? Every year the government milks my profits to a point where . . ." Red in the face, he whirls and stares out the window. The label "Bureau of Internal Revenue" cuts loose emotions that stop the general manager's listening.

In the meantime, the accountant may go on to say that there is a chance to save $3,000 this year if the general manager will take a few simple steps. The fuming general manager may hear this—if the accountant presses hard enough—but the chances are he will fail to comprehend it.

When emotions make listening too easy, it usually results from hearing something which supports the deeply rooted inner feelings that we hold. When we hear such support, our mental barriers are dropped and everything is welcomed. We ask few questions about what we hear; our critical faculties are put out of commission by our emotions. Thinking drops to a minimum because we are hearing thoughts that we have harbored for years in support of our inner feelings. It is good to hear someone else think those thoughts, so we lazily enjoy the whole experience.

What can we do about these emotional filters? The solution is not easy in practice, although it can be summed up in this simple admonition: *hear the man out*. Following are two pointers that often help in training people to do this:

1. *Withhold evaluation*—This is one of the most important principles of learning, especially learning through the ear. It requires self-control, sometimes more than many of us can muster, but with persistent practice it can be turned into a valuable habit. While listening, the main object is to comprehend each point made by the talker. Judgments and decisions should be reserved until after the talker has finished. At that time, and only then, review his main ideas and assess them.

2. *Hunt for negative evidence*—When we listen, it is human to go on a militant search for evidence which proves us right in what we believe. Seldom do we make a search for evidence to prove ourselves wrong. The latter type of effort is not easy, for behind its application must lie a generous spirit and real breadth of outlook. However, an important part of listening comprehension is found in the search for negative evidence in what we hear. If we make up our minds to seek out the ideas that might prove us wrong, as well as those that might prove us right, we are less in danger of missing what people have to say.

## Benefits in Business

The improvement of listening, or simply an effort to make people aware of how important their listening ability is, can be of great value in today's business. When people in business fail to hear and understand each other, the results can be costly. Such things as numbers, dates, places, and names are especially easy to confuse, but the most straightforward agreements are often subjects of listening errors, too. When these mistakes are compounded, the resulting cost and inefficiency in business communication become serious. Building awareness of the importance of listening among employees can eliminate a large percentage of this type of aural error.

What are some of the specific problems which better listening can help solve?

## LESS PAPER WORK

For one thing, it leads to economy of communication. Incidents created by poor listening frequently give businessmen a real fear of oral communication. As a result, they insist that more and more communication should be put into writing. A great deal of communication needs to be on the record, but the pressure to write is often carried too far. The smallest detail becomes "memoed." Paper work piles higher and higher and causes part of the tangle we call red tape. Many times less writing and more speaking would be advisable—*if* we could plan on good listening.

Writing and reading are much slower communication elements than speaking and listening. They require more personnel, more equipment, and more space than do speaking and listening. Often a stenographer and a messenger are needed, to say nothing of dictating machines, typewriters, and other writing materials. Few people ever feel it is safe to throw away a written communication; so filing equipment is needed, along with someone to do the filing.

In oral communication there are more human senses at work than in the visual; and if there is good listening, more can often be communicated in one message. And, perhaps most important of all, there is the give-and-take feature of oral communication. If the listener does not understand a message, he has the opportunity to straighten matters out then and there.

## UPWARD COMMUNICATION

The skill of listening becomes extremely important when we talk about "upward communication." There are many avenues through which management can send messages downward through a business organization, but there are few avenues for movement of information in the upward direction. Perhaps the most obvious of the upward avenues is the human chain of people talking to people: the man working at the bench talks to his foreman, the foreman to his superintendent, the superintendent to his boss; and, relayed from person to person, the information eventually reaches the top.

This communication chain has potential, but it seldom works well because it is full of bad listeners. There can be failure for at least three reasons:

> Without good listeners, people do not talk freely and the flow of communication is seldom set in motion.
>
> If the flow should start, only one bad listener is needed to stop its movement toward the top.
>
> Even if the flow should continue to the top, the messages are likely to be badly distorted along the way.

It would be absurd to assume that these upward communication lines could be made to operate without hitches, but there is no reason to think that they cannot be improved by better listening. But the first steps must be taken by top management people. More and better listening on their part can prime the pumps that start the upward flow of information.

## HUMAN RELATIONS

People in all phases of business need to feel free to talk to their superiors and to know they will be met with sympathetic understanding. But too many superiors—although they announce that their doors are always open—fail to listen; and their subordinates, in the face of this failure, do not feel free to say what they want to say. As a result, subordinates withdraw from their superiors more and more. They fail to talk about important problems that should be aired for both parties' benefit. When such problems remain unaired, they often turn into unrealistic monsters that come back to plague the superior who failed to listen.

The remedy for this sort of aural failure—and it should be applied when subordinates feel the need to talk—is what we have called "nondirective listening." The listener hears, really tries to understand, and later shows understanding by taking action if it is required. Above all, during an oral discourse, the listener refrains from firing his own thoughts back at the person talking or from indicating his displeasure or disapproval by his mannerisms or gestures; he speaks up only to ask for clarification of a point.

Since the listener stands the chance of hearing that his most dearly held notions and ideas may be wrong, this is not an easy thing to do. To listen nondirectively without fighting back requires more courage than most of us can muster. But when nondirective listening can be applied, the results are usually worth the effort. The persons talking have a chance to unburden themselves. Equally important, the odds are better that the listener can counsel or act effectively when the time comes to make a move.

Listening is only one phase of human relations, only one aspect of the administrator's job; by itself it will solve no major problems. Yet the past experience of many executives and organizations leaves no doubt, in our opinion, that better listening can lead to a reduction of the human frictions which beset many businesses today.

## LISTENING TO SELL

High-pressure salesmanship is rapidly giving way to low-pressure methods in the marketing of industrial and consumer goods. Today's successful salesman is likely to center his attention on the customer-problem approach to selling.

To put this approach to work, the skill of listening becomes an essential tool for the salesman, while his vocal agility becomes less important. *How* a salesman talks turns out to be relatively unimportant because *what* he says, when it is guided by his listening, gives power to the spoken word. In other words, the salesman's listening becomes an on-the-spot form of customer research that can immediately be put to work in formulating any sales talk.

Regardless of the values that listening may hold for people who live by selling, a great many sales organizations seem to hold to the conviction that glibness has magic. Their efforts at improvement are aimed mainly at the talking side of salesmanship. It is our conviction, however, that with the typical salesman the ability to talk will almost take care of itself, but the ability to listen is something in real need of improvement.

## IN CONFERENCE

The most important affairs in business are conducted around conference tables. A great deal has been said and written about how to talk at a conference, how to compromise, how to get problem-centered, and how to cope with certain types of individuals. All these things can be very important, but too frequently the experts forget to say, "First and foremost you must learn to listen at a conference."

The reason for this is simple when we think of the basic purpose for holding almost any conference. People get together to contribute their different viewpoints, knowledge, and experience to members of the group, which then seeks the best of all the conferees' thinking to solve a common problem. If there is far more talking than listening at a conference, however, the oral contributions made to the group are hardly worth the breath required to produce them.

More and better listening at any conference is certain to facilitate the exchange of ideas so important to the success of a meeting. It also offers many other advantages; for example, when participants do a good job of listening, their conference is more likely to remain centered on the problem at hand and less likely to go off on irrelevant tangents.

The first steps toward improved conference listening can be taken by the group leader. If he will simply make an opening statement calling attention to the importance of listening, he is very likely to increase the participants' aural response. And if the leader himself does a good job of listening, he stands the chance of being imitated by the others in his group.

## Conclusion

Some businessmen may want to take steps to develop a listening improvement program in their companies. Here are 14 suggestions designed to carry on what we hope this article has already started to do—build awareness of listening.

1. Devote an executive seminar, or seminars, to a discussion of the roles and functions of listening as a business tool.

2. Use the filmed cases now becoming available for management training programs.[3] Since these cases present the problem as it would appear in reality, viewers are forced to practice good listening habits in order to be sure of what is going on—and this includes not only hearing the sound track but also watching the facial mannerisms, gestures, and motions of the actors.

3. If possible, bring in qualified speakers and ask them to discuss

listening with special reference to how it might apply to business. Such speakers are available at a number of universities where listening is being taught as a part of communication training.

4. Conduct a self-inventory by the employees regarding their listening on the job. Provide everyone with a simple form divided into spaces for each hour of the day. Each space should be further divided to allow the user to keep track of the amount of time spent in reading, writing, speaking, and listening. Discuss the results of these forms after the communication times have been totaled. What percentage of the time do people spend listening? What might improved listening mean in terms of job effectiveness?

5. Give a test in listening ability to people and show them the scores that they make. There is at least one standardized test for this purpose.[4] Discuss the meaning of the scores with individuals tested.

6. Build up a library of spoken-word records of literature, speeches, and so forth (many can be purchased through record stores), and make them available in a room that has a record player. Also, lend the records to employees who might wish to take them home to enjoy them at their leisure. For such a library, material pertinent to the employees' jobs might be recorded so that those who are interested can listen for educational purposes.

7. Record a number of actual briefing sessions that may be held by plant superintendents or others. When new people go to work for the company, ask them to listen to these sessions as part of their initial training. Check their comprehension of what they hear by means of brief objective tests. Emphasize that this is being done because listening is important on the new jobs.

8. Set up role-playing situations wherein executives are asked to cope with complaints comparable to those that they might hear from subordinates. Ask observers to comment on how well an executive seems to listen. Do his remarks reflect a good job of listening? Does he keep himself from becoming emotionally involved in what the subordinate says? Does the executive listen in a way which would encourage the subordinate to talk freely?

9. Ask salesmen to divide a notebook into sections, one for each customer. After making a call, a salesman should write down all useful information received aurally from the customer. As the information grows, he should refer to it before each return visit to a customer.

10. Where a sales organization has a number of friendly customers, invite some of the more articulate ones to join salesmen in a group discussion of sales techniques. How do the customers feel about talk-

ing and listening on the part of salesmen? Try to get the customers to make listening critiques of salesmen they encounter.

11. In a training session, plan and hold a conference on a selected problem and tape-record it. Afterwards, play back the recording. Discuss it in terms of listening. Do the oral contributions of different participants reflect good listening? If the conference should go off the track, try to analyze the causes in terms of listening.

12. If there is time after a regularly scheduled conference, hold a listening critique. Ask each member to evaluate the listening attention that he received while talking and to report his analysis of his own listening performance.

13. In important management meetings on controversial issues try Irving J. Lee's "Procedure for 'Coercing' Agreement."[5] Under the ground rules for this procedure, which Lee outlined in detail in his article, the chairman calls for a period during which proponents of a hotly debated view can state their position without interruption; the opposition is limited to (a) the asking of questions for clarification; (b) requests for information concerning the peculiar characteristics of the proposal being considered; and (c) requests for information as to whether it is possible to check the speakers' assumptions or predictions.

14. Sponsor a series of lectures for employees, their families, and their friends. The lectures might be on any number of interesting topics that have educational value as well as entertainment features. Point out that these lectures are available as part of a listening improvement program.

Not all of these suggestions are applicable to every situation, of course. Each firm will have to adapt them to its own particular needs. The most important thing, however, may not be what happens when a specific suggestion is followed, but rather simply what happens when people become aware of the problem of listening and of what improved aural skills can do for their jobs and their businesses.

## Notes

1. See E.J. Kramar and Thomas R. Lewis, "Comparison of Visual and Nonvisual Listening," *Journal of Communication*, November 1951, p. 16; and Arthur W. Heilman, "An Investigation in Measuring and

Improving Listening Ability of College Freshmen," *Speech Monographs*, November 1951, p. 308.

2. See Wendell Johnson, "The Fateful Process of Mr. A Talking to Mr. B," *Harvard Business Review*, January–February 1953, p. 49.

3. See George W. Gibson, "The Filmed Case in Management Training," *Harvard Business Review*, May–June 1957, p. 123.

4. Brown-Carlsen Listening Comprehension Test (Yonkers-on-Hudson, World Book Company).

5. *Harvard Business Review*, January–February 1954, p. 39.

# 3
# ABCs of Job Interviewing

## James M. Jenks and Brian L.P. Zevnik

Your organization is looking over several candidates for a vacancy in its managerial ranks, and you have the final say in the decision. You are getting ready to interview the applicants.

Are you well prepared for this task? Poorly conducted interviews can come back to haunt you—you may hire someone who doesn't work out or reject someone with star potential. Or in these litigious days, you may risk being slapped with a lawsuit and hauled into court.

Unlike your human resources people, you interview applicants only occasionally. You don't catch that duty often enough to hone your skills. The candidates themselves are likely to be more adroit than you. Often they have received careful instructions from the recruiting firms that sent them your way. Recent experience on the job trail may have taught them all the right things to ask and say.

Then there are the personal attributes that you bring to the interview. The aggressive characteristics that helped put you in an executive position also put obstacles in your way to becoming an expert interviewer—learning how to ask, to watch, and to listen. The take-charge attitude of many top executives makes it hard for them to keep their ears open and mouths shut—two critical characteristics of the expert interviewer.

On the other hand, you know the job and the qualities you're looking for. Furthermore, your concern over having a good fit between individual and organization is your greatest advantage: with the proper preparation, it will give you an edge in the interview.

## Prepping for the Interviews

Before the interviews begin, write out a job profile based on the job description. The purpose is to translate duties and responsibilities into the personal characteristics the manager must have to do the job.

Take the job description for a national sales manager for a life insurance company. One duty is, "Reviews data to calculate sales potential and customer desires and to recommend prices and policies to meet sales goals." From that you distill these requirements for your profile: powers of analysis, managerial skills, commitment. Another duty, "Prepares periodic sales reports showing potential sales and actual results," calls for skill in writing and in oral communication.

Now you get down to specifics. For every duty or responsibility, you list the characteristics or qualities your candidate must possess to do the job. For instance, regarding powers of analysis: "Finds information in such publications as *Insurance and Tax News* and interprets it to show how sales agents can use tax law changes to sell life insurance policies." And concerning written communication: "Writes copy for advertising department to prepare new sales brochures for agents describing benefits of various types of life insurance for young singles, young newly marrieds, and mature empty nesters."

Naturally, you'll find that many requirements for different jobs are alike. Your human resources department can help in determining the most important characteristics and otherwise preparing you for the interviews.

Once you've listed the job requirements, put them in black and white: prepare a written interview guide. Using such a guide doesn't mean that you lack verbal facility, smoothness in meeting people, or deftness in leading a discussion; rather, it contributes substantially to a wise assessment of applicants with whom you must go one-on-one. Here is a checklist of items as a basis for an interview guide:

Consult the applicant's resume and application for jobs, experience, accomplishments that are most relevant to your job requirements.

Plan questions touching on the qualities you are looking for. In the interviews with applicants for insurance company national sales manager, if you know that a candidate indeed reads journals like *Insurance and Tax News*, you might probe: "Tell me how you've interpreted information from such publications for sales purposes."

Prepare a step-by-step scenario of how to present the position.

Do the same for your company, division, and department.

Seek examples of behavior by focusing on what the applicant has done, not on what he or she might do. Of the life insurance sales manager applicant, you might ask: "Can you show me samples of brochures, sales letters, or articles you've developed?"

An interview guide will help you to be consistent and focused in your questioning, thus ensuring each applicant a fair shake, steering you clear of improper questions, and preventing you from putting applicants on the defensive. Moreover, an interview guide keeps you in control of the conversation.

## Past Performance

It has long been established that a person's past behavior is the surest guide to future performance. To determine an applicant's fit with the people in your company (including you) requires questions that uncover personality characteristics.

How can you make a judgment as to whether an applicant will do the job and fit in well? You are looking for a particular kind of behavior for every critical requirement you've listed for the job. The question to keep in mind is, What has this candidate done in the past to meet these requirements? So make a list of questions that are relevant to your concerns about them.

The following examples illustrate the kinds of questions that reveal willingness to do the job as well as style and personality:

*Your concern*: In this era of DINK (double income, no kids) couples, you may wonder about the prospective employee's motivation to work. Will this person put in the hours necessary to get the job done?

*Faulty question*: "Is your spouse employed?"

*Comment*: Such a question makes for amiable conversation, but it doesn't meet your concern. It has little to do with the candidate's motivation to work.

*Improved questions*: "Can you tell me about any project you had to tackle where you had to meet a hard deadline? What did you do to get the work out on time?"

When the individual you seek is one who can make an appreciable difference in the company, simply meeting the position's technical qualifications is not enough. You're not just filling a slot, you're hiring someone who is flexible, who will do what the job requires.

*Your concern*: How well this candidate will meet the demands of the position.

*Faulty question*: "Did you ever drop the ball on your last job and get bawled out by your boss?"

*Comment*: There are several problems with this question. For one thing, it can be answered with a single word—"yes" or "no." And a single-word answer (whichever it is) does nothing to get at your concern. Secondly, you're asking for a confession of failure, which is difficult for anyone to make. Finally, the question is unrelated to any requirement of the position and therefore gives you no behavioral matches.

*Improved question*: "Tell me about a task you took on in your previous job that would prepare you for handling the requirements we're discussing here."

Naturally, you want to consider how well the applicant will get along with colleagues as well as top executives—if the job opening is at a high level.

*Your concern*: How well the candidate will fit in your organization.

*Faulty questions*: "You need a lot of personal PR in this position. Do you get along well with people? What clubs do you belong to?"

*Comment*: No matter how strong the candidates or how expert in their fields, if they don't work well in your particular environment, they'll fail. Some interviewers ask about hobbies and clubs to ascertain fit. But such questions stray into irrelevant areas. What does being a good tennis player have to do with getting along with peers or superiors?

*Improved question*: "Tell me about any incident in your last job that caused a conflict with another manager; what did you do to smooth things out?"

Assessment of how well candidates have mastered human relations skills is difficult. Interviewers often ask questions about activities that are at best only dimly connected to the position's requirements.

*Your concern*: On paper, your candidate for a professional position is well qualified. But the person selected will also direct a staff that includes several supervisors, so you need to find a candidate with good people-managing skills.

*Faulty question*: "What do you do on your own time, say, with clubs, associations, or groups of people?"

*Comment*: This question is designed to find out if the candidate is congenial and well rounded, but it promises to uncover nothing valuable about the candidate's behavior.

*Improved questions*: "We all run into instances where two people disagree on how to get a job done. Can you tell me how you handled a particular argument or disagreement about operations that came up among the people you managed in your last job? How about disputes between colleagues?"

## Wrong and Right Tacks

Doing your homework thoroughly will help you maintain control of the dialogue and avoid pitfalls that interviewers often run into. Here are some "don'ts" in the art of interviewing.

Don't telegraph the response you're seeking. Suppose you are exploring the candidate's ability to work with departments that he or she would have no control over. "Do you think you'll be able to get cooperation from managers in other areas of the company?" you ask. The applicant smoothly replies, "No problem. I get along with everybody."

Your question not only allows a sharp interviewee to give you the response you want to hear but also gives you zero help in finding out what you really want to know. We suggest something like: "Tell me about a time when you had to gain the cooperation of a group you had no authority over. What did you do?"

Don't get defensive if an interviewee directs a tough question right back at you. You may be concerned, for example, about the person's steady availability. So you ask, "Do you have any small children at home?" She replies easily, "I think you'll agree that my experience and education clearly show I'm qualified. I'm not at all sure why you asked that question. Can you explain?" The applicant has neatly lobbed the ball back into your court and put you on the defensive. (And since the question is rarely asked of males, it borders on illegality anyway.) (See "Shooting the Rapids.")

## Shooting the Rapids

The principle of fairness in employment, which has become the law of the land, does not ignore the seemingly straightforward job interview. Not only must you be sure that your hiring practices conform to legal specs but you must also take great care in your questions.

The dangerous questions aren't those that reflect overt discrimination. In any case, the law and its enforcers are more concerned with the effects of employers' actions than with their intentions. The dangerous questions are those meant to discover something interviewers *think* they need to know, something it would be *nice* to know, or even something intended to put the applicant at ease, like questions about family or nationality.

Executives ask irrelevant questions because they reason that the information may be useful should the job seeker become an employee. Questions that can be asked after hire, concerning age and marital status, for example, may be illegal during pre-employment interviews. (Technically, a question by itself usually isn't illegal. It's when the answers are improperly used that the *gendarmes* swarm in.)

Suppose an executive asks a female applicant this seemingly innocuous question: "What kind of work does your husband do?" He wants to put her at ease and at the same time get an inkling about how long the candidate might want to stay on the job. But the question is patently discriminatory because it is seldom asked of males. Moreover, it is irrelevant to the job requirements or the person's qualifications.

Our society seems intent on using the courts as the first resort, not the last, to redress suffering. Corporations and executives are being dragged into court with dismaying frequency, and juries are awarding enormous sums—even into the millions—against both "deep pockets" corporations and individual executives.

The key to preventing discrimination claims lies in one simple policy. If a question is not directly related to the hiring decision and relevant to the job, don't ask it.

A better approach would be: "I don't know if you're aware of this, but we need managers at your level to be at work by 8 A.M. At unscheduled times each month, you'll have to come to executive committee meetings beginning at 5 P.M. and lasting several hours. How do you feel about that kind of unpredictable schedule?"

Don't get into a joust. Some people revel in one-upmanship or competitive tilting. You wonder whether this candidate is willing to work what are usually leisure hours to complete projects within deadline, so you ask, "Would you work weekends and holidays when necessary?" Your applicant fires back, "Absolutely. I can keep up with anybody else's schedule."

Implicit in this thrust is the claim that he or she can do anything you can do. Feel your hackles rising? Avoid that kind of behavior with straightforward business questions. Keep your feelings in check and your combativeness on a short leash. A better tack would be, "How do you plan your week's activities? Tell me what you do in your current job when you can't meet your planned schedule."

Finally, don't get uptight if the applicant gets uptight. You control the situation, it's your show. Part of your job is to make the interview an informative meeting, not a trip to the dentist's chair. Remember too that part of your task is to sell your organization to a top-notch candidate. You do that with convincing descriptions of the position, the opportunities, and the organization itself; also by how you come across—natural, prepared, professional. Furthermore, if you get uptight, you're liable to do too much talking and not enough listening.

Hiring is like a contest, especially when you're engaging skillful players who are the kind you always want on your managerial team. Choosing the right applicants for important management slots is a key to achieving exceptional results for you and your company. Behavioral-match, performance-oriented questions, buttressed by careful preparation, give you the best chance of finding talented candidates who will do more than just fill those slots well.

# 4
# How to Meet the Press

**Chester Burger**

Why cannot business find a way to tell its story through the news media? Is the press really dominated by hostile, anti-establishment reporters? Are leftist editors biting the business hand that feeds them?

Many corporate spokesmen are convinced that today's news media, or at least their young reporters, are imbued with a fundamental bias against business.

Journalist Edith Efron believes, for example, that American newsmen are hostile to business, to capitalism itself. Referring specifically to television, she writes: "The antagonism to capitalism on the nation's airwaves, the deeply entrenched prejudice in favor of state control over the productive machinery of the nation, is not a subjective assessment. It is a hard cultural fact."

That, however, is an assessment with which one can reasonably disagree. As NBC commentator David Brinkley reminds us, "When a reporter asks questions, he is not working for the person being questioned, whether businessman, politician, or bureaucrat, but he is working for the readers and listeners."

If indeed the working press, reporters, and correspondents bear an antibusiness animosity, opinion polls tell us that such attitudes are quite representative of public opinion generally in the United States today. Rather than dismissing newsmen and news media as hostile, these may be the very ones to whom business ought to increase its communication, because they typify the attitudes of millions of Americans.

Further, while the corporate president often finds his life and circle

of personal contacts circumscribed within the territory of his management team, his luncheon club, and his country club, the working
reporter's duties bring him into daily contact with broad strata of the
population, ranging from politicians to factory workers and activist
leaders. He cannot be dismissed lightly. Nor should he be written off.

So it would seem essential for corporate presidents and spokesmen
to learn how to tell their stories effectively to the press, radio, and
television reporters. But there is more to it than that. Unless one
knows how to tell what CBS commentator Eric Sevareid calls "the
simple truth," one may fail to communicate. Although businessmen
are as intelligent as members of the working press, they are unskilled
in the art of effective communication.

As Bos Johnson, president of the Radio-Television News Directors
Association, says, "Businessmen are often so frightened or wary of the
reporters that they come across looking suspicious. And there's no
reason to be. They should put their best foot forward, speak out
candidly, assuming they have nothing to hide."

A corporate president is not chosen for his outstanding ability to
articulate corporate problems. He is selected by his board of directors
because of his management know-how, or his financial expertise, or
his legal proficiency, or whatever particular combination of these talents may be required by the immediate problems facing the company.
In utilizing his own skills, he is usually very good indeed.

But the skills of management are not the same as those required to
deal with the news media. Reporters, whether they are employed by
television (where most people get their news these days), newspapers,
magazines, or radio are trained in the skills of interviewing. They excel
in their ability to talk with someone and unearth a newsworthy story,
one that will stimulate their viewers or readers. That is why they were
selected; that is their surpassing talent; and that is precisely what
unnerves corporate managers who choose to face their questions.

The elaborate files of newspapers and the film and tape libraries of
television stations are replete with examples of boners, indiscretions,
and insensitive statements voiced by corporate spokesmen. My own
experience, first as a television network news executive and later as a
management consultant, convinces me that there is no more mysteri-
ous reason for management's failure to communicate effectively with
the news media than that it simply does not know how.

Businessmen, rarely fearful of meeting their stockholders or their
bankers, tremble before the newsman for fear he will accidentally or
deliberately misquote them or pull their words out of context.

This can indeed happen, and it occasionally does. But every reporter knows that if he sins or errs more than once or twice, his job will be endangered. Newspapers do not like to print corrections of their errors—only a few do—but editors like even less to see errors break into print or be broadcast on radio or television.

The problem usually is not with the reporters. They try to get things straight. More and more these days, in fact, they are showing up for interviews armed with cassette tape recorders. This is an encouraging trend for the businessman because it ensures more accurate quotation. It also frees the newsman from the note-taking burden so that he can concentrate on the subject under discussion.

But a recorded interview is hell for the executive who says the wrong things. If he puts his foot in his mouth, his words will be quotable and, most likely, quoted. No longer will he be able to blame the reporter for misquotation.

Business managers know from experience that newsmen will not hesitate to cover (i.e., write or film) a story that may be damaging to their company. From this perception, it is easy to conclude that the reporters are basically hostile to business. However, management often fails to understand that the reporter's first responsibility is to produce a newsworthy story that will interest his audience. The reporter frankly does not care whether that "public interest story" will help or hinder the company. The reporter will select, from his bag of techniques, whatever method he believes will produce an interesting and informative story.

So the lesson is clear: if the corporate executive has something to say, he must present it to the reporter in an interesting way. A skilled reporter, hot on the trail of a noteworthy story, uses standard techniques to get it. Businessmen ought to know what these techniques are, and to decide that it is worth the effort to learn to cope with them. Kerryn King, Texaco's senior vice president–public affairs, put it sharply and well when he told a recent public relations conference:

Industry, and especially the petroleum industry, has an urgent need to dispel its reputation for secrecy and its reputation for indifference to public opinion that this supposed secrecy implies. I believe that when you once lay the full facts before a journalist, he is less likely to be taken in by critics who know less about your business than he does.

The more information you can get out, the more light you can shed, especially on misunderstood economic matters, the better your standing with the public, in my opinion.

A principal reason that people become frightened during a crisis is misinformation or noninformation. That is what moves them to action, whether that action be violence or demands for nationalization.

## The Rules of the "Game"

Rather than abandon the field to misinformation, it is better to learn the rules of critics, journalistic or otherwise. These guidelines are simple, and they can be learned. Hundreds, and probably several thousand corporate managers have learned them. They have discovered that when you know the rules of the reporter's "game," you can communicate your story effectively and truthfully, with no post-mortems necessary.

For the businessman to be successful in speaking with press or public, there are two general criteria and ten specific guidelines to learn and remember. I shall present these respectively in the balance of this article.

### GENERAL CRITERIA

First, it is necessary to have a sound attitude. That attitude is not one of either arrogance or false humility. Rather, it is an attitude in which the business executive respects his own competence and greater knowledge of his own subject, but realistically recognizes that the reporter or critic is skilled in the art of asking provocative questions, hopefully to elicit provocative, interesting, and perhaps controversial answers.

Second, it is always wise to prepare carefully for a press interview. Never should an executive walk into a meeting with the press, planning to "play it by ear" (i.e., to improvise). Preparation is essential. The best preparation consists of anticipating the most likely questions, attempting to research the facts, and structuring effective answers to be held ready for use. Probably it is unwise to carry such notes into the interview. It would be better instead to have the answers well in mind, although not literally memorized.

**SPECIFIC GUIDELINES**

Let us now turn to the ten specific rules of effective communication found most useful by corporate executives.

1. *Talk from the viewpoint of the public's interest, not the company's.*

This important rule presents difficulties for most corporate presidents and senior executives. Their difficulty is understandable. When you have spent years struggling to manage the company, it is difficult to step back and look at your problem and your own company from a different perspective.

For example, often during negotiations for a new union contract, corporate spokesmen will tell the press, in effect, "We can't afford the increase the union is asking." That may be true, but why should the public be concerned with the company's financial problems? Employees often respond with hostility and resentment. It is much better to say, "We'd like to give our employees the increase they seek. But if our costs go up too much, our customers won't buy. That will hurt us, and in the end, it will endanger our employees' jobs."

Or an electric utility challenged, say, on its policy of requiring deposits from new customers, may respond, since it is a truthful answer, "We don't like to ask for deposits because they annoy our customers; they're a nuisance to us. Also, we have to pay interest on the money.

"But we don't think it fair that you should have to pay part of someone else's electric bill when he fails to pay. And that's just what happens: the cost of his service is passed along to all other users. If a new customer pays his bills promptly for six months, we refund his deposit, and we're glad to do it."

Sometimes, in their efforts to present their story from the public viewpoint, companies seem to assume the pose of philanthropic institutions. They claim to be acting in and serving the public interest in whatever course of action they are following. And indeed this may be true.

But to a skeptical public, such talk falls on unhearing ears. The public knows, or believes, that a company primarily acts in its own self-interest. When this self-interest is not frankly admitted, credibility is endangered.

So it is desirable always to indicate your company's position in a given course of action. The soft-drink bottler who launches a campaign for collecting and recycling of its containers can frankly admit that it does not want to irritate the public by having its product's packaging strewn across the landscape. Because this is the truth, the public will find the entire story of the company's environmental efforts more credible.

Every industry has its own language, its own terminology. When a corporate spokesman uses company lingo, he knows exactly what he means. But the public generally does not. So speak in terms the ordinary citizen can understand.

Instead of saying, "Our management is considering whether to issue equity or debt," it might be better to say, "We are considering whether to sell more stock in our company, or to try to borrow money by issuing bonds."

*2. Speak in personal terms whenever possible.*

Any corporation, even one of modest size, involves many people in decision making and other activities. So corporate executives early in their careers learn never to say "I," but rather "we" or "the company."

When dozens or a hundred people have worked on developing a new product or adopting a new policy, it becomes difficult if not impossible for anyone connected with the project to say "I." Yet the words "the company" or "we" only reinforce the public image of corporations as impersonal monoliths in which no one retains his individuality or has any individual responsibility.

To avoid reinforcing this impression, if an executive has participated in a project he is proud of, he should be encouraged to speak in the first person and to reflect that pride. For example, "I was one of the team that worked on this product. My job involved the product design." Of course, it is wrong to claim personal credit where it has not been earned. But the top executive who can speak in terms of his personal experience will always make a favorable impression.

Executives sometimes even hesitate to use the term "we" because they are reluctant to speak officially on behalf of the company. Unless they have been properly authorized by management, their reluctance is justified. But when middle-level or even lower-level managers have been carefully briefed and know the answers to the questions under discussion, they often make quite effective company spokesmen.

One telephone company, for example, invited its chief operators to speak to the press on its behalf in small communities where their position had considerable esteem. In this case, if a chief operator discussed local matters within her range of responsibility, such as changes in local telephone rates, she would provide considerable credibility. The press and public would rightfully assume she knew from personal involvement what she was talking about. But if she were to discuss overall corporate financing, obviously her credibility would vanish.

3. *If you do not want some statement quoted, do not make it.*

Corporate spokesmen should avoid "off-the-record" statements. There is no such thing as "off the record." If a company president tells something to a reporter off the record, it may not be used with his name attached. But it may well turn up in the same published article, minus his name, and with a qualifying phrase added, "Meanwhile, it has been learned from other sources that. . . ." The damage is done.

Therefore, an experienced company officer quickly learns that if he does not want something published or used, he should not divulge it to the reporter on any basis. And although naive company officials sometimes assume that an invisible line divides informal conversation from the beginning of the formal interview, no such dividing line exists in the reporter's mind. What is said may be used, either directly or as a basis for further probing elsewhere.

The same off-the-record rule applies to telephone conversations with the media: whether or not you hear a beep, your words may be recorded. A recording makes it impossible for you to deny later what the reporter has taped in your own voice.

4. *State the most important fact at the beginning.*

Years of training and experience, often without conscious thought, have accustomed the typical corporate executive to respond to questions in a particular way. If the executive is asked, "What should we do about our new product?" he will frequently respond along these lines, "We are facing shortages of plastics. And their cost is rising so fast I don't think we can price the product at an attractive level. Moreover, we have a labor shortage in the plant. So I recommend we don't take any action now to develop the product."

The executive's format lists the facts that lead to his final conclusion and recommendation. But such organization of his material will fail when it is used in talking with the news media. There are both psychological and technical reasons why.

Psychologically, we tend to remember most clearly the first thing that is said, not the last. So when you speak to a reporter, you should turn your statement around to begin with the conclusion, "We don't plan to develop the product. We are facing materials shortages. Our costs are going up, and we also have a shortage of skilled labor." In such a reverse format, the most important statement is likely to be best remembered: "We don't plan to develop the new product."

Technical considerations in printing and production are also an important reason for giving your conclusion first. The newspaper reporter who writes the story seldom knows in advance how much space will be available for its publication. So he has been trained to put the most important fact at the beginning, using subsequent paragraphs to report items of declining importance. If the most important fact is buried at the bottom of the story, it may simply be chopped off in the composing room to fit the available space.

On television, time pressures and broadcast deadlines often make it impossible to screen all filmed material for selection of the best footage; frequently, program producers or news editors are compelled to select segments from the beginning of a film. So, I repeat, the most important fact should be stated first. Afterward, it can be explained at whatever length is necessary; but even if the full explanation is cut, the initial statement will survive.

5. *Do not argue with the reporter or lose your cool.*

Understand that the newsman seeks an interesting story and will use whatever techniques he needs to obtain it. An executive cannot win an argument with the reporter in whose power the published story lies. Since the executive has initially allowed himself to be interviewed, he should use the interview as an opportunity to answer questions in a way that will present his story fairly and adequately.

If a reporter interrupts the executive, it is not rudeness; it is a deliberate technique that means he is not satisfied with the corporate response he is hearing. The solution is for the executive to respond more directly and more clearly.

An executive should never ask questions of the reporter out of his own anger and frustration. I remember the following example:

Reporter: How many black executives do you have in your company?

Executive: [Irritated] Damn it, how many black editors do you have on your paper?

Reporter: I'm here to ask *you* the questions.

An executive may occasionally win the battle with that sort of tactic, but he will always lose the war. The reporter, not the executive, will write the story. The published interview will reflect the reporter's own hostility.

6. *If a question contains offensive language or simply words you do not like, do not repeat them, even to deny them.*

Reporters often use the gambit of putting words into the subject's mouth. It is easy. Politicians do it, too. The technique works like this: the reporter includes colorful, provocative language in his question. For example, "Mr. Jones, wouldn't you describe your oil company's profits this year as a bonanza?" If Mr. Jones bites, he will answer, "No, our profits are not a bonanza."

When Senator Abraham Ribicoff asked a similar question during the 1974 Senate Committee hearings, President Harry Bridges of Shell Oil Company (USA) was trapped. That is exactly how he did answer. And his answer was headlined "Oil Profits No Bonanza, Executive Says." Even though Bridges denied the charge, in the public's mind he associated the word "oil profits" with "bonanza." He might have answered the question this way: "Senator, our profits aren't high enough. To build more refineries and increase oil supply, we're going to need to earn much more money."

Most executives have never noticed, but the reporter knows well that his questions will not be quoted in his article; only the interviewee's answers will be. It is not important, therefore, whether a reporter asks a question loaded with hostile and inaccurate language; the important thing is how the question is answered. As long as an executive does not repeat the offensive language, even to deny it, it will not appear in the published report.

On some occasions, overzealous reporters have even been known, with dubious ethics, to ask an executive to comment on a so-called fact, which may be an outright untruth. The quoted "fact" has the ring of plausibility.

For example, one reporter asked a plant manager, *"Ecology Magazine* says your plant is one of the worst polluters in this state. Would you care to comment on that?"

The manager immediately became defensive and insisted to the reporter that his plant did not really pollute too badly, considering all the other sources of pollution in the local river. The manager did not know that no magazine called *Ecology* exists. The false quotation had been manufactured by the reporter. But it served its purpose. It put the manager on the defensive and induced him to talk. The reporter's false "quotation" was never published.

If you are asked a question based on a "fact" about which you are uncertain, be wary of a trap. The so-called fact may indeed be a fact, but if you are not sure, it is better to dissociate yourself from it. You might say, "I'm not familiar with that quotation," and then proceed to answer the question in your own positive way.

*7. If the reporter asks a direct question, he is entitled to an equally direct answer.*

Sometimes, executives who have been interviewed complain afterward that they answered all the questions the reporter asked, but that they never got a chance to make their points in a positive way. They fail to make the points they wanted to make, and then they blame the reporter. Usually, it is their own fault. They have been playing what is called the "ping-pong game." The reporter asks a question; they answer it. He asks another; they answer it. Back and forth the ball bounces, but the executive does not know how to squeeze in what he regards as *his* important points.

This common error in dealing with the press is one the executive is particularly prone to make. Management training accustoms executives to answer questions directly, without undue amplification. Such conduct is appropriate when talking with the boss, but it is inappropriate when talking with a reporter. Here amplification is often in order.

Corporate officers incorrectly assume that they somehow protect themselves by giving simple yes or no answers to questions. Their theory is that the less said, the better. The yes or no answer is not, however, interesting to a reporter. Usually, he will react by provoking the executive in the hope of obtaining a more informative and colorfully expressed response.

This rule is not intended to suggest that an executive answer with either evasion or wordiness. But interviewees should not stop with a one-word response. Instead, they should amplify the point until they have said what they want to say.

For example, suppose a reporter asks, "Aren't you still polluting the air and river?" The answer should be positive and broad, rather than simply "No." A factory manager might respond, "Protecting the environment in Jonesville concerns us greatly. We've eliminated the major sources of pollution. The smoke from our factories is gone; we spent $3 million to purify the exhaust fumes from our furnaces. We've added filters to remove waste from water that flows back into the river. But we still haven't solved the problem of cooling our waste water, and we are working hard on that."

8. *If an executive does not know the answer to a question, he should simply say, "I don't know, but I'll find out for you."*

His response does not make the executive look ignorant. Nor is his lack of knowledge newsworthy. Even in an interview filmed for television, such an answer would find itself "on the cutting room floor."

However, if the executive replies simply, "I don't know," it might appear to the reporter or viewer that he is being evasive. So executives are advised never to answer "I don't know" alone, but always to qualify the answer with a phrase like, "I'll put you in touch with someone else who can answer that for you," or similar words. Of course, the executive then assumes the responsibility of following through to ensure that the requested information is provided promptly.

Occasionally, a reporter will ask a question which the executive does not wish to answer. There may be a legal reason, say, because the company is in registration in connection with a new securities issue. Or the requested information may be a proprietary company secret. In such circumstances, the recommended course is to respond directly, without evasion or excuses, "I'm sorry. I can't give you that information."

However, if the question seems appropriate, and it usually is, it is desirable to explain to the reporter why his question cannot be answered. Executives are cautioned never to "play dumb," deny knowledge, or give anything other than a forthright refusal.

9. *Tell the truth, even if it hurts.*

In this era of skepticism, hostility, and challenge, the fact remains that the most difficult task of all sometimes is simply telling the truth. This rule can be embarrassing for the executive and the company.

Neither individuals nor corporations (groups of individuals) like to be embarrassed. So to avoid embarrassment, they sometimes tell the press and public half-truths (which are half-lies).

Understandably, nobody likes to admit that business is bad, that employees must be laid off, that a new product introduction has been unsuccessful, that the company has "goofed" in one way or another. Yet telling the truth remains the best answer.

How much truth should a company tell? My experience answers, "As much as the reporter wants to know." When an executive change is announced, probably 99 out of 100 reporters will be satisfied with that bare fact, and ask nothing more. But once in a while a keen reporter may respond, "Mr. Jones, I've heard that you held Mr. Smith responsible for the severe drop in earnings your company had last year. Is that true?"

First of all, if the allegation were true, I would not deny it; denial would only lead to a loss of credibility later when the reporter confirmed it from another source. But neither would I invite a libel suit from Mr. Smith by blaming him for the company's problems. So the question might be answered, factually but tactfully, "When economic conditions are difficult, companies frequently make management changes and that's what we've done."

Executives, already fearful of the power of the press, find themselves terrified at the thought of having to report bad tidings. Countless examples can be found in the business press of attempts to conceal, or to grudgingly admit only portions of the truth, when it is unfavorable to the company.

My experience, however, convinces me that while the press and public do not like to hear bad news and will judge the company or its management adversely because of it, fair-minded people will understand that the difficulties of management make unavoidable a certain number of errors in judgment. Thoughtful people understand that no one is perfect; that each of us makes errors despite his or her best judgments and best efforts.

What the public will not understand or tolerate, however, is dishonesty. Concealment and lying will be neither forgotten nor forgiven by the press and public alike. Evidence exists to confirm this. An example can be found in the aviation industry.

In earlier years, whenever a commercial airliner crashed, certain airlines had standing policies to rush work crews to the site and to paint out the company name and emblems on the wrecked aircraft before photographs were permitted.

Today, that policy has changed. Most carriers currently cooperate fully with the media, furnish all available information, and provide all assistance needed for news coverage. The theory, and I believe it is the correct one, is that the crash will be reported anyway; the name of the airline will be headlined anyway; so it is better to cooperate with the press and get the story covered and forgotten as quickly as possible.

10. *Do not exaggerate the facts.*

The American Bakers Association may have done just that. The president of the Public Relations Society of America, James F. Fox of New York, commented in a 1974 speech:

> Last winter, we heard a great deal about an imminent wheat shortage and bread at a dollar a loaf this spring. Well, spring has about two weeks to go; the cost of wheat is down a little, and bread is nowhere near one dollar a loaf. What was that all about? Under Secretary of Agriculture J. Phil Campbell suggested that the bakers' move to reinstitute stockpiling was motivated by the desire to have government maintain wheat reserves to carry inventory for the industry and lower its costs.
>
> I don't know whether that's the whole story or even a part of it. It isn't necessary that we settle the facts here; whether, as Campbell implies, the industry's self-interest overcame its discretion, or it was depending in good faith on bad information or inadequate projections.
>
> What does concern us is that the American Bakers Association looks a little foolish now. It's going to be that much harder for them to make themselves heard and believed next time, when they might just be right.

Telling the business story to an apathetic or hostile nation is not easy, but it is worth doing, and it can be done successfully. As one senior executive in an engineering company told me:

> I've been interviewed frequently over the past 20 years, and every time afterward, I felt sorry for myself. But now, I realize that I just didn't know the rules of the reporter's game. Since I started playing the game too, I've had a much better press. In one case, I even got a sympathetic newspaper editorial in one of our plant communities, where we always used to get clobbered. It's convinced me to look on a press interview as an opportunity, rather than as a cause for fear.

# PART

# III

# Managing Successful Meetings

# 1
# How to Run a Meeting

Antony Jay

Why have a meeting anyway? Why indeed? A great many important matters are quite satisfactorily conducted by a single individual
who consults nobody. A great many more are resolved by a letter, a
memo, a phone call, or a simple conversation between two people.
Sometimes five minutes spent with six people separately is more
effective and productive than a half-hour meeting with them all together.

Certainly a great many meetings waste a great deal of everyone's
time and seem to be held for historical rather than practical reasons;
many long-established committees are little more than memorials to
dead problems. It would probably save no end of managerial time if
every committee had to discuss its own dissolution once a year, and
put up a case if it felt it should continue for another twelve months.
If this requirement did nothing else, it would at least refocus the minds
of the committee members on their purposes and objectives.

But having said that, and granting that "referring the matter to a
committee" can be a device for diluting authority, diffusing responsibility, and delaying decisions, I cannot deny that meetings fulfill a deep
human need. Man is a social species. In every organization and every
human culture of which we have record, people come together in
small groups at regular and frequent intervals, and in larger "tribal"
gatherings from time to time. If there are no meetings in the places
where they work, people's attachment to the organizations they work
for will be small, and they will meet in regular formal or informal
gatherings in associations, societies, teams, clubs, or pubs when work
is over.

This need for meetings is clearly something more positive than just a legacy from our primitive hunting past. From time to time, some technomaniac or other comes up with a vision of the executive who never leaves his home, who controls his whole operation from an all-electronic, multichannel, microwave, fiber-optic video display dream console in his living room. But any manager who has ever had to make an organization work greets this vision with a smile that soon stretches into a yawn.

There is a world of science fiction, and a world of human reality; and those who live in the world of human reality know that it is held together by face-to-face meetings. A meeting still performs functions that will never be taken over by telephones, teleprinters, Xerox copiers, tape recorders, television monitors, or any other technological instruments of the information revolution.

## Functions of a Meeting

At this point, it may help us understand the meaning of meetings if we look at the six main functions that meetings will always perform better than any of the more recent communication devices:

1. In the simplest and most basic way, a meeting defines the team, the group, or the unit. Those present belong to it; those absent do not. Everyone is able to look around and perceive the whole group and sense the collective identity of which he or she forms a part. We all know who we are—whether we are on the board of Universal International, in the overseas sales department of Flexitube, Inc., a member of the school management committee, on the East Hampton football team, or in Section No. 2 of Platoon 4, Company B.

2. A meeting is the place where the group revises, updates, and adds to what it knows *as a group*. Every group creates its own pool of shared knowledge, experience, judgment, and folklore. But the pool consists only of what the individuals have experienced or discussed as a group—i.e., those things which every individual knows that all the others know, too. This pool not only helps all members to do their jobs more intelligently, but it also greatly increases the speed and efficiency of all communications among them. The group knows that all special nuances and wider implications in a brief statement will be immediately clear to its members. An enormous amount of material can be left unsaid that would have to be made explicit to an outsider.

But this pool needs constant refreshing and replenishing, and occasionally the removal of impurities. So the simple business of exchanging information and ideas that members have acquired separately or in smaller groups since the last meeting is an important contribution to the strength of the group. By questioning and commenting on new contributions, the group performs an important "digestive" process that extracts what's valuable and discards the rest.

Some ethologists call this capacity to share knowledge and experience among a group "the social mind," conceiving it as a single mind dispersed among a number of skulls. They recognize that this "social mind" has a special creative power, too. A group of people meeting together can often produce better ideas, plans, and decisions than can a single individual, or a number of individuals, each working alone. The meeting can of course also produce worse outputs or none at all, if it is a bad meeting.

However, when the combined experience, knowledge, judgment, authority, and imagination of a half dozen people are brought to bear on issues, a great many plans and decisions are improved and sometimes transformed. The original idea that one person might have come up with singly is tested, amplified, refined, and shaped by argument and discussion (which often acts on people as some sort of chemical stimulant to better performance), until it satisfies far more requirements and overcomes many more objections than it could in its original form.

3. A meeting helps every individual understand both the collective aim of the group and the way in which his own and everyone else's work can contribute to the group's success.

4. A meeting creates in all present a commitment to the decisions it makes and the objectives it pursues. Once something has been decided, even if you originally argued against it, your membership in the group entails an obligation to accept the decision. The alternative is to leave the group, but in practice this is very rarely a dilemma of significance. Real opposition to decisions within organizations usually consists of one part disagreement with the decision to nine parts resentment at not being consulted before the decision. For most people on most issues, it is enough to know that their views were heard and considered. They may regret that they were not followed, but they accept the outcome.

And just as the decision of any team is binding on all the members, so the decisions of a meeting of people higher up in an organization carry a greater authority than any decision by a single executive. It is much harder to challenge a decision of the board than of the chief executive acting on his own. The decision-making authority of a meeting is of special importance for long-term policies and procedures.

5. In the world of management, a meeting is very often the only occasion where the team or group actually exists and works as a group, and the only time when the supervisor, manager, or executive is actually perceived as the leader of the team, rather than as the official to whom individuals report. In some jobs the leader does guide his team through his personal presence—not just the leader of a pit gang or construction team, but also the chef in the hotel kitchen and the maître d'hôtel in the restaurant, or the supervisor in a department store. But in large administrative headquarters, the daily or weekly meeting is often the only time when the leader is ever perceived to be guiding a team rather than doing a job.

6. A meeting is a status arena. It is no good to pretend that people are not or should not be concerned with their status relative to the other members in a group. It is just another part of human nature that we have to live with. It is a not insignificant fact that the word *order* means (a) hierarchy or pecking order; (b) an instruction or command; and (c) stability and the way things ought to be, as in "put your affairs in order," or "law and order." All three definitions are aspects of the same idea, which is indivisible.

Since a meeting is so often the only time when members get the chance to find out their relative standing, the "arena" function is inevitable. When a group is new, has a new leader, or is composed of people like department heads who are in competition for promotion and who do not work in a single team outside the meeting, "arena behavior" is likely to figure more largely, even to the point of dominating the proceedings. However, it will hardly signify with a long-established group that meets regularly.

Despite the fact that a meeting can perform all of the foregoing main functions, there is no guarantee that it will do so in any given situation. It is all too possible that any single meeting may be a waste of time, an irritant, or a barrier to the achievement of the organization's objectives.

## What Sort of Meeting?

While my purpose in this article is to show the critical points at which most meetings go wrong, and to indicate ways of putting them right, I must first draw some important distinctions in the size and type of meetings that we are dealing with.

Meetings can be graded by *size* into three broad categories: (1) the assembly—100 or more people who are expected to do little more than listen to the main speaker or speakers; (2) the council—40 or 50 people who are basically there to listen to the main speaker or speakers but who can come in with questions or comments and who may be asked to contribute something on their own account and (3) the committee—up to 10 (or at the most 12) people, all of whom more or less speak on an equal footing under the guidance and control of a chairman.

We are concerned in this article only with the "committee" meeting though it may be described as a committee, a subcommittee, a study group, a project team, a working party, a board, or by any of dozens of other titles. It is by far the most common meeting all over the world, and can perhaps be traced back to the primitive hunting band through which our species evolved. Beyond doubt it constitutes the bulk of the 11 million meetings that—so it has been calculated—take place every day in the United States.

Apart from the distinction of size, there are certain considerations regarding the *type* of meeting that profoundly affect its nature. For instance:

*Frequency*—A daily meeting is different from a weekly one, and a weekly meeting from a monthly one. Irregular, ad hoc, quarterly, and annual meetings are different again. On the whole, the frequency of meetings defines—or perhaps even determines—the degree of unity of the group.

*Composition*—Do the members work together on the same project, such as the nursing and ancillary staff on the same ward of a hospital? Do they work on different but parallel tasks, like a meeting of the company's plant managers or regional sales managers? Or are they a diverse group—strangers to each other, perhaps—united only by the meeting itself and by a common interest in realizing its objectives?

*Motivation*—Do the members have a common objective in their work, like a football team? Or do they to some extent have a competitive working relationship, like managers of subsidiary companies at a meeting with the chief executive, or the heads of research, production, and marketing discussing finance allocation for the coming year? Or does the desire for success through the meeting itself unify them, like a neighborhood action group or a new product design committee?

*Decision process*—How does the meeting group ultimately reach its decisions? By a general consensus, "the feeling of the meeting"? By a majority vote? Or are the decisions left entirely to the chairman himself, after he has listened to the facts, opinions, and discussions?

## KINDS OF MEETINGS

The experienced meeting-goer will recognize that, although there seem to be five quite different methods of analyzing a meeting, in practice there is a tendency for certain kinds of meetings to sort themselves out into one of three categories. Consider:

The *daily meeting*, where people work together on the same project with a common objective and reach decisions informally by general agreement.

The *weekly* or *monthly meeting*, where members work on different but parallel projects and where there is a certain competitive element and a greater likelihood that the chairman will make the final decision himself.

The *irregular, occasional,* or *"special project"* meeting, composed of people whose normal work does not bring them into contact and whose work has little or no relationship to the others'. They are united only by the project the meeting exists to promote and motivated by the desire that the project should succeed. Though actual voting is uncommon, every member effectively has a veto.

Of these three kinds of meeting, it is the first—the workface type—that is probably the most common. It is also, oddly enough, the one most likely to be successful. Operational imperatives usually ensure that it is brief, and the participants' experience of working side by side ensures that communication is good.

The other two types are a different matter. In these meetings all sorts of human crosscurrents can sweep the discussion off course, and errors of psychology and technique on the chairman's part can defeat its purposes. Moreover, these meetings are likely to bring together the more senior people and to produce decisions that profoundly affect the efficiency, prosperity, and even survival of the whole organization. It is, therefore, toward these higher-level meetings that the lessons of this article are primarily directed.

## Before the Meeting

The most important question you should ask is: "What is this meeting intended to achieve?" You can ask it in different ways—"What would be the likely consequences of not holding it?" "When it is over, how shall I judge whether it was a success or a failure?"—but unless you have a very clear requirement from the meeting, there is a grave danger that it will be a waste of everyone's time.

### DEFINING THE OBJECTIVE

You have already looked at the six main functions that all meetings perform, but if you are trying to use a meeting to achieve definite objectives, there are in practice only certain types of objectives it can really achieve. Every item on the agenda can be placed in one of the following four categories, or divided up into sections that fall into one or more of them:

1 *Informative-digestive*—Obviously, it is a waste of time for the meeting to give out purely factual information that would be better circulated in a document. But if the information should be heard from a particular person, or if it needs some clarification and comment to make sense of it, or if it has deep implications for the members of the meeting, then it is perfectly proper to introduce an item onto the agenda that requires no conclusion, decision, or action from the meeting; it is enough, simply, that the meeting should receive and discuss a report.

The "informative-digestive" function includes progress reports—to keep the group up to date on the current status of projects it is responsible for or that affect its deliberations—and review of completed projects in order to come to a collective judgment and to see what can be learned from them for the next time.

2. *Constructive-originative*—This "What shall we do?" function embraces all items that require something new to be devised, such as a new policy, a new strategy, a new sales target, a new product, a new

marketing plan, a new procedure, and so forth. This sort of discussion asks people to contribute their knowledge, experience, judgment, and ideas. Obviously, the plan will probably be inadequate unless all relevant parties are present and pitching in.

3. *Executive responsibilities*—This is the "How shall we do it?" function, which comes after it has been decided what the members are going to do; at this point, executive responsibilities for the different components of the task have to be distributed around the table. Whereas in the second function the contributors' importance is their knowledge and ideas, here their contribution is the responsibility for implementing the plan. The fact that they and their subordinates are affected by it makes their contribution especially significant.

It is of course possible to allocate these executive responsibilities without a meeting, by separate individual briefings, but several considerations often make a meeting desirable:

First, it enables the members as a group to find the best way of achieving the objectives.

Second, it enables each member to understand and influence the way in which his own job fits in with the jobs of the others and with the collective task.

Third, if the meeting is discussing the implementation of a decision taken at a higher level, securing the group's consent may be of prime importance. If so, the fact that the group has the opportunity to formulate the detailed action plan itself may be the decisive factor in securing its agreement, because in that case the final decision belongs, as it were, to the group. Everyone is committed to what the group decides and is collectively responsible for the final shape of the project, as well as individually answerable for his own part in it. Ideally, this sort of agenda item starts with a policy, and ends with an action plan.

4. *Legislative framework*: Above and around all considerations of "What to do" and "How to do it," there is a framework—a departmental or divisional organization—and a system of rules, routines, and procedures within and through which all the activity takes place. Changing this framework and introducing a new organization or new procedures can be deeply disturbing to committee members and a threat to their status and long-term security. Yet leaving it unchanged can stop the organization from adapting to a changing world. At

whatever level this change happens, it must have the support of all the perceived leaders whose groups are affected by it.

The key leaders for this legislative function must collectively make or confirm the decision; if there is any important dissent, it is very dangerous to close the discussion and make the decision by decree. The group leaders cannot expect quick decisions if they are seeking to change the organization framework and routines that people have grown up with. Thus they must be prepared to leave these items unresolved for further discussion and consultation. As Francis Bacon put it—and it has never been put better—"Counsels to which time hath not been called, time will not ratify."

## MAKING PREPARATIONS

The four different functions just discussed may of course be performed by a single meeting, as the group proceeds through the agenda. Consequently, it may be a useful exercise for the chairman to go through the agenda, writing beside each item which function it is intended to fulfill. This exercise helps clarify what is expected from the discussion and helps focus on which people to bring in and what questions to ask them.

PEOPLE. The value and success of a committee meeting are seriously threatened if too many people are present. Between 4 and 7 is generally ideal, 10 is tolerable, and 12 is the outside limit. So the chairman should do everything he can to keep numbers down, consistent with the need to invite everyone with an important contribution to make.

The leader may have to leave out people who expect to come or who have always come. For this job he may need tact; but since people generally preserve a fiction that they are overworked already and dislike serving on committees, it is not usually hard to secure their consent to stay away.

If the leader sees no way of getting the meeting down to a manageable size, he can try the following devices: (a) analyze the agenda to see whether everyone has to be present for every item (he may be able to structure the agenda so that some people can leave at half time and others can arrive); (b) ask himself whether he doesn't really need two separate, smaller meetings rather than one big one; and (c) determine whether one or two groups can be asked to thrash some of the topics out in advance so that only one of them needs to come in with its proposals.

Remember, too, that a few words with a member on the day before a meeting can increase the value of the meeting itself, either by ensuring that an important point is raised that comes better from the floor than from the chair or by preventing a time-wasting discussion of a subject that need not be touched on at all.

PAPERS. The agenda is by far the most important piece of paper. Properly drawn up, it has a power of speeding and clarifying a meeting that very few people understand or harness. The main fault is to make it unnecessarily brief and vague. For example, the phrase "development budget" tells nobody very much, whereas the longer explanation "To discuss the proposal for reduction of the 1976–1977 development budget now that the introduction of our new product has been postponed" helps all committee members to form some views or even just to look up facts and figures in advance.

Thus the leader should not be afraid of a long agenda, provided that the length is the result of his analyzing and defining each item more closely, rather than of his adding more items than the meeting can reasonably consider in the time allowed. He should try to include, very briefly, some indication of the reason for each topic to be discussed. If one item is of special interest to the group, it is often a good idea to single it out for special mention in a covering note.

The leader should also bear in mind the useful device of heading each item "For information," "For discussion," or "For decision" so that those at the meeting know where they are trying to get to.

And finally, the chairman should not circulate the agenda too far in advance, since the less organized members will forget it or lose it. Two or three days is about right—unless the supporting papers are voluminous.

Other "paper" considerations: The order of items on the agenda is important. Some aspects are obvious—the items that need urgent decision have to come before those that can wait till next time. Equally, the leader does not discuss the budget for the reequipment program before discussing whether to put the reequipment off until next year. But some aspects are not so obvious. Consider:

The early part of a meeting tends to be more lively and creative than the end of it, so if an item needs mental energy, bright ideas, and clear heads, it may be better to put it high up on the list. Equally, if there is one item of great interest and concern to everyone, it may be a good idea to hold it back for a while and get some other useful work done first. Then the star item can be introduced to carry the meeting over the attention lag that sets in after the first 15 to 20 minutes of the meeting.

Some items unite the meeting in a common front while others divide the members one from another. The leader may want to start with unity before entering into division, or he may prefer the other way around. The point is to be aware of the choice and to make it consciously, because it is apt to make a difference to the whole atmosphere of the meeting. It is almost always a good idea to find a unifying item with which to end the meeting.

A common fault is to dwell too long on trivial but urgent items, to the exclusion of subjects of fundamental importance whose significance is long-term rather than immediate. This can be remedied by putting on the agenda the time at which discussion of the important long-term issue will begin—and by sticking to it.

Very few business meetings achieve anything of value after two hours, and an hour and a half is enough time to allocate for most purposes.

It is often a good idea to put the finishing time of a meeting on the agenda as well as the starting time.

If meetings have a tendency to go on too long, the chairman should arrange to start them one hour before lunch or one hour before the end of work. Generally, items that ought to be kept brief can be introduced ten minutes from a fixed end point.

The practice of circulating background or proposal papers along with the minutes is, in principle, a good one. It not only saves time, but it also helps in formulating useful questions and considerations in advance. But the whole idea is sabotaged once the papers get too long; they should be brief or provide a short summary. If they are circulated, obviously the chairman has to read them, or at least must not be caught not having read them.

(One chairman, more noted for his cunning than his conscientiousness, is said to have spent 30 seconds before each meeting going through all the papers he had not read with a thick red pen, marking lines and question marks in the margins at random, and making sure these were accidentally made visible to the meeting while the subject was being discussed.)

If papers are produced at the meeting for discussion, they should obviously be brief and simple, since everyone has to read them. It is a supreme folly to bring a group of people together to read six pages of closely printed sheets to themselves. The exception is certain kinds of

financial and statistical papers whose function is to support and illustrate verbal points as reference documents rather than to be swal-
lowed whole: these are often better tabled at the meeting.

All items should be thought of and thought about in advance if they
are to be usefully discussed. Listing "Any other business" on the
agenda is an invitation to waste time. This does not absolutely preclude the chairman's announcing an extra agenda item at a meeting
if something really urgent and unforeseen crops up or is suggested to
him by a member, provided it is fairly simple and straightforward. Nor
does it preclude his leaving time for general unstructured discussion
after the close of the meeting.

The chairman, in going through the agenda items in advance, can
usefully insert his own brief notes of points he wants to be sure are
not omitted from the discussion. A brief marginal scribble of "How
much notice?" or "Standby arrangements?" or whatever is all that is
necessary.

## The Chairman's Job

Let's say that you have just been appointed chairman of the committee. You tell everyone that it is a bore or a chore. You also tell them
that you have been appointed "for my sins." But the point is that you
tell them. There is no getting away from it: some sort of honor or glory
attaches to the chairman's role. Almost everyone is in some way
pleased and proud to be made chairman of something. And that is
three quarters of the trouble.

### MASTER OR SERVANT?

Their appointment as committee chairman takes people in different
ways. Some seize the opportunity to impose their will on a group that
they see themselves licensed to dominate. Their chairmanship is a
harangue, interspersed with demands for group agreement.

Others are more like scoutmasters, for whom the collective activity
of the group is satisfaction enough, with no need for achievement.
Their chairmanship is more like the endless stoking and fueling of a
campfire that is not cooking anything.

And there are the insecure or lazy chairmen who look to the meeting for reassurance and support in their ineffectiveness and inactivity,

so that they can spread the responsibility for their indecisiveness among the whole group. They seize on every expression of disagreement or doubt as a justification for avoiding decision or action.

But even the large majority who do not go to those extremes still feel a certain pleasurable tumescence of the ego when they take their place at the head of the table for the first time. The feeling is no sin: the sin is to indulge it or to assume that the pleasure is shared by the other members of the meeting.

It is the chairman's self-indulgence that is the greatest single barrier to the success of a meeting. His first duty, then, is to be aware of the temptation and of the dangers of yielding to it. The clearest of the danger signals is hearing himself talking a lot during a discussion.

One of the best chairmen I have ever served under makes it a rule to restrict her interventions to a single sentence, or at most two. She forbids herself ever to contribute a paragraph to a meeting she is chairing. It is a harsh rule, but you would be hard put to find a regular attender of her meetings (or anyone else's) who thought it was a bad one.

There is, in fact, only one legitimate source of pleasure in chairmanship, and that is pleasure in the achievements of the meeting—and to be legitimate it must be shared by all those present. Meetings are *necessary* for all sorts of basic and primitive human reasons, but they are *useful* only if they are seen by all present to be getting somewhere—and somewhere they know they could not have gotten to individually.

If the chairman is to make sure that the meeting achieves valuable objectives, he will be more effective seeing himself as the servant of the group rather than as its master. His role then becomes that of assisting the group toward the best conclusion or decision in the most efficient manner possible: to interpret and clarify; to move the discussion forward; and to bring it to a resolution that everyone understands and accepts as being the will of the meeting, even if the individuals do not necessarily agree with it.

His true source of authority with the members is the strength of his perceived commitment to their combined objective and his skill and efficiency in helping and guiding them to its achievement. Control and discipline then become not the act of imposing his will on the group but of imposing the group's will on any individual who is in danger of diverting or delaying the progress of the discussion and so from realizing the objective.

Once the members realize that the leader is impelled by his commitment to their common objective, it does not take great force of personality for him to control the meeting. Indeed, a sense of urgency and a clear desire to reach the best conclusion as quickly as possible are a much more effective disciplinary instrument than a big gavel. The effective chairman can then hold the discussion to the point by indicating that there is no time to pursue a particular idea now, that there is no time for long speeches, that the group has to get through this item and on to the next one, rather than by resorting to pulling rank.

There are many polite ways the chairman can indicate a slight impatience even when someone else is speaking—by leaning forward, fixing his eyes on the speaker, tensing his muscles, raising his eyebrows, or nodding briefly to show the point is taken. And when replying or commenting, the chairman can indicate by the speed, brevity, and finality of his intonation that "we have to move on." Conversely, he can reward the sort of contribution he is seeking by the opposite expressions and intonations, showing that there is plenty of time for that sort of idea, and encouraging the speaker to develop the point.

After a few meetings, all present readily understand this nonverbal language of chairmanship. It is the chairman's chief instrument of educating the group into the general type of "meeting behavior" that he is looking for. He is still the servant of the group, but like a hired mountain guide, he is the one who knows the destination, the route, the weather signs, and the time the journey will take. So if he suggests that the members walk a bit faster, they take his advice.

This role of servant rather than master is often obscured in large organizations by the fact that the chairman is frequently the line manager of the members: this does not, however, change the reality of the role of chairman. The point is easier to see in, say, a neighborhood action group. The question in that case is, simply, "Through which person's chairmanship do we collectively have the best chance of getting the children's playground built?"

However, one special problem is posed by this definition of the chairman's role, and it has an extremely interesting answer. The question is: How can the chairman combine his role with the role of a member advocating one side of an argument?

The answer comes from some interesting studies by researchers who sat in on hundreds of meetings to find out how they work. Their consensus finding is that most of the effective discussions have, in fact, two leaders: one they call a "team," or "social," leader; the other a "task," or "project," leader.

Regardless of whether leadership is in fact a single or a dual function, for our purposes it is enough to say that the chairman's best role is that of social leader. If he wants a particular point to be strongly advocated, he ensures that it is someone else who leads off the task discussion, and he holds back until much later in the argument. He might indeed change or modify his view through hearing the discussion, but even if he does not it is much easier for him to show support for someone else's point later in the discussion, after listening to the arguments. Then, he can summarize in favor of the one he prefers.

The task advocate might regularly be the chairman's second-in-command, or a different person might advocate for different items on the agenda. On some subjects, the chairman might well be the task advocate himself, especially if they do not involve conflict within the group. The important point is that the chairman has to keep his "social leadership" even if it means sacrificing his "task leadership." However, if the designated task advocate persists in championing a cause through two or three meetings, he risks building up quite a head of antagonism to lılm among the other members. Even so, this antagonism harms the group less by being directed at the "task leader" than at the "social leader."

## STRUCTURE OF DISCUSSION

It may seem that there is no right way or wrong way to structure a committee meeting discussion. A subject is raised, people say what they think, and finally a decision is reached, or the discussion is terminated. There is some truth in this. Moreover, it would be a mistake to try and tie every discussion of every item down to a single immutable format.

Nevertheless, there is a logical order to a group discussion, and while there can be reasons for not following it, there is no justification for not being aware of it. In practice, very few discussions are inhibited, and many are expedited, by a conscious adherence to the following stages, which follow exactly the same pattern as a visit to the doctor:

*"What seems to be the trouble?"* The reason for an item being on a meeting agenda is usually like the symptom we go to the doctor with: "I keep getting this pain in my back" is analogous to "Sales have risen in Germany but fallen in France." In both cases it is clear that something is wrong and that something ought to be done to put it right.

But until the visit to the doctor, or the meeting of the European marketing committee, that is about all we really know.

*"How long has this been going on?"* The doctor will start with a case history of all the relevant background facts, and so will the committee discussion. A solid basis of shared and agreed-on facts is the best foundation to build any decision on, and a set of pertinent questions will help establish it. For example, when did French sales start to fall off? Have German sales risen exceptionally? Has France had delivery problems, or less sales effort, or weaker advertising? Have we lost market share, or are our competitors' sales falling too? If the answers to all these questions, and more, are not established at the start, a lot of discussion may be wasted later.

*"Would you just lie down on the couch?"* The doctor will then conduct a physical examination to find out how the patient is now. The committee, too, will want to know how things stand at this moment. Is action being taken? Do long-term orders show the same trend? What are the latest figures? What is the current stock position? How much money is left in the advertising budget?

*"You seem to have slipped a disc."* When the facts are established, you can move toward a diagnosis. A doctor may seem to do this quickly, but that is the result of experience and practice. He is, in fact, rapidly eliminating all the impossible or far-fetched explanations until he leaves himself with a short list. The committee, too, will hazard and eliminate a variety of diagnoses until it homes in on the most probable—for example the company's recent energetic and highly successful advertising campaign in Germany plus new packaging by the market leader in France.

*"Take this round to the druggist."* Again, the doctor is likely to take a shortcut that a committee meeting may be wise to avoid. The doctor comes out with a single prescription, and the committee, too, may agree quickly on a single course of action.

But if the course is not so clear, it is better to take this step in two stages: (a) construct a series of options—do not, at first, reject any suggestions outright but try to select and combine the promising elements from all of them until a number of thought-out, coherent, and sensible suggestions are on the table; and (b) only when you have generated these options do you start to choose among them. Then you can discuss and decide whether to pick the course based on repackaging and point-of-sale promotion, or the one based on advertising and a price cut, or the one that bides its time and saves the money for heavier new-product promotion next year.

If the item is at all complex or especially significant, it is important for the chairman not only to have the proposed course of the discussion in his own head, but also to announce it so that everyone knows. A good idea is to write the headings on an easel pad with a felt pen. This saves much of the time wasting and confusion that result when people raise items in the wrong place because they were not privy to the chairman's secret that the right place was coming up later on in the discussion.

## Conducting the Meeting

Just as the driver of a car has two tasks, to follow his route and to manage his vehicle, so the chairman's job can be divided into two corresponding tasks, dealing with the subject and dealing with the people.

### DEALING WITH THE SUBJECT

The essence of this task is to follow the structure of discussion as just described in the previous section. This, in turn, entails listening carefully and keeping the meeting pointed toward the objective.

At the start of the discussion of any item, the chairman should make it clear where the meeting should try to get to by the end. Are the members hoping to make a clear decision or firm recommendation? Is it a preliminary deliberation to give the members something to go away with and think about? Are they looking for a variety of different lines to be pursued outside the meeting? Do they have to approve the proposal, or merely note it?

The chairman may give them a choice: "If we can agree on a course of action, that's fine. If not, we'll have to set up a working party to report and recommend before next month's meeting."

The chairman should make sure that all the members understand the issue and why they are discussing it. Often it will be obvious, or else they may have been through it before. If not, then he or someone he has briefed before the meeting should give a short introduction, with some indication of the reason the item is on the agenda; the story so far; the present position; what needs to be established, resolved, or proposed; and some indication of lines of inquiry or courses of action that have been suggested or explored, as well as arguments on both sides of the issue.

If the discussion is at all likely to be long or complex, the chairman should propose to the meeting a structure for it with headings (written up if necessary), as I stated at the end of the section on "Structure of discussion." He should listen carefully in case people jump too far ahead (e.g., start proposing a course of action before the meeting has agreed on the cause of the trouble), or go back over old ground, or start repeating points that have been made earlier. He has to head discussion off sterile or irrelevant areas very quickly (e.g., the rights and wrongs of past decisions that it is too late to change, or distant prospects that are too remote to affect present actions).

It is the chairman's responsibility to prevent misunderstanding and confusion. If he does not follow an argument or understand a reference, he should seek clarification from the speaker. If he thinks two people are using the same word with different meanings, he should intervene (e.g., one member using *promotion* to mean point-of-sale advertising only, and another also including media publicity).

He may also have to clarify by asking people for facts or experience that perhaps influence their view but are not known to others in the meeting. And he should be on the lookout for points where an interim summary would be helpful. This device frequently takes only a few seconds, and acts like a life belt to some of the members who are getting out of their depth.

Sometimes a meeting will have to discuss a draft document. If there are faults in it, the members should agree on what the faults are and the chairman should delegate someone to produce a new draft later. The group should never try to redraft around the table.

Perhaps one of the most common faults of chairmanship is the failure to terminate the discussion early enough. Sometimes chairmen do not realize that the meeting has effectively reached an agreement, and consequently they let the discussion go on for another few minutes, getting nowhere at all. Even more often, they are not quick enough to close a discussion *before* agreement has been reached.

A discussion should be closed once it has become clear that (a) more facts are required before further progress can be made, (b) discussion has revealed that the meeting needs the views of people not present, (c) members need more time to think about the subject and perhaps discuss it with colleagues, (d) events are changing and likely to alter or clarify the basis of the decision quite soon, (e) there is not going to be enough time at this meeting to go over the subject properly, or (f) it is becoming clear that two or three of the members can settle this outside the meeting without taking up the time of the rest. The fact that the decision is difficult, likely to be disputed, or going to be unwelcome to somebody, however, is not a reason for postponement.

At the end of the discussion of each agenda item, the chairman should give a brief and clear summary of what has been agreed on. This can act as the dictation of the actual minutes. It serves not merely to put the item on record, but also to help people realize that something worthwhile has been achieved. It also answers the question "Where did all that get us?" If the summary involves action by a member of the meeting, he should be asked to confirm his acceptance of the undertaking.

## DEALING WITH THE PEOPLE

There is only one way to ensure that a meeting starts on time, and that is to start it on time. Latecomers who find that the meeting has begun without them soon learn the lesson. The alternative is that the prompt and punctual members will soon realize that a meeting never starts until ten minutes after the advertised time, and they will also learn the lesson.

Punctuality at future meetings can be wonderfully reinforced by the practice of listing late arrivals (and early departures) in the minutes. Its ostensible and perfectly proper purpose is to call the latecomer's attention to the fact that he was absent when a decision was reached. Its side effect, however, is to tell everyone on the circulation list that he was late, and people do not want that sort of information about themselves published too frequently.

There is a growing volume of work on the significance of seating positions and their effect on group behavior and relationships. Not all the findings are generally agreed on. What does seem true is that:

Having members sit face to face across a table facilitates opposition, conflict, and disagreement, though of course it does not turn allies into enemies. But it does suggest that the chairman should think about whom he seats opposite himself.

Sitting side by side makes disagreements and confrontation harder. This in turn suggests that the chairman can exploit the friendship value of the seats next to him.

There is a "dead man's corner" on the chairman's right, especially if a number of people are seated in line along from him (it does not apply if he is alone at the head of the table).

As a general rule, proximity to the chairman is a sign of honor and favor. This is most marked when he is at the head of a long, narrow table. The greater the distance, the lower the rank—just as the lower-status positions were "below the salt" at medieval refectories.

**CONTROL THE GARRULOUS.**    In most meetings someone takes a long time to say very little. As chairman, your sense of urgency should help indicate to him the need for brevity. You can also suggest that if he is going to take a long time it might be better for him to write a paper. If it is urgent to stop him in full flight, there is a useful device of picking on a phrase (it really doesn't matter what phrase) as he utters it as an excuse for cutting in and offering it to someone else: "Inevitable decline—that's very interesting. George, do you agree that the decline is inevitable?"

**DRAW OUT THE SILENT.**    In any properly run meeting, as simple arithmetic will show, most of the people will be silent most of the time. Silence can indicate general agreement, or no important contribution to make, or the need to wait and hear more before saying anything, or too good a lunch, and none of these need worry you. But there are two kinds of silence you must break:

1. The silence of diffidence. Someone may have a valuable contribution to make but be sufficiently nervous about its possible reception to keep it to himself. It is important that when you draw out such a contribution, you should express interest and pleasure (though not necessarily agreement) to encourage further contributions of that sort.

2. The silence of hostility. This is not hostility to ideas, but to you as the chairman, to the meeting, and to the process by which decisions are being reached.
This sort of total detachment from the whole proceedings is usually the symptom of some feeling of affront. If you probe it, you will usually find that there is something bursting to come out, and that it is better out than in.

**PROTECT THE WEAK.** Junior members of the meeting may provoke the disagreement of their seniors, which is perfectly reasonable. But if the disagreement escalates to the point of suggesting that they have no right to contribute, the meeting is weakened. So you may have to take pains to commend their contribution for its usefulness, as a pre-emptive measure. You can reinforce this action by taking a written note of a point they make (always a plus for a member of a meeting) and by referring to it again later in the discussion (a double-plus).

**ENCOURAGE THE CLASH OF IDEAS.** But, at the same time, discourage the clash of personalities. A good meeting is not a series of dialogues between individual members and the chairman. Instead, it is a cross-flow of discussion and debate, with the chairman occasionally guiding, meditating, probing, stimulating, and summarizing, but mostly letting the others thrash ideas out. However, the meeting must be a contention of *ideas*, not people.

If two people are starting to get heated, widen the discussion by asking a question of a neutral member of the meeting, preferably a question that requires a purely factual answer.

**WATCH OUT FOR THE SUGGESTION-SQUASHING REFLEX.** Students of meetings have reduced everything that can be said into questions, answers, positive reactions, and negative reactions. Questions can only seek, and answers only supply, three types of response: information, opinion, and suggestion.

In almost every modern organization, it is the suggestions that contain the seeds of future success. Although very few suggestions will ever lead to anything, almost all of them need to be given every chance. The trouble is that suggestions are much easier to ridicule than facts or opinions. If people feel that making a suggestion will provoke the negative reaction of being laughed at or squashed, they will soon stop. And if there is any status-jostling going on at the meeting, it is all too easy to use the occasion of someone's making a suggestion as the opportunity to take him down a peg. It is all too easy and a formula to ensure sterile meetings.

The answer is for you to take special notice and show special warmth when anyone makes a suggestion, and to discourage as sharply as you can the squashing-reflex. This can often be achieved by requiring the squasher to produce a better suggestion on the spot. Few suggestions can stand up to squashing in their pristine state: your reflex must be to pick out the best part of one and get the other committee members to help build it into something that might work.

**COME TO THE MOST SENIOR PEOPLE LAST.** Obviously, this cannot be a rule, but once someone of high authority has pronounced on a topic, the less senior members are likely to be inhibited. If you work up the pecking order instead of down it, you are apt to get a wider spread of views and ideas. But the juniors who start it off should only be asked for contributions within their personal experience and competence. ("Peter, you were at the Frankfurt Exhibition—what reactions did you pick up there?")

**CLOSE ON A NOTE OF ACHIEVEMENT.** Even if the final item is left unresolved, you can refer to an earlier item that was well resolved as you close the meeting and thank the group.

If the meeting is not a regular one, fix the time and place of the next one before dispersing. A little time spent with appointment diaries at the end, especially if it is a gathering of five or more members, can save hours of secretarial telephoning later.

## FOLLOWING THE MEETING

Your secretary may take the minutes (or better still, one of the members), but the minutes are your responsibility. They can be very brief, but they should include these facts:

The time and date of the meeting, where it was held, and who chaired it.

Names of all present and apologies for absence.

All agenda items (and other items) discussed and all decisions reached. If action was agreed on, record (and underline) the name of the person responsible for the assignment.

The time at which the meeting ended (important, because it may be significant later to know whether the discussion lasted 15 minutes or 6 hours).

The date, time, and place of the next committee meeting.

# 2
# Meetings That Work: Plans Bosses Can Approve

**Paul D. Lovett**

With his business under severe pressure, a group vice president went into his annual strategic-plan meeting with top management carrying nothing more than a large, pencil-draft spread sheet. He brought along no plan document, no overhead slides, and none of his operating staff. But using that simple spread sheet, he identified the difficult options facing his ailing subsidiary and presented his plan. The company's top half-dozen executives hotly debated the proposal, peppering him with questions. Finally, the chairman overruled his aides and opted to continue to invest in the business.

Of the many meetings I attended as manager of corporate planning for a $2 billion industrial gas products company, that one taught me the most about how planning decisions are made—and not made—in a large corporation.

Clearly, there is a substantial gap between planning theory and its practice. Planning meetings are typified by players concerned mostly with covering their own rear ends—too busy putting out fires to think about the future and afraid to nail down a decision that would mean accountability. Decision makers are as often motivated by friendships, concerns for popularity, and self-interest as by the cold, hard facts gleaned from rigorous analysis. Planning documents too often ignore what's really at stake among participants and fail to establish a logical, agreed-on course of action.

My first task as manager of planning, in fact, was to redesign the bulky forms the company used in its annual planning exercise. At that time, the company generated plan *books*, and by the end of the planning cycle, the president would have a foot-high stack of these thick, three-ring binders crammed with facts, figures, charts, and endless prose about markets and competitors. The problem was, top decision makers didn't read the plan books because they weren't helpful as a guide for action.

I soon discovered that it wasn't just the plan books that didn't work. Almost nothing formally written down or presented worked. Strategic plans were not read, presentations seldom inspired a creative exchange of ideas, portfolio analysis was disregarded, and financial forecasts had no credibility. Managers were only going through the planning process because corporate had asked them to fill in some forms or make a presentation. They saw no value in it for themselves.

The document-oriented planning process did not take into account that key executives spend much of their time in meetings, not writing long documents or reading them, and the more senior the position, the more exaggerated this phenomenon becomes.

The VP of that crisis-ridden subsidiary understood the hidden agendas and preoccupations of his superiors when he reduced his proposal to its essentials. The simple lesson he taught me was that the meeting is where the plan becomes real—where the decision up or down is made. If you want your bosses to approve your idea, you have to sell them on it. You first must get them to focus on the elements you deem important—your vision and your plan of action. And that requires simplicity. Nobody is going to focus on a dull recitation of turgid mush. They certainly won't remember it, and if people can't remember what was said at the meeting, then no planning got done.

This article, then, is really about meetings more than plans, meetings where a decision is sought from the boss—approval of a capital budget, the purchase of a piece of equipment, an increase in the work force.

Over the years I have come to realize that chief executive officers want four questions answered before they will approve a plan:

1. What is the plan?
2. Why is the plan recommended?
3. What are the goals?
4. How much will it cost to implement the plan?

If you satisfactorily answer these questions for the decision maker, chances are you'll get your decision.

You should limit the written presentation of each of the four points to one page. It may be tough to summarize the programs for a $500 million business on a single sheet of paper, but I've found it is usually possible. Moreover, it will make you focus on what you want and why you want it.

This four-part approach to planning is straightforward enough, but the real planning must occur *before* the meeting when you and your staff shape the agenda and package the information to make your case convincing. It is at these earlier meetings, too, that you and your staff accept responsibility for the plan and for making it a reality. And you can use these meetings not only for planning but also for building your network of supporters.

A divisional manager of a $40 million specialty business used the four-step process to develop his plan, and at each preparatory meeting he included the managers from R&D, manufacturing, sales, and marketing. By the time the plan was finally presented to his boss, each member of the task force felt a part of the team and was already prepared to implement the plan. The preparation had created the impetus for approval and for execution once approval was given.

## What Is the Plan?

Answering this question requires a positive and specific future-tense statement of strategy that the CEO can accept or reject: "The auto products division will acquire a chain of muffler shops." Then you list the actions that will support the plan, like studying the kinds of acquisitions sought and the market areas and hiring an investment banker to help pursue the right deals. Programs at this level might lay the groundwork for a series of capital expenditures that you will request the following year. They might propose a major reorganization, establish a pricing policy, or target a market segment. The statement and list are enough to get the discussion started.

While all this may seem basic enough, I have found that many presentations don't discuss the plan itself. They'll forecast performance and describe environments, but they won't sketch out the action to be taken.

Sometimes, to avoid confrontation, presenters use general statements that may sound like a strategy. "Margins will be increased by focusing on the high-growth segments of the market" is one often-used statement. Now who would deny the wisdom of that approach? If you think about it, it's a good approach for the other business units in the division or for the whole company, in fact for nearly all units in every company, everywhere. It's not a strategy, however. It's not specific enough to provide guidance for anything. How will the unit raise its margins, by how much, and in what time frame? What are the high-growth segments of the market?

Often, business managers won't volunteer answers to such questions. Why should they take the risk, after all? It's tough to call the future, and they'd rather wait to see how things turn out. But by then, of course, it will be too late to implement an effective strategy for taking advantage of the situation.

The following statement, still very short, provides far greater insight into the intentions of the business unit: "The sales staff will be doubled so we can expand into the New York–New Jersey electronics market." Now there is something to discuss with the president. The high-potential market segment is identified, and the means and magnitude of the proposed solution are outlined.

To be effective, those who report directly to the decision maker must establish *their* plan—not one that is simply a conglomeration of subordinate-unit plans but one that establishes priorities among those units. At the industrial gas company, the group VPs who reported to the president were seldom central participants in the process. Most saw it as an opportunity to parade their staff in front of senior management. The group VP assumed the role of the reviewing party rather than the party under review. Consequently, the president was not getting the group VP's plan but what could be more aptly described as a laundry list of items that the business managers wanted to accomplish. After the meetings, the operating execs would frequently complain about the president meddling with the details of their business. But how could he do otherwise until they stopped delivering the details and started presenting a strategically oriented message?

## Why Is the Plan Recommended?

The definitive programs, once established, will be successful only as long as the boss remains confident that the opportunity is attractive and that there is a basis for competitive advantage. It is crucial, therefore, to make the plan's rationale clear to the decision maker. You're laying out what the situation is.

Even fail-safe ideas need to be thoroughly supported. One VP went into a plan meeting with the president and asked for permission to open an office in Southeast Asia. To the VP, the need for the company's presence on the Pacific Rim was obvious, and the cost was so low—only $1 million—that he thought approval was in the bag. But he hadn't studied the market or hypothesized a rate of return, so he couldn't demonstrate the value of the investment. The president told him no. "But it's only $1 million," the surprised vice president said. "A million dollars is a lot of money, even for us," the president responded.

Operating managers rarely face the CEO to discuss planning issues and may think they need to brief him or her on every last fact about the market and the situation. This only results in the rationale getting muddled, either by too much detail or by a failure to delve into real operations issues. Remember, CEOs don't have the time to address the details of any one subject. It's up to the manager, therefore, to synthesize the rationale in such a way as to give the CEO confidence in the information and conclusions. And that requires thorough research—of the markets, competition, costs, and whatever else is important to the logic of the proposal. You've got to know the environment in which your programs will be operating.

To control the tendency toward overkill, some companies insist managers draw up a list of key issues that will help establish the rationale for a plan. This part of the process can generate a high level of interest. But even here, the temptation is to discuss the issues so thoroughly that no time is left to decide what to do about them, what programs to create.

The more prevalent problem is that the boss doesn't get *enough* synthesized information. People want to know what the boss thinks before they play their cards. In effect, they want the CEO to tell them what the solution is instead of the other way around. It thus seems much easier to state the concern as a question: "What are we going to do about the fluctuating price of oil? Will a new competitor enter the market? What will be the rate of growth of the product?"

The implication is that any actions the manager will propose depend on the results of the question. Frequently, in fact, the stated issues are about things over which the unit manager has no control (take a second look at the questions above). Presenters highlight the price of oil or the economy as an issue because they know there is no correct solution against which they can later be evaluated.

Managers may also try to avoid confronting senior management with real issues and definitive programs. Here is an example. At each annual planning meeting, the VP of the international division would discuss budgets and projections of all his units, including the one in South Africa. Despite public pressure on U.S. companies with operations there, the VP would not focus on the question, "Should we maintain our position in South Africa or change it?" As a consequence, the key executives deferred debate on an exit strategy, leaving little time to evaluate the costs and benefits of getting out or looking at prospective buyers. Two years later, the unit was sold, but from a far more disadvantageous bargaining position.

All meeting participants bear a certain responsibility. If the meeting is to be useful, everyone needs to view the proposal as something to be negotiated and agreed on. Gaining consensus on the presenter's outline of programs is the primary objective of the entire planning exercise. Without consensus there is no plan.

Managers will get good feedback only if they propose specific programs that map out well-defined courses of action. Both presenter and staff should be able to proceed from the meeting with the confidence that senior management will be supportive. When strategies and programs are not specific, managers will have to qualify anew each individual initiative as it arises in succeeding months—negating the intended purpose of the planning exercise.

For their part, when executives have doubts, they have the responsibility to question their subordinates' conclusions. Unless the doubts are aired, there will be no shared commitment to the plan, and it will be doomed to failure—either because the doubts were valid or because in the long run the boss simply will not support the tactical programs necessary to carry out the plan.

Executives must also feel responsible for accepting or rejecting the various parts of the proposal, rather than just reviewing them—or interjecting their own off-the-cuff proposal, such as what happened at one top-level plan meeting.

Near the end, the president mentioned two new industries that had not been discussed but that he believed should get marketing attention. Even though nobody had investigated those industries, the group VP's concluding remark was, "Okay, we will give attention to those markets but let's remember what we said when budget time comes." His implication was that people or monetary resources would be applied to the new industries. Yet he and the president had not agreed on goals or a level of expenditure for the program. Consequently, nothing was done. Even the president's program had to wait until it had more definition.

## What Are the Goals?

The goals are what you expect to happen if the plan is adopted. A planning system requiring managers to identify and defend specific goals yields more realistic forecasts because managers realize their success can be carefully monitored. While this makes the plan presenter less comfortable, it gives senior management better control over the operation.

It is possible, in fact necessary, to limit the financial detail to a few important numbers. First, get the conversation focused on the unit of measure, not the numerical values. Is the business manager's objective to increase earnings or to gain an improved share position? A simple chart can then illustrate what the goals are and how they compare with the present situation. In some special cases, a list of milestones may summarize the goal better than a numerical target.

Just a few numbers are enough to focus the goals discussion on the right issues. For example, how is the business doing today in terms of share position, sales, and earnings, and how do we expect to be doing five years from now in each of these categories?

Often, though, when executives speak of their goals, they are mistakenly thinking about just their financial forecasts. A unit manager, therefore, will push responsibility for developing the plan onto the controller. The manager may hold a perfunctory meeting to establish a sales scenario, and then will shuffle onto the controller the burden of working up the details and perhaps even presenting the plan. Controllers invest significant time and effort into forecasting sales, detailing costs, and projecting net incomes. So the numbers become the principal output of the plan.

There is one problem: the numbers are frequently worthless. Controllers struggle to get next year's budget close; they cannot be expected to project reasonable numbers five years out. Moreover, business managers typically want the numbers to show increased share, the introduction of new products, and increased profitability all at the same time. The industrial gas company's 1980 plan, which was based on all the units' projections, reflects what often happens. Sales would reach $3 billion in five years and profits, $246 million, the plan said. The results were not even close. Sales in 1985, a good year, were $1.8 billion; earnings were $143 million. A year later, a major write-down left earnings at only $5 million.

The numbers, then, are only a part of the proposal, and by overfocusing on them, a unit is prone to overlook market realities. The industrial gas company, for example, holding a highly profitable leadership position in the U.S. market for hydrogen, foresaw an opportunity to enter the European market. At the time, there was no commercial distributor of the product in Europe. The company had a choice of two goals: (1) establish market leadership by making an early preemptive investment of $40 million in plant and equipment, or (2) attempt to win an upcoming major European space agency contract as a base load for the facility, a process that would take two years.

To establish market leadership, it would be necessary to sell products at cost to generate demand from commercial and industrial buyers. The investment would be justified then, on the basis that customers once signed on would stay as customers as prices later rose to provide an acceptable level of profitability. The necessary early years of low earnings, however, would result in a projected return below the corporate hurdle rate. So by default, the second goal became the operable one. Unfortunately, a French company—also seeing the value of the space agency business—fought tenaciously and won the contract on its home turf.

In the end, the U.S. company revised its market forecast and invested in a European plant anyway. But by then, two years had passed and the French were in the market with their own plant. The company had lost an opportunity to make strong, long-term profits; number crunching had gotten in the way of sound strategic judgment.

## How Much Will the Plan Cost?

As a fourth and final step, the business manager must request the resources necessary to carry out the plan. Having established the plan, its rationale, and the goals, the manager now has to "cut the deal." In other words, for there to be real consensus and commitment, sufficient funds and personnel have to be allocated.

Failure to establish agreement on resources—monetary, human, and others—usually means the program will not be sustained. A major division presented a plan which called for making a $50 million acquisition in a closely related industry. There was no discussion, however, about creating the search and evaluation team needed to make the acquisition. Consequently, while the president accepted the program, no human resources were allocated to accomplish the task. No acquisition was ever made.

The plan meeting is really the first step in the budget process. Does your CEO support programs during the plan meeting but cut back those same programs at budget time? The fact is, business managers frequently don't emphasize the cost impact of their initiatives, worried that the project might get killed before it gets off the ground. These are the same managers who complain of a lack of feedback and who cry foul when their budget requests are rejected.

I was once helping a divisional VP prepare the documentation for his annual meeting when it became obvious that he was uncomfortable with the spending level projected for a new initiative, about $3 million. If the planning process had been working effectively, he would either have gone back to the unit manager and negotiated a change or presented it to the president to get his opinion on the acceptable spending level. In this case, he did neither. He eliminated the initiative from his discussion. This "solution" actually undermined the plan. The business manager and the VP were left with neither the guidance nor the authority to carry it out.

The presenter must identify his or her current year's expenditures and compare them with the request for next year and for following years. Here, a financial staff is obviously not just a help in preparing the request; it's mandatory. There shouldn't be any surprises, and a budget increase should be linked to some specified payback—higher growth or an expanded market share.

Resource allocation discussions are about the short as well as the long term. They should address next year's budget for the project. Based on the CEO's response to anticipated spending levels, the business unit can better allocate its funding. Of course, it's not all engraved in stone. You'll have opportunities to reestablish the need for parts of the program that are to come in later years.

## The Payoff

The payoff from the preliminary meetings is an agenda that will get your boss to focus on the initiatives you have in mind. You should minimize the written requirements and encourage informality in your discussions.

All four agenda points should be addressed at the same meeting with the boss. I've seen managers talk about their plan and get agreement on goals, only to find out later that the money wasn't there or that the strategy was so vaguely worded that participants had conflicting interpretations of it. To know that you're on the same wavelength on all four points, they must all be resolved together.

This four-step procedure has been successfully used by business owners with $500,000 in sales and by divisional vice presidents representing $500 million. With such an agenda, the boss, the CEO—the decision maker—will be able to participate in the construction of your plan without spending an inordinate amount of time. Chances are, you'll get a decision. Moreover, the meeting's results will be simply stated so they can be communicated informally and rapidly to lower level managers, thus setting the backdrop for actions to be taken by the enterprise.

# 3
# Creative Meetings through Power Sharing

**George M. Prince**

Meetings are obviously an important part of a manager's life. In face-to-face encounters with one or more of his subordinates or peers, problems are brought up, information is shared, presentations are made, new ideas are developed, and, often, decisions are made.

One would think that meetings are an exciting and rewarding component of business life. But this is the case far too seldom. Most meetings are notable for hidden agendas, lack of candor, and waste of talent. This produces a high level of frustration and boredom for participants and a low level of accomplishment, both for the company and for those persons present.

One reason why meetings so often seem to accomplish so little—and by "meeting" I am thinking particularly of a gathering involving two or more persons where there is a superior-subordinate relationship—is that those present never forget that the organization's system of reward and punishment is still operating. To put it more precisely, the manager (the superior) does not let them forget.

Most managers operate with a style that I call judgmental. It is characterized by an emphasis on the power and right of the manager to pass judgment on actions of his subordinates.

The manager may keep hands off as subordinates prepare proposals for presentation to him. Such useful devices as delegation of authority, management by objectives, and participative management attempt to augment the autonomy of the subordinate, but meaningful decisions are usually reserved to managers well up the corporate ladder. In fact, one's right to make important decisions is the single most telling measure of status and power.

As a result, there is heavy emphasis on getting and guarding the power to decide important issues. This view of power as the right to make decisions about and comment more or less freely on actions, ideas, and proposals of subordinates puts the manager in a judgmental posture.

But as a judgmental manager he places himself in a different situation: if he maintains detachment in order to be fair to his subordinates, he removes himself somewhat from the action. On the other hand, if he uses his experience and skills in the usual way to involve himself in the discussion leading up to the decision to be made, he becomes a partisan. Then he is competing with his subordinates rather than playing his superior role as a manager/decision maker. In either case, much of the satisfaction of cooperative accomplishment is denied him.

In practice, the manager often walks a devious middle path. He uses persuasion and informal rewards and punishments to lead his subordinates to propose only what he can decide on favorably. But they resent his manipulation of them if they realize it. The result is misunderstanding and suspicion that make wholehearted cooperation difficult.

In my view, there is a better way of dealing with subordinates in order to obtain cooperation and further the organization's goals. But the better way cannot be imposed from above; it requires a collaborative effort between superiors and subordinates. I shall describe an approach to establishing a climate that encourages new ideas and innovation.

## Conditioned Responses

An organization's informal reward and punishment system is less visible than the formal one of salaries, bonuses, and promotions, but no less real. It is based on the tacit dependence of subordinate on superior. Each subordinate must often—perhaps several times a day—try to guess what action will be acceptable to his manager. To win acceptance rather than suffer rejection, he soon becomes conditioned to anticipating how his boss will react to an idea or a proposal.

On the face of it, this appears to be a good way for a subordinate to learn how to perform well in his job. In fact, it has a quite different effect, because it stifles initiative and leads to organizational inertia. This condition can create rather ludicrous situations, such as this case:

The marketing vice president of a company was asked why he did not make himself more available to his sales managers, so that they could benefit from his considerable talent and experience. "The problem is," he said, "that they listen to me too hard. For instance, I'll be just speculating that a red can might increase shelf visibility and suddenly the cans *are* red."

Nearly every manager will deny that he conditions his subordinates. But he should ask himself whether *his* manager lets him forget the superior-subordinate relationship and his explicit power to pass judgment on ideas and recommendations presented to him.

Let me make it clear that I believe controls and guidance to be appropriate and necessary. What concerns me is the destructive conditioning that pervades our organizational climate.

The hierarchical organization makes such apparent sense and has been so productive that it is hard to recognize the destructiveness of this manipulative force. But talk candidly to younger managers and you will observe that they—and, increasingly, older managers too—are very vocal in their frustration over the "Mickey Mouse" methods that corporations employ in the name of efficiency and the welfare of the organization.

## Rejection and Approval

If you could watch and listen to video and sound tapes of business meetings, you would note the pervasiveness of the judgmental managerial style in corporate life. In watching and listening to hundreds of these tapes over many years, I have been impressed again and again by these observations:

Even mild rejection has a significant negative effect on people.

Pointing out flaws in the ideas and actions of others occupies much of the time.

Approval has a positive effect on people and creates a climate for resolution of the problem.

In this section I shall discuss these phenomena in terms of business meetings.

## EFFECTS OF REJECTION

There is a widespread belief that in maturity one learns to take the slings and arrows of fortune with equanimity. And to some extent this is true. As one matures, he becomes more philosophical and learns to keep in perspective the daily ups and downs that occur.

One also learns to conceal his true feelings from others. While hurt feelings may not surface at all, more often they are translated unconsciously into uncooperative or even aggressive behavior aimed at the person who has stepped on one's toes. In a meeting, such action is usually disguised as a rational and potentially useful contribution to the dialogue. It is considered mature to view such behavior in this light, so it is easy to forget how sensitive to rejection mature people are.

Let us study the effects of rejection by dissecting the interaction that takes place at a meeting. (To illustrate more clearly my points about rejection and acceptance, I shall not include a superior-subordinate relationship here, but in a later vignette.) Let us suppose a group of four is working to improve one of their company's products, the familiar director's chair, which consists of a wooden frame and two slings.

*Mr. First*: Let's replace the canvas with nylon.

This is an *offer*. Its chief characteristics are that it contains information and (sometimes or) an idea. More important for our purposes, the person who makes it gets a feeling of worth and satisfaction from it.

*Mr. Second*: I think that's a good idea because it will give us better weathering characteristics.

This is an *acceptance*. It conveys credit and approval to the offerer and gives a reason why the idea merits approval. The originator of an acceptance tends to get pleasure from this action. In addition, the acceptance reinforces Mr. First's feeling of worth and satisfaction. He also views Mr. Second as an ally and a man of taste and perception—a person to pay attention to.

*Mr. Third*: Will nylon take the bright dyes that we use?

This is a *query*, and it is a slippery, chameleon-like element. A friendly query is perceived by Mr. First, the offerer, as clearly seeking information. He sifts words, tone, and nonverbal signals to determine whether this is a friendly query. If he perceives it to be so, he retains his positive feelings and speculates comfortably and openly with Mr. Third. If, however, he considers the query unfriendly, it constitutes a *rejection* and he reacts defensively or perhaps aggressively. Participants in a dialogue often use questions to make an offerer either defend his contribution or see the folly of it.

*Mr. Fourth*: That's a good idea, First, but nylon will stretch much more than canvas and the user will hit the supports.

This is another kind of rejection. What appears at the start to be an acceptance proves to be just sugarcoating of the pill. The chief characteristic of a rejection is its negativeness. Regardless of how politely conveyed and how factually accurate and even necessary this negative information is, the offerer perceives it as a put-down. His sense of worth and satisfaction is injured.

The feelings of the rejector are mixed. Even if the information he offers in support of his rejection is important and necessary, the satisfaction of giving it is eroded by the knowledge that he has used his information to put someone else down.

**PUNISHMENT AND BACKLASH.** Nearly everything that happens in conversation can be described in terms of these elements. There are thousands of ways to reject. Through use of the proper (or improper) tone an acceptance or query can be turned into a flat rejection. For example, a question such as "Are you seriously suggesting we do that?" is clearly a rejection. The same can be accomplished by a counter-suggestion, silence, changing the subject, and countless other actions, many of them nonverbal.

In a meeting of several people, typically about half of the transactions involve rejections. In the rough-and-tumble of the usual discussion, many of the rejections pass unnoticed. If one asks a participant if he perceived some negative action toward him as a rejection, he will nearly always say *no*. We are all thoroughly conditioned to appear to accept rejection, since that is considered to be mature behavior.

Often a participant is unaware that he is hurt and angry over a rejection. But if he is carefully observed, his nonverbal reactions may tell a different story. The signals are faint: an animated face turns into a poker face, the arms cross, or the head jerks backward slightly.

Better evidence may come later, if the rejected offerer tries to justify his offer or pay back his adversary in kind, rather than responding to the substance of the rejection. Let us continue the dialogue.

*Mr. Fourth*: I have an idea! We could double over this part of the fabric and—

*Mr. First*: That would increase our costs too much.

Mr. First rejects Mr. Fourth's idea before he can possibly know what Mr. Fourth has in mind.

The most important aspect of a rejection is the transformation of any transaction or exchange from potentially rewarding to punishing. If a manager is unaware of the dynamics of his transactions, he will tend to rely heavily on pointing out flaws or presenting countersuggestions. Both of these are usually perceived as rejections. So the manager is unintentionally punishing and conditioning subordinates to offer ideas or take action very cautiously—if at all.

## POINTING OUT FLAWS

In meetings called to attack particular problems, this sequence can be repeatedly observed: one member suggests an idea containing some elements that will help solve the problem. It is not, however, a completely acceptable solution. The manager and the other participants focus on the failings of the idea and firmly point them out. The group discards it to search for a new and better idea.

This series of reactions is considered rational and useful because ideas are judged good and worth pursuing or unhelpful and weeded out quickly. Time is not wasted on ideas that cannot stand up to this early testing.

The flaw in this reasoning has become apparent in an experiment which I have conducted hundreds of times with different groups. Of, say, ten groups working to solve the same difficult problem, nine fail to develop a concept to solve it. The tenth considers an idea discarded by the other nine and is intrigued by it, although it fails to meet some of the specifications of the problem. The group struggles with these shortcomings and somehow, making modifications as it goes along, transforms the bad idea into a good one that meets the specifications.

In analyzing the results of this reiterated experiment, I have pinpointed seven ideas that are regularly weeded out and discarded because they fail the early testing. Yet each of these unacceptable ideas can be transformed into an acceptable solution, and has been by the odd group (about one in ten) that becomes interested in it and struggles cooperatively to overcome its weaknesses.

While watching video tapes of these experiments, I have observed how often members of a group choose to focus on the flaws of an idea rather than on overcoming the flaws. The evidence from one incident, or several, might lead one to conclude, "Pointing out a flaw is the first step in overcoming it." This can, of course, be true. But when, in thousands of incidents, the second step seldom follows, one questions the benign intent behind pointing out a flaw.

One can then identify other evidence that suggests that this behavior serves some other purpose: the tone of voice may be unfriendly and may be accompanied by expressions or gestures that indicate disdain, impatience, or satisfaction in catching the offerer in sloppy thinking. Very seldom does pointing out a flaw convey helpful concern.

What other purpose does it serve? I believe that such behavior is an attempt to exercise power over another person. Implicit is the notion that one's co-workers are adversaries in an unending competition, and that one wins (or at least cuts his losses) by rendering someone else's idea worthless. The manager is not exempt from these feelings. When he is operating with subordinates, however, his stakes are much lower; he can always win.

## CLIMATE OF APPROVAL

The beginning of improvement in conditions comes when the manager recognizes that for productivity's sake, at least, he must avoid transactions between individuals that arouse defensive or revengeful reactions. Instead, he must establish a climate in which it is appropriate to voice imperfect thoughts and ideas. In this climate all ideas are explored and used by the group. Flaws are dealt with, but as drawbacks to be overcome by everyone.

In my experience, when this climate is present, rejections, unfriendly queries, and pointing-out-a-flaw behavior are practically eliminated. Idea production rises dramatically. Every idea is noted and explored to some extent. According to the participants, they often come out of these meetings feeling exhilarated, pleased with having made worthwhile contributions, and sometimes even personally enriched.

The concrete results of this style of meeting are more difficult to evaluate. The participants consistently rate this type of meeting as more productive and useful than a traditional meeting. But one cannot quantify solutions to problems per meeting; the most important results emerge gradually out of the clarifying effect of disciplined cooperation. These results take the form of more frequent individual and group accomplishment and increased satisfaction and motivation.

## The Judicious Manager

Since there are so many drawbacks to judgmental management, why does anyone use this style? I suggested earlier that in our culture there is little apparent choice. Given the heavy emphasis on productivity and profit, it appears that an effective manager must use his power to govern important matters.

Another limiting factor in choice of styles is a lack of models. Among one's teachers, managers, peers, and subordinates, it is difficult to find someone who is not judgmental.

Also, the fact that this style tends to be punishing to subordinates may even reinforce its use. As Walter Nord says, "Punishment is the most widely used technique in our society for behavior control."[1] He goes on to suggest that because punishment immediately stops the undesired response, the punisher is rewarded or reinforced for punishing. If negativeness and pointing out a flaw are seen as punishing, one can understand the manager's attraction to a judgmental posture.

The kind of manager who, in contrast, relies on affirmation and collaboration to get results I call the judicious manager. He holds different assumptions about power, efficiency, roles, and decision making. The contrasting assumptions are summarized in Exhibit I. (These propositions owe much to Abraham Maslow, Douglas McGregor, Gordon Lippitt, and the other giants of humanistic psychology.)

Obviously, I am not discussing merely managerial styles, but attitudes toward others and how people interact. People are quite consistent in the ways they act; the strategies one uses in a meeting tend to be the same as those one uses in other situations. For example, a manager who uses humor to try to soften his criticism of ideas and behavior in a meeting probably does the same in any situation where

## *Exhibit I  Contrasting the assumptions of a judgment manager and a judicious manager*

| Judgmental manager | Judicious manager |
|---|---|
| The most efficient mode is to have one boss call the shots. | The most efficient mode is to make use cooperatively of the varied talents available. |
| I must protect my power to make decisions. | The best decision will emerge if I combine my power with that of the implementers. |
| I decide every course of action where I am authorized to decide. | I enlist my subordinates to devise courses of action, and contribute my thoughts as matters progress. |
| I must exercise all the autonomy my power permits. | I must use my power to help each subordinate develop his or her autonomy. |
| I use my power for my own growth. | I share my power so that my subordinates can grow as I grow. |
| I motivate people. | Accomplishment motivates people. I can provide opportunities for accomplishment. |
| I review, oversee, and control the efforts of my subordinates. | I use my experience, power, and skill to aid subordinates in accomplishing the task. |
| I take credit for the results of the groups I manage. | I explicitly recognize the accomplishments of subordinates. |
| To get results I must spot flaws and have them corrected. | To get results we must help each other overcome flaws. |
| When subordinates express themselves or act in ways unacceptable to me, I point out the flaws. | When subordinates express themselves or act in unacceptable ways, I assume they had reasons that made sense to them and explore the action from that point of view. |
| As mature people we are able to "take" put-downs and criticism without destructive consequences. | Even mature people are distressed to some degree by put-downs and criticism, and this makes cooperation difficult. |
| My role is to define the mission of my group. | My role in mission definition is to facilitate discovery by my subordinates and myself. |
| My role is to make judgments about the actions of my subordinates while they are carrying out our mission. | My role is to join my subordinates to make sure they succeed. |

he exercises power over others. A manager who uses questions in meetings to mask his rejections does the same in other contexts.

Changing from a system of informal punishment and rewards is difficult because of the confusions in our present judgmental system. For example, autonomy and cooperation may seem antithetical. In reality they are not. The autonomous person has less need to be defensive and competitive and is therefore free to use his power to appreciate, support, and build on the action or idea of another.

Situations and people are changing continuously. Each of us has bad days, makes mistakes, and some days is less able to cope. Misunderstanding and confusion are an everyday part of this reality. That is why the manager must carry on a continuous clarification of roles and expectations.

## Recognize Others' Value

Meetings provide an ideal way of carrying out this mission. The best way of using the meeting to redefine roles and expectations is to tape record them (video tape is best, if available, but sound tape is satisfactory too). It is too difficult to reconstruct the fast action of a meeting without having a tape of it. Later the participants can analyze the tape. Thus each member of the group can take his turn analyzing parts where he made offers.

To illustrate, I shall analyze a simple episode, in which a manager and two subordinates at a food-processing company are discussing how they might reduce shipping costs.

*Mr. A*: You know, if we decentralize our manufacturing, we could cut shipping costs.

*Mr. B*: A more practical way would be to get some more competition among our carriers.

*Manager*: You remember we had a dispute with AA Trucking about eight months ago and got some bids from others. It would be worth examining that possibility again.

The following pluses and minuses can be identified in this exchange:

*Plus*—Two different offers were quickly forthcoming.
*Plus*—Everyone is focusing on an aspect of the same problem.

*Plus*—The manager accepted one.

*Minus*—Mr. A's offer is rejected when the others ignore it.

*Minus*—Mr. B suggests that Mr. A is not practical.

*Minus*—The manager puts subordinates in a competitive, win-lose position.

The next step is for the group to take each minus, rephrase it as a problem, and come up with a solution.

Let us consider the problem of how to avoid rejection of Mr. A's offer. The manager wants to encourage idea generation, but his action has the opposite effect on Mr. A. Though the manager knows that he should acknowledge every offer and assume that the idea it contains has some value, he gave it short shrift.

Why? From the little evidence we have here, it appears that the manager heard two offers almost at once, which, of course, often happens in meetings. He evidently selected the one that seemed more realistic to him in light of the company's experience. But what seemed to him to be perfectly reasonable action was to Mr. A arbitrary rejection of his idea, without enlightenment as to the manager's grounds.

So we note a discrepancy between the manager's perception of the episode and Mr. A's. Such discrepancies lead to misunderstanding and confusion. The victim wastes energy in speculating about their meaning or, worse, feels resentful and, perhaps unconsciously, determines to "get even."

A useful procedure for avoiding rejections is based on the assumption that an idea made some sort of sense to the person who expressed it—no matter what flaws leaped immediately to the listener's mind. So the burden is on the listener to speculate first about the useful aspects of the idea.

Only after exercising his wit and imagination on the constructive elements may he air his concerns or speak of flaws he sees. Even then, if he can word his concerns and flaws as subproblems to be worked on, he will keep the group's energy focused on building a solution.

Here is how the shipping-cost meeting might go if everyone knew and used this technique.

*Mr. A*: You know, if we decentralize our manufacturing, we could cut shipping costs.

*Manager*: Decentralizing would do some nice things for us. It *would* save on shipping and it would give us smaller, faster-moving manufacturing units. Another thing I like about the idea is that it would break up this huge, centralized operation and spread responsibilities in the organization. *(Having acknowledged the value in Mr. A's thinking and revealed some of his values too, the manager shifts to his own concerns.)* I have some problems here to consider—how to decentralize without any capital expense, for one. Another is how to retain both economies of scale and the advantages of small plants.

*Mr. B:* I have an idea about keeping capital expenses down. We could take a whole packing line and farm it out to someone in the area we want to operate it. We could contract with him to work for us on an exclusive basis.

*Manager:* Yeah, that would get around the capital problem—we might lease the equipment to a supplier—and it would get us out from under the production problems. It also puts the emphasis on our marketing strengths, where we are superior. But I have a couple of concerns here. How do we persuade the chairman—you know how he loves the production end—and how do we maintain quality control?

*Mr. A:* What this suggests to me is that we might keep production here and control it as usual—just condense our stews and soups and have reconstituting or repackaging stations at decentralized locations.

*Manager:* Sure, we could ship the condensed product in tank cars and just decentralize our packaging. I like this line of thought. Perhaps we wouldn't even have to condense if we were using bulk shipping. Now let's see, we have two things to explore, the condense-and-reconstitute idea and the bulk shipment with decentralized packaging. Anyone have any other approaches?

Another way of recognizing value in subordinates and of clarifying expectations is to delegate the decision making to the one who is to be the direct implementer of the undertaking. The purpose of the meeting (or a portion of it) is to provide him with alternatives. The manager must take care to maintain his participatory role and to avoid taking over the decision making. If he has concerns about an alternative being developed, he should state first what is useful in the developing idea and then turn to the problems he sees.

Finally, the subordinate selects among the alternatives. He may select an alternative which the manager considers acceptable but not the best one available. At times like these the manager proves his mettle. Accepting the subordinate's decision is not easy, since he knows that the ultimate responsibility is his. He may be asked by *his* boss to account for the results of a "second best" decision. However, a judicious manager knows that this is the risk he must repeatedly take if his subordinates are to grow in commitment and autonomy.

In these ways the manager can make a profound change in how he is perceived. He is relying on his experience and wisdom, not to judge and impose the accept-reject alternatives, but to encourage, teach, guide, and capitalize on the powers of his subordinates. He is very much into and a part of the action. Meetings can become a place where there are many rewards for the offering and few punishments.

## Concluding Note

Dealing with problems is the everyday job of a manager. By shifting from the judgmental to the judicious mode, the manager frees himself to contribute all his skill, experience, and knowledge without relegating subordinates to the position of lackeys. In doing this, he does not relinquish his responsibilities of guidance and control.

In short, the judicious manager enjoys his job more while he makes a much larger contribution and helps his subordinates do the same.

## Note

1. "Beyond the Teaching Machine: The Neglected Area of Operant Conditioning in the Theory and Practice of Management," *Organizational Behavior and Human Performance*, Vol. 4, 1969, p. 383.

# PART
# IV
## Writing with Confidence

# 1

# "What Do You Mean You Don't Like My Style?"

## John S. Fielden

In large corporations all over the country, people are playing a game of paddleball—with drafts of letters instead of balls. Volley after volley goes back and forth between those who sign the letters and those who actually write them. It's a game nobody likes, but it continues, and we pay for it. The workday has no extra time for such unproductiveness. What causes this round robin of revision?

Typos? Factual misstatements? Poor format? No. *Style* does. Ask yourself how often you hear statements like these:

"It takes new assistants about a year to learn my style. Until they do, I have no choice but to bounce letters back for revision. I won't sign a letter if it doesn't sound like me."

"I find it difficult, almost impossible, to write letters for my boss's signature. The boss's style is different from mine."

In companies where managers primarily write their own letters, confusion about style also reigns. Someone sends out a letter and hears later that the reaction was not at all the one desired. It is reported that the reader doesn't like the writer's "tone." A colleague looks over a copy of the letter and says, "No wonder the reader doesn't like this letter. You shouldn't have said things the way you did. You used the wrong style for a letter like this." "Style?" the writer says. "What's wrong with my style?" "I don't know" is the response. "I just don't like the way you said things."

Everybody talks about style, but almost nobody understands the meaning of the word in the business environment. And this lack of understanding hurts both those who write letters for another's signature and those who write for themselves. Neither knows where to turn for help. Strunk and White's marvelous book *The Elements of Style* devotes only a few pages to a discussion of style, and that concerns only literary style.[1] Books like the Chicago *Manual of Style*[2] seem to define style as all the technical points they cover, from abbreviations and capitalizations to footnotes and bibliographies. And dictionary definitions are usually too vague to be helpful.

Even such a general definition as this offers scant help, although perhaps it comes closest to how business people use the word:

> Style is "the way something is said or done, as distinguished from its substance."[3]

Managers signing drafts written by subordinates, and the subordinates themselves, already know that they have trouble agreeing on "the way things should be said." What, for instance, is meant by "way"? In trying to find that way, both managers and subordinates are chasing a will-o'-the-wisp. There *is* no magical way, no perfect, universal way of writing things that will fend off criticism of style. There is no one style of writing in business that is appropriate in all situations and for all readers, even though managers and subordinates usually talk and behave as if there were.

But why all the confusion? Isn't style really the way we say things? Certainly it is. Then writing style must be made up of the particular words we select to express our ideas and the types of sentences and paragraphs we put together to convey those ideas. What else could it be? Writing has no tone of voice or body gesture to impart additional meanings. In written communication, tone comes from what a reader reads into the words and sentences used.

Words express more than *denotations*, the definitions found in dictionaries. They also carry *connotations*. In the feelings and images associated with each word lies the capacity a writing style has for producing an emotional reaction in a reader. And in that capacity lies the tone of a piece of writing. Style is largely a matter of tone. The writer uses a style; the reader infers a communication's tone. Tone comes from what a reader reads into the words and sentences a writer uses.

In the business environment, tone is especially important. Business writing is not literary writing. Literary artists use unique styles to "express" themselves to a general audience. Business people write to particular persons in particular situations, not so much to express themselves as to accomplish particular purposes, "to get a job done." If a reader doesn't like a novelist's tone, nothing much can happen to the writer short of failing to sell some books. In the business situation, however, an offensive style may not only prevent a sale but may also turn away a customer, work against a promotion, or even cost you a job.

While style can be distinguished from substance, it cannot be divorced from substance. In business writing, style cannot be divorced from the circumstances under which something is written or from the likes, dislikes, position, and power of the reader.

A workable definition of style in business writing would be something like this:

> Style is that choice of words, sentences, and paragraph format which by virtue of being appropriate to the situation and to the power positions of both writer and reader produces the desired reaction and result.

## Which Style Is Yours?

Let's take a case and see what we can learn from it. Assume that you are an executive in a very large information-processing company. You receive the following letter:

Mr.(Ms.) Leslie J. Cash
XYZ Corporation
Main Street
Anytown, U.S.A.

Dear Leslie:

As you know, I respect your professional opinion highly. The advice your people have given us at ABC Corporation as we have moved into a comprehensive information system over the past three years has been very helpful. I'm writing to you now, however, in my role as chairman of the executive committee of the trustees of our hospital. We at Community General Hospital have decided to establish a skilled volunteer data processing evaluation team to assess proposals to automate our hospital's information flow.

I have suggested your name to my committee. I know you could get real satisfaction from helping your community as a member of this evaluation team. Please say yes. I look forward to being able to count on your advice. Let me hear from you soon.

Frank J. Scalpel
Chairman
Executive Committee
Community General Hospital
Anytown, U.S.A.

If you accepted the appointment mentioned in this letter, you would have a conflict of interest. You are an executive at XYZ, Inc. You know that XYZ will submit a proposal to install a comprehensive information system for the hospital. Mr. Scalpel is the vice president of finance at ABC Corp., a very good customer of yours. You know him well since you have worked with him on community programs as well as in the business world.

I can think of four typical responses to Scalpel's letter. Each says essentially the same thing, but each is written in a different business style:

**Response 1**

Mr. Frank J. Scalpel
Chairman, Executive Committee
Community General Hospital
Anytown, U.S.A.
Dear Frank,

As you realize, this litigious age often makes it necessary for large companies to take stringent measures not only to avoid conflicts of interest on the part of their employees but also to preclude even the very suggestion of conflict. And, since my company intends to submit a proposal with reference to automating the hospital's information flow, it would not appear seemly for me to be part of an evaluation team assessing competitors' proposals. Even if I were to excuse myself from consideration of the XYZ proposal, I would still be vulnerable to charges that I gave short shrift to competitors' offerings.

If there is any other way that I can serve the committee that will not raise this conflict-of-interest specter, you know that I would find it pleasurable to be of service, as always.

Sincerely,

**Response 2**

Dear Frank,

Your comments relative to your respect for my professional opinion are most appreciated. Moreover, your invitation to serve on the hospital's data processing evaluation team is received with gratitude, albeit with some concern.

The evaluation team must be composed of persons free of alliance with any of the vendors submitting proposals. For that reason, it is felt that my services on the team could be construed as a conflict of interest.

Perhaps help can be given in some other way. Again, please be assured that your invitation has been appreciated.

Sincerely,

### Response 3

Dear Frank,

Thank you for suggesting my name as a possible member of your data processing evaluation team. I wish I could serve, but I cannot.

XYZ intends, naturally, to submit a proposal to automate the hospital's information flow. You can see the position of conflict I would be in if I were on the evaluation team.

Just let me know of any other way I can be of help. You know I would be more than willing. Thanks again for the invitation.

Cordially,

### Response 4

Dear Frank,

Thanks for the kind words and the invitation. Sure wish I could say yes. Can't, though.

XYZ intends to submit a sure-fire proposal on automating the hospital's information. Shouldn't be judge and advocate at the same time!

Any other way I can help, Frank—just ask. Thanks again.

Cordially,

### WHAT DO YOU THINK OF THESE LETTERS?

Which letter has the style you like best? Check off the response you prefer.

| Response | 1 | 2 | 3 | 4 |
|----------|---|---|---|---|
| | ☐ | ☐ | ☐ | ☐ |

Which letter has the style resembling the one you customarily use?
Again, check off your choice.

Response             1            2            3            4
                     ☐            ☐            ☐            ☐

Which terms best describe the style of each letter? Check the appropriate boxes.

Response 1        ☐ Colorful      ☐ Passive       ☐ Personal
                  ☐ Dull          ☐ Forceful      ☐ Impersonal

Response 2        ☐ Colorful      ☐ Passive       ☐ Personal
                  ☐ Dull          ☐ Forceful      ☐ Impersonal

Response 3        ☐ Colorful      ☐ Passive       ☐ Personal
                  ☐ Dull          ☐ Forceful      ☐ Impersonal

Response 4        ☐ Colorful      ☐ Passive       ☐ Personal
                  ☐ Dull          ☐ Forceful      ☐ Impersonal


## LET'S COMPARE REACTIONS

Now that you've given your reactions, let's compare them with
some of mine.

**Response 1** seems cold, impersonal, complex. Most business people
would, I think, react somewhat negatively to this style because it
seems to push the reader away from the writer. Its word choice has a
cerebral quality that, while flattering to the reader's intelligence, also
parades the writer's.

**Response 2** is fairly cool, quite impersonal, and somewhat complex. Readers' reactions will probably be neither strongly positive nor
strongly negative. This style of writing is "blah" because it is heavily
passive. Instead of saying "I appreciate your comments," it says "Your
comments are most appreciated"; instead of "I think that my services
could be construed as a conflict of interest," it says "It is felt that my
services could be construed. . . ." The use of the passive voice subordinates writers modestly to the back of sentences or causes them to
disappear.

This is the impersonal, passive style of writing that many with
engineering, mathematics, or scientific backgrounds feel most comfortable using. It is harmless, but it is certainly not colorful; nor is it
forceful or interesting.

**Response 3** illustrates the style of writing that most high-level executives use. It is simple; it is personal; it is warm without being syrupy; it is forceful, like a firm handshake. Almost everybody in business likes this style, although lower-level managers often find themselves afraid to write so forthrightly (and, as a result, often find themselves retreating into the styles of responses 1 and 2—the style of 1 to make themselves look "smart" to superiors and the style of 2 to appear unbossy and fairly impersonal). Persons who find response 2 congenial may feel a bit dubious about the appropriateness of response 3. (Although I have no way of proving this judgment, I would guess that more readers in high positions—perhaps more owner-managers—would like response 3 than would readers who are still in lower positions.)

**Response 4** goes beyond being forceful; it is annoyingly self-confident and breezy. It is colorful and conversational to an extreme, and it is so intensely personal and warm that many business people would be offended, even if they were very close acquaintances of Frank Scalpel's. "It sounds like an advertising person's chitchat," some would probably say.

## Strategy Is Part of Style

As you compared your responses with mine, did you say, "What difference does it make which style *I* like or which most resembles *my* customary style? What matters is which style will go over best with Mr. Scalpel in this situation"? If you did, we're getting somewhere.

Earlier, when we defined business writing style, some may have wanted to add, "And that style should sound like me." This was left out for a good reason. Circumstances not only alter cases; they alter the "you" that it is wise for your style to project. Sometimes it's wise to be forceful; at other times it's suicidal. Sometimes being sprightly and colorful is appropriate; at other times it's ludicrous. There are times to be personal and times to be impersonal.

Not understanding this matter of style and tone is why the big corporation game of paddleball between managers and subordinates goes on and on. The subordinate tries to imitate the boss's style, but in actuality—unless the boss is extremely insensitive—he or she has no single style for all circumstances and for all readers. What usually happens is that after several tries, the subordinate writes a letter that the boss signs. "Aha!" the subordinate says. "So that's what the boss wants!" And then the subordinate tries to use that style for all situations and readers. Later, the superior begins rejecting drafts written in the very style he or she professed liking before. Both parties throw up their hands.

This volleying is foolish and wasteful. Both superior and subordinate have to recognize that in business writing, style cannot be considered apart from the given situation or from the person to whom the writing is directed. Expert writers select the style that fits a particular reader and the type of writing situation with which they are faced. In business, people often face the following writing situations:

**Positive situations.**

Saying yes or conveying good news.

**Situations where some action is asked of the reader.**

Giving orders or persuading someone to do as requested.

**Information-conveying situations.**

Giving the price of ten widgets, for example.

**Negative situations.**

Saying no or relaying bad news.

In each of these situations, the choice of style is of strategic importance.

In positive situations, a writer can relax on all fronts. Readers are usually so pleased to hear the good news that they pay little attention to anything else. Yet it is possible for someone to communicate good news in such a cold, impersonal, roundabout, and almost begrudging way that the reader becomes upset.

Action-request situations involve a form of bargaining. In a situation where the writer holds all the power, he or she can use a forceful commanding style. When the writer holds no power over the reader, though, actions have to be asked for and the reader persuaded, not ordered. In such cases, a forceful style will not be suitable at all.

In information-conveying situations, getting the message across forcefully and straightforwardly is best. Such situations are not usually charged emotionally.

In negative situations, diplomacy becomes very important. The right style depends on the relative positions of the person saying no and the person being told no.

For instance, if you were Leslie Cash, the person in the example at the beginning of the article whom Frank Scalpel was inviting to serve on a hospital's evaluation team, you would be in a situation of having to say no to a very important customer of your company. You would also be in a doubly sensitive situation because it is unlikely that Mr. Scalpel would fail to recognize that he is asking you to enter a conflict-of-interest situation. He is probably asking you *anyway*. Therefore, you would not only have to tell him no, but you would have to avoid telling him that he has asked you to do something that is highly unethical. In this instance, you would be faced with communicating two negative messages at once.

## Suit Your Style to the Situation

Now that we've thought about the strategic implications of style, let's go back to look at each of the responses to Scalpel's request and ask ourselves which is best.

Do we *want* to be personal and warm? Usually yes. But in this situation? Do we want to communicate clearly and directly and forcefully? Usually yes. But here? Do we want to appear as if we're brushing aside the conflict, as the third response does? Or do we want to approach that issue long-windedly, as in the first response, or passively, as in the second? What is the strategically appropriate style?

In the abstract, we have no way of knowing which of these responses will go over best with Mr. Scalpel. The choice is a matter of judgment in a concrete situation. Judging the situation accurately is what separates successful from unsuccessful executive communicators.

Looking at the situation with strategy in mind, we note that in the first response, the writer draws back from being close, knowing that it is necessary to reject not only one but two of the reader's requests. By using legalistic phraseology and Latinate vocabulary, the writer lowers the personal nature of the communication and transforms it into a formal statement. It gives an abstract, textbooklike response that removes the tone of personal rejection.

The very fact that response 1 is difficult to read and dull in impact may be a strategic asset in this type of negative situation. But if in this situation a subordinate presented response 1 to you for your signature, would it be appropriate for you to reject it because it is not written in the style *you* happen to *like* best in the abstract—say, the style of response 3?

Now let's look at response 2. Again, we see that a lack of personal warmth may be quite appropriate to the situation at hand. Almost immediately, the letter draws back into impersonality. And by using the passive constantly, the writer avoids the need to say "I must say no." Furthermore, the term *construed* reinforces the passive in the second paragraph. This term is a very weak but possibly a strategically wise way of implying that *some* persons (*other* people, not the writer) could interpret Scalpel's request as an invitation to participate in an improper action. Now we can see that, instead of seeming dull and lacking in personal warmth as it did in the abstract, response 2 may be the type of letter we would be wise to send out, that is, when we have taken the whole situation into careful consideration and not just our personal likes and dislikes.

The third response, and to an even greater extent the fourth, have styles that are strategically inappropriate for this situation. In fact, Scalpel might well regard the colorful style of the fourth response as highly offensive. Both responses directly and forcefully point out the obvious conflict, but by being so direct each runs the risk of subtly offending him. (The third response is "You can see the position of conflict I'd be in if I were on the evaluation team," and the fourth is "Shouldn't be judge and advocate at the same time!") We could make a pretty strong argument that the direct, forceful, candid style of the third response and the breezy, warm, colorful, intensely personal "advertising" style of the fourth response may both prove ineffectual in a delicate, negative situation such as this.

## What Effect Do You Want?

At this point, readers may say, "All right. I'm convinced. I need to adjust my style to what is appropriate in each situation. And I also need to give directions to others to let them know how to adjust their styles. But I haven't the foggiest notion of how to do either!" Some suggestions for varying your writing style follow. I am not implying that a communication must be written in one style only. A letter to be read aloud at a colleague's retirement party, for instance, may call not only for a warm, personal style but for colorfulness as well. A long analytic report may require a passive, impersonal style, but the persuasive cover letter may call for recommendations being presented in a very forceful style.

### FOR A FORCEFUL STYLE

This style is usually appropriate only in situations where the writer has the power, such as in action requests in the form of orders or when you are saying no firmly but politely to a subordinate.

Use the active voice. Have your sentences do something to people and to objects, not just lie there having things done to them; have them give orders: "Correct this error immediately" (you-understood is the subject) instead of "A correction should be made" (which leaves the reader wondering, made by whom).

Step up front and be counted: "I have decided not to recommend you for promotion" instead of "Unfortunately, a positive recommendation for your promotion is not forthcoming."

Do not beat around the bush or act like a politician. If something needs to be said, say it directly.

Write most of your sentences in subject-verb-object order. Do not weaken them by putting namby-pamby phrases before the subject:

"I have decided to fund your project" instead of "After much deliberation and weighing of the pros and cons, I have decided to fund your project."

Do not weaken sentences by relegating the point or the action to a subordinate clause:

If your point is that your company has won a contract, say "Acme won the contract, although the bidding was intense and highly competitive," not "Although Acme won the contract, the bidding was intense and highly competitive."

Adopt a tone of confidence and surety about what you say by avoiding weasel words like:

"Possibly," "maybe," "perhaps."

"It could be concluded that. . . ."

"Some might conclude that. . . ."

## FOR A PASSIVE STYLE

This style is often appropriate in negative situations and in situations where the writer is in a lower position than the reader.

Avoid the imperative—never give an order:

Say "A more effective and time-conserving presentation of ideas should be devised before our next meeting" as opposed to "Do a better job of presenting your ideas at our next meeting. Respect my time and get right to the point."

Use the passive voice heavily because it subordinates the subject to the end of the sentence or buries the subject entirely. The passive is especially handy when you are in a low-power position and need to convey negative information to a reader who is in a higher position (an important customer, for instance):

Say "Valuable resources are being wasted" instead of "Valuable resources are being wasted by your company" or, even worse, "You are wasting valuable resources."

Avoid taking responsibility for negative statements by attributing them to faceless, impersonal "others":

Say "It is more than possible that several objections to your proposed plans might be raised by some observers" or "Several objections might be raised by those hostile to your plans" instead of "I have several objections to your plans."

Use weasel words, especially if the reader is in a high-power position and will not like what you are saying.

Use long sentences and heavy paragraphs to slow down the reader's comprehension of sensitive or negative information.

### FOR A PERSONAL STYLE

This style is usually appropriate in good-news and persuasive action-request situations.

Use the active voice, which puts you, as the writer, at the front of sentences:

"Thank you very much for your comments" or "I appreciated your comments" instead of "Your comments were very much appreciated by me" or the even more impersonal "Your comments were very much appreciated."

Use persons' names (first names, when appropriate) instead of referring to them by title:

"Bill James attended the meeting" instead of "Acme's director attended the meeting."

Use personal pronouns—especially "you" and "I"—when you are saying positive things:

"I so much appreciate the work you've done" as opposed to "The work you've done is appreciated."

Use short sentences that capture the rhythm of ordinary conversation:

"I discussed your proposal with Frank. He's all for it!" as opposed to "This is to inform you that your proposal was taken up at Friday's meeting and that it was regarded with favor."

Use contractions ("can't," "won't," "shouldn't") to sound informal and conversational.

Direct questions to the reader:

"Just ask yourself, how would your company like to save $10,000?"

Interject positive personal thoughts and references that will make the reader know that this letter is really to him or her and not some type of form letter sent to just anyone.

## FOR AN IMPERSONAL STYLE

This style is usually appropriate in negative and information-conveying situations. It's always appropriate in technical and scientific writing and usually when you are writing to technical readers.

Avoid using persons' names, especially first names. Refer to people, if at all, by title or job description.

"I would like to know what you think of this plan" instead of "What do you think of this, Herb?" "Our vice president of finance" or "the finance department," not "Ms. Jones."

Avoid using personal pronouns, especially "you" and "I" ("we" may be all right because the corporate we is faceless and impersonal):

"The logistics are difficult, and the idea may not work" instead of "I think you have planned things so that the logistics are difficult and your idea may not work." "We wonder if the idea will work" rather than "I don't think the idea will work."

Use the passive voice to make yourself conveniently disappear when desirable:

"An error in the calculations has been made" instead of "I think your calculations are wrong."

Make some of your sentences complex and some paragraphs long; avoid the brisk, direct, simple-sentence style of conversation.

## FOR A COLORFUL STYLE

Sometimes a lively style is appropriate in good-news situations. It is most commonly found in the highly persuasive writing of advertisements and sales letters.

Insert some adjectives and adverbs:

Instead of "This proposal will save corporate resources," write "This (hard-hitting) (productivity-building) (money-saving) proposal will (easily) (surely) (quickly) (immediately) save our (hard-earned) (increasingly scarce) (carefully guarded) corporate resources."

If appropriate, use a metaphor (A is B) or a simile (A is like B) to make a point:

"Truly this program is a *miracle* of logical design." "Our solution strikes at the very *root* of Acme's problems." "This program is like *magic* in its ability to. . . ."

**FOR A LESS COLORFUL STYLE**

By avoiding adjectives, adverbs, metaphors, and figures of speech, you can make your style less colorful. Such a style is appropriate for ordinary business writing and also results from:

Blending the impersonal style with the passive style.

Employing words that remove any semblance of wit, liveliness, and vigor from the writing.

Please bear in mind that these six styles are not mutually exclusive. There is some overlap. A passive style is usually far more impersonal than personal and also not very colorful. A forceful style is likely to be more personal than impersonal, and a colorful style is likely to be fairly forceful. Nevertheless, these styles are distinct enough to justify talking about them. If we fail to make such distinctions, style becomes a catchall term that means nothing specific. Even if not precise, these distinctions enable us to talk about style and its elements and to learn to write appropriately for each situation.

## Discuss Needs First

What conclusions can we draw from this discussion? Simply that, whether you write your own letters or have to manage the writing of subordinates, to be an effective communicator, you must realize that:

1. Each style has an impact on the reader.
2. Style communicates to readers almost as much as the content of a message.
3. Style cannot be isolated from a situation.
4. Generalizing about which style is the best in all situations is impossible.
5. Style must be altered to suit the circumstances.
6. Style must be discussed sensibly in the work situation.

These conclusions will be of obvious help to managers who write their own letters. But what help will these conclusions be to managers who direct assistants in the writing of letters? In many instances, writing assignments go directly to subordinates for handling. Often, manager and assistant have no chance to discuss style strategy together. In such cases, rather than merely submitting a response for a signature, the subordinate would be wise to append a note: e.g., "This is a very sensitive situation, I think. Therefore, I deliberately drew back into a largely impersonal and passive style." At least, the boss will not jump to the conclusion that the assistant has written a letter of low impact by accident.

When they do route writing assignments to assistants, superiors could save much valuable time and prevent mutual distress if they told the subordinates what style seemed strategically wise in each situation. Playing guessing games also wastes money.

And if, as is often the case, neither superior nor subordinate has a clear sense of what style is best, the two can agree to draft a response in one style first, and if that doesn't sound right, to adjust the style appropriately.

Those who write their own letters can try drafting several responses to tough but important situations, each in a different style. It's wise to sleep on them and then decide which sounds best.

Whether you write for yourself or for someone else, it is extremely unlikely that in difficult situations a first draft will be signed by you or anyone else. Only the amateur expects writing perfection on the first try. By learning to control your style and to engineer the tone of your communications, you can make your writing effective.

## Notes

1. William Strunk, Jr. and E.B. White, *The Elements of Style* (New York: Macmillan, 1979).
2. *A Manual of Style* (Chicago: University of Chicago Press, 1969).
3. *The American Heritage Dictionary of the English Language* (Boston: American Heritage and Houghton Mifflin, 1969).

# 2
# Clear Writing Means Clear Thinking Means . . .

**Marvin H. Swift**

If you are a manager, you constantly face the problem of putting words on paper. If you are like most managers, this is not the sort of problem you enjoy. It is hard to do, and time consuming; and the task is doubly difficult when, as is usually the case, your words must be designed to change the behavior of others in the organization.

But the chore is there and must be done. How? Let's take a specific case.

Let's suppose that everyone at X Corporation, from the janitor on up to the chairman of the board, is using the office copiers for personal matters; income tax forms, church programs, children's term papers, and God knows what else are being duplicated by the gross. This minor piracy costs the company a pretty penny, both directly and in employee time, and the general manager—let's call him Sam Edwards—decides the time has come to lower the boom.

Sam lets fly by dictating the following memo to his secretary:

To: All Employees
From: Samuel Edwards, General Manager
Subject: Abuse of Copiers

It has recently been brought to my attention that many of the people who are employed by this company have taken advantage of their positions by availing themselves of the copiers. More specifically, these machines are being used for other than company business.

Obviously, such practice is contrary to company policy and must cease and desist immediately. I wish therefore to inform all concerned—

those who have abused policy or will be abusing it—that their behavior cannot and will not be tolerated. Accordingly, anyone in the future who is unable to control himself will have his employment terminated.

If there are any questions about company policy, please feel free to contact this office.

Now the memo is on his desk for his signature. He looks it over; and the more he looks, the worse it reads. In fact, it's lousy. So he revises it three times, until it finally is in the form that follows:
To: All Employees
From: Samuel Edwards, General Manager
Subject: Use of Copiers

We are revamping our policy on the use of copiers for personal matters. In the past we have not encouraged personnel to use them for such purposes because of the costs involved. But we also recognize, perhaps belatedly, that we can solve the problem if each of us pays for what he takes.

We are therefore putting these copiers on a pay-as-you-go basis. The details are simple enough. . . .

*Samuel Edwards*

This time Sam thinks the memo looks good, and it *is* good. Not only is the writing much improved, but the problem should now be solved. He therefore signs the memo, turns it over to his secretary for distribution, and goes back to other things.

## From Verbiage to Intent

I can only speculate on what occurs in a writer's mind as he moves from a poor draft to a good revision, but it is clear that Sam went through several specific steps, mentally as well as physically, before he had created his end product:
He eliminated wordiness.
He modulated the tone of the memo.
He revised the policy it stated.

Let's retrace his thinking through each of these processes.

## ELIMINATING WORDINESS

Sam's basic message is that employees are not to use the copiers for their own affairs at company expense. As he looks over his first draft, however, it seems so long that this simple message has become diffused. With the idea of trimming the memo down, he takes another look at his first paragraph:

It has recently been brought to my attention that many of the people who are employed by this company have taken advantage of their positions by availing themselves of the copiers. More specifically, these machines are being used for other than company business.

He edits it like this:
*Item*: "recently"
*Comment to himself*: Of course; else why write about the problem? So delete the word.

*Item*: "It has been brought to my attention"
*Comment*: Naturally. Delete it.

*Item*: "the people who are employed by this company"
*Comment*: Assumed. Why not just "employees"?

*Item*: "by availing themselves" and "for other than company business"
*Comment*: Since the second sentence repeats the first, why not coalesce?

And he comes up with this:

Employees have been using the copiers for personal matters.

He proceeds to the second paragraph. More confident of himself, he moves in broader swoops, so that the deletion process looks like this:

Obviously, such practice is contrary to company policy and ~~must cease and desist immediately. I wish therefore to inform all concerned those who have abused policy or will be abusing it that their behavior cannot and will not be tolerated. Accordingly, anyone in the future~~

~~who is unable to control himself will have his employment terminated.~~ will result in dismissal.

The final paragraph, apart from "company policy" and "feel free," looks all right, so the total memo now reads as follows:

To: All Employees
From: Samuel Edwards, General Manager
Subject: Abuse of Copiers

Employees have been using the copiers for personal matters. Obviously, such practice is contrary to company policy and will result in dismissal.

If there are any questions, please contact this office.

Sam now examines his efforts by putting these questions to himself:
*Question*: Is the memo free of deadwood?
*Answer*: Very much so. In fact, it's good, tight prose.
*Question*: Is the policy stated?
*Answer*: Yes—sharp and clear.
*Question*: Will the memo achieve its intended purpose?
*Answer*: Yes. But it sounds foolish.
*Question*: Why?
*Answer*: The wording is too harsh; I'm not going to fire anybody over this.
*Question*: How should I tone the thing down?

To answer this last question, Sam takes another look at the memo.

**CORRECTING THE TONE**

What strikes his eye as he looks it over? Perhaps these three words:
Abuse . . .
Obviously . . .
. . . dismissal . . .
The first one is easy enough to correct: he substitutes "use" for "abuse." But "obviously" poses a problem and calls for reflection. If the policy is obvious, why are the copiers being used? Is it that people

are outrightly dishonest? Probably not. But that implies the policy isn't obvious; and whose fault is this? Who neglected to clarify policy? And why "dismissal" for something never publicized?

These questions impel him to revise the memo once again:

To: All Employees
From: Samuel Edwards, General Manager
Subject: Use of Copiers

Copiers are not to be used for personal matters. If there are any questions, please contact this office.

## REVISING THE POLICY ITSELF

The memo now seems courteous enough—at least it is not discourteous—but it is just a blank, perhaps overly simple, statement of policy. Has he really thought through the policy itself?

Reflecting on this, Sam realizes that some people will continue to use the copiers for personal business anyhow. If he seriously intends to enforce the basic policy (first sentence), he will have to police the equipment, and that raises the question of costs all over again.

Also, the memo states that he will maintain an open-door policy (second sentence)—and surely there will be some, probably a good many, who will stroll in and offer to pay for what they use. His secretary has enough to do without keeping track of affairs of that kind.

Finally, the first and second sentences are at odds with each other. The first says that personal copying is out, and the second implies that it can be arranged.

The facts of organizational life thus force Sam to clarify in his own mind exactly what his position on the use of copiers is going to be. As he sees the problem now, what he really wants to do is put the copiers on a pay-as-you-go basis. After making that decision, he begins anew:

To: All Employees
From: Samuel Edwards, General Manager
Subject: Use of copiers

We are revamping our policy on the use of copiers . . . .

This is the draft that goes into distribution and now allows him to turn his attention to other problems.

## The Chicken or the Egg?

What are we to make of all this? It seems a rather lengthy and tedious report of what, after all, is a routine writing task created by a problem of minor importance. In making this kind of analysis, have I simply labored the obvious?

To answer this question, let's drop back to the original draft. If you read it over, you will see that Sam began this kind of thinking:

"The employees are taking advantage of the company."
"I'm a nice guy, but now I'm going to play Dutch uncle."
"I'll write them a memo that tells them to shape up or ship out."

In his final version, however, his thinking is quite different:

"Actually, the employees are pretty mature, responsible people. They're capable of understanding a problem."
"Company policy itself has never been crystallized. In fact, this is the first memo on the subject."
"I don't want to overdo this thing—any employee can make an error in judgment."
"I'll set a reasonable policy and write a memo that explains how it ought to operate."

Sam obviously gained a lot of ground between the first draft and the final version, and this implies two things. First, if a manager is to write effectively, he needs to isolate and define, as fully as possible, all the critical variables in the writing process and scrutinize what he writes for its clarity, simplicity, tone, and the rest. Second, he may find that what he has written is not what has to be said. In this sense, writing is feedback and a way for the manager to discover himself. What are his real attitudes toward that amorphous, undifferentiated gray mass of employees "out there"? Writing is a way of finding out. By objectifying his thoughts in the medium of language, he gets a chance to see what is going on in his mind.

In other words, *if the manager writes well, he will think well.* Equally, the more clearly he has thought out his message before he starts to dictate, the more likely he is to get it right on paper the first time round. In other words, *if he thinks well, he will write well.*

Hence we have a chicken-and-the-egg situation: writing and thinking go hand in hand; and when one is good, the other is likely to be good.

## Revision Sharpens Thinking

More particularly, rewriting is the key to improved thinking. It demands a real openmindedness and objectivity. It demands a willingness to cull verbiage so that ideas stand out clearly. And it demands a willingness to meet logical contradictions head on and trace them to the premises that have created them. In short, it forces a writer to get up his courage and expose his thinking process to his own intelligence.

Obviously, revising is hard work. It demands that you put yourself through the wringer, intellectually and emotionally, to squeeze out the best you can offer. Is it worth the effort? Yes, it is—if you believe you have a responsibility to think and communicate effectively.

# 3

# How to Write a Winning Business Plan

**Stanley R. Rich and David E. Gumpert**

A comprehensive, carefully thought-out business plan is essential to the success of entrepreneurs and corporate managers. Whether you're starting up a new business, seeking additional capital for existing product lines, or proposing a new activity in a corporate division, you will never face a more challenging writing assignment than the preparation of a business plan.

Only a well-conceived and well-packaged plan can win the necessary investment and support for your idea. It must describe the company or proposed project accurately and attractively. Even though its subject is a moving target, the plan must detail the company or the project's present status, current needs, and expected future. You must present and justify ongoing and changing resource requirements, marketing decisions, financial projections, production demands, and personnel needs in logical and convincing fashion.

Because they struggle so hard to assemble, organize, describe, and document so much, it's not surprising when managers overlook the fundamentals. We have found that the most important one is the accurate reflection of the viewpoints of three constituencies, as follows:

1. The market, including both existing and prospective clients, customers, and users of the planned product or service.
2. The investors, whether of financial or other resources.
3. The producer, whether the entrepreneur or the inventor.

Too many business plans are written from the viewpoint of the third constituency—the producer. They describe the underlying technology or creativity of the proposed product or service in glowing terms and at great length. They neglect the constituencies that give the venture its financial viability—the market and the investor.

Take the case of five executives seeking financing to establish their own engineering consulting firm. In their business plan, they listed a dozen types of specialized engineering services and estimated their annual sales and profit growth at 20%. But the executives did not determine which of the proposed dozen services their potential clients really needed and which would be most profitable. By neglecting to examine these issues closely, they ignored the possibility that the marketplace might want some services not among the dozen listed.

Moreover, they failed to indicate the price of new shares or the percentage available to investors. Dealing with the investor's perspective was important because—for a new venture, at least—backers seek a return of 40% to 60% on their capital, compounded annually. The expected sales and profit growth rates of 20% couldn't provide the necessary return unless the founders gave up a substantial share of the company.

In fact, the executives had only considered their own perspective—including the new company's services, organization, and projected results. Because they hadn't convincingly demonstrated why potential customers would buy the services or how investors would make an adequate return (or when and how they could cash out), their business plan lacked the credibility necessary for raising the investment funds needed.

We have had experience in both evaluating business plans and organizing and observing presentations and investor responses at sessions of the MIT Enterprise Forum over the past seven years (see "The MIT Enterprise Forum"). We believe that business plans must deal convincingly with marketing and investor considerations. This article identifies and evaluates those considerations and explains how business plans can be written to satisfy them.

### The MIT Enterprise Forum

Organized under the auspices of the Massachusetts Institute of Technology Alumni Association in 1978, the MIT Enterprise Forum offers business at a critical stage of development an opportunity to obtain counsel from a panel of experts on steps to take to achieve their goals.

In monthly evening sessions the forum evaluates the business plans of companies accepted for presentation during 60- to 90-minute segments in which no holds are barred. The format allows each presenter 20 minutes to summarize a business plan orally. Each panelist reviews the written business plan in advance of the sessions. Then each of four panelists— who are venture capitalists, bankers, marketing specialists, successful entrepreneurs, MIT professors, or other experts—spends five to ten minutes assessing the strengths and weaknesses of the plan and the enterprise and suggesting improvements.

In some cases, the panelists suggest a completely new direction. In others, they advise more effective implementation of existing policies. Their comments range over the spectrum of business issues.

Sessions are open to the public and usually draw about 300 people, most of them financiers, business executives, accountants, lawyers, consultants, and others with special interest in emerging companies. Following the panelists' evaluations, audience members can ask questions and offer comments.

Presenters have the opportunity to respond to the evaluations and suggestions offered. They also receive written evaluations of the oral presentation from audience members. (The entrepreneur doesn't make the written plan available to the audience.) These monthly sessions are held primarily for companies that have advanced beyond the start-up stage. They tend to be from one to ten years old and in need of expansion capital.

The MIT Enterprise Forum's success at its home base in Cambridge, Massachusetts has led MIT alumni to establish forums in New York, Washington, Houston, Chicago, and Amsterdam, among other cities.

## Emphasize the Market

Investors want to put their money into market-driven rather than technology-driven or service-driven companies. The potential of the product's market, sales, and profit is far more important than its attractiveness or technical features.

You can make a convincing case for the existence of a good market by demonstrating user benefit, identifying marketplace interest, and documenting market claims.

## SHOW THE USER'S BENEFIT

It's easy even for experts to overlook this basic notion. At an MIT Enterprise Forum session an entrepreneur spent the bulk of his 20-minute presentation period extolling the virtues of his company's product—an instrument to control certain aspects of the production process in the textile industry. He concluded with some financial projections looking five years down the road.

The first panelist to react to the business plan—a partner in a venture capital firm—was completely negative about the company's prospects for obtaining investment funds because, he stated, its market was in a depressed industry.

Another panelist asked, "How long does it take your product to pay for itself in decreased production costs?" The presenter immediately responded, "Six months." The second panelist replied, "That's the most important thing you've said tonight."

The venture capitalist quickly reversed his original opinion. He said he would back a company in almost any industry if it could prove such an important user's benefit—and emphasize it in its sales approach. After all, if it paid back the customer's cost in six months, the product would after that time essentially "print money."

The venture capitalist knew that instruments, machinery, and services that pay for themselves in less than one year are mandatory purchases for many potential customers. If this payback period is less than two years, it's a probable purchase; beyond three years, they don't back the product.

The MIT panel advised the entrepreneur to recast his business plan so that it emphasized the short payback period and played down the self-serving discussion about product innovation. The executive took the advice and rewrote the plan in easily understandable terms. His company is doing very well and has made the transition from a technology-driven to a market-driven company.

## FIND OUT THE MARKET'S INTEREST

Calculating the user's benefit is only the first step. An entrepreneur must also give evidence that customers are intrigued with the user's benefit claims and that they like the product or service. The business plan must reflect clear positive responses of customer prospects to the question "Having heard our pitch, will you buy?" Without them, an investment usually won't be made.

How can start-up businesses—some of which may have only a prototype product or an idea for a service—appropriately gauge market reaction? One executive of a smaller company had put together a prototype of a device that enables personal computers to handle telephone messages. He needed to demonstrate that customers would buy the product, but the company had exhausted its cash resources and was thus unable to build and sell the item in quantity.

The executives wondered how to get around the problem. The MIT panel offered two possible responses. First, the founders might allow a few customers to use the prototype and obtain written evaluations of the product and the extent of their interest when it became available.

Second, the founders might offer the product to a few potential customers at a substantial price discount if they paid part of the cost—say one-third up front—so that the company could build it. The company could not only find out whether potential buyers existed but also demonstrate the product to potential investors in real-life installations.

In the same way, an entrepreneur might offer a proposed new service at a discount to initial customers as a prototype if the customers agreed to serve as references in marketing the service to others.

For a new product, nothing succeeds as well as letters of support and appreciation from some significant potential customers along with "reference installations." You can use such third-party statements—from would-be customers to whom you've demonstrated the product, initial users, sales representatives, or distributors—to show that you have indeed discovered a sound market that needs your product or service.

You can obtain letters from users even if the product is only in prototype form. You can install it experimentally with a potential user to whom you will sell it at or below cost in return for information on its benefits and an agreement to talk to sales prospects or investors. In an appendix to the business plan or in a separate volume, you can include letters attesting to the value of the product from experimental customers.

## DOCUMENT YOUR CLAIMS

Having established a market interest, you must use carefully analyzed data to support your assertions about the market and the growth rate of sales and profits. Too often, executives think "If we're smart, we'll be able to get about 10% of the market" and "Even if we only get 1% of such a huge market, we'll be in good shape."

Investors know that there's no guarantee a new company will get any business, regardless of market size. Even if the company makes such claims based on fact—as borne out, for example, by evidence of customer interest—they can quickly crumble if the company doesn't carefully gather and analyze supporting data.

One example of this danger surfaced in a business plan that came before the MIT Enterprise Forum. An entrepreneur wanted to sell a service to small businesses. He reasoned that he could have 170,000 customers if he penetrated even 1% of the market of 17 million small enterprises in the United States. The panel pointed out that anywhere from 11 million to 14 million of such so-called small businesses were really sole proprietorships or part-time businesses. The total number of full-time small businesses with employees was actually between 3 million and 6 million and represented a real potential market far beneath the company's original projections—and prospects.

Similarly, in a business plan relating to the sale of certain equipment to apple growers, you must have U.S. Department of Agriculture statistics to discover the number of growers who could use the equipment. If your equipment is useful only to growers with 50 acres or more, then you need to determine how many growers have farms of that size, that is, how many are minor producers with only an acre or two of apple trees.

A realistic business plan needs to specify the number of potential customers, the size of their businesses, and which size is most appropriate to the offered products or services. Sometimes bigger is not better. For example, a saving of $10,000 per year in chemical use may be significant to a modest company but unimportant to a DuPont or a Monsanto.

Such marketing research should also show the nature of the industry. Few industries are more conservative than banking and public utilities. The number of potential customers is relatively small, and industry acceptance of new products or services is painfully slow, no matter how good the products and services have proven to be. Even so, most of the customers are well known and while they may act slowly, they have the buying power that makes the wait worthwhile.

At the other end of the industrial spectrum are extremely fast-growing and fast-changing operations such as franchised weight-loss clinics and computer software companies. Here the problem is reversed. While some companies have achieved multimillion dollar sales in just a few years, they are vulnerable to declines of similar proportions from competitors. These companies must innovate constantly so that potential competitors will be discouraged from entering the marketplace.

You must convincingly project the rate of acceptance for the product or service—and the rate at which it is likely to be sold. From this marketing research data, you can begin assembling a credible sales plan and projecting your plant and staff needs.

## Address Investors' Needs

The marketing issues are tied to the satisfaction of investors. Once executives make a convincing case for their market penetration, they can make the financial projections that help determine whether investors will be interested in evaluating the venture and how much they'll commit and at what price.

Before considering investors' concerns in evaluating business plans, you will find it worth your while to gauge who your potential investors might be. Most of us know that for new and growing private companies, investors may be professional venture capitalists and wealthy individuals. For corporate ventures, they are the corporation itself. When a company offers shares to the public, individuals of all means become investors along with various institutions.

But one part of the investor constituency is often overlooked in the planning process—the founders of new and growing enterprises. By deciding to start and manage a business, they are committed to years of hard work and personal sacrifice. They must try to stand back and evaluate their own businesses in order to decide whether the opportunity for reward some years down the road truly justifies the risk early on.

When an entrepreneur looks at an idea objectively rather than through rose-colored glasses, the decision whether to invest may change. One entrepreneur who believed in the promise of his scientific instruments company faced difficult marketing problems because the product was highly specialized and had, at best, few customers. Because of the entrepreneur's heavy debt, the venture's chance of eventual success and financial return was quite slim.

The panelists concluded that the entrepreneur would earn only as much financial return as he would have had holding a job during the next three to seven years. On the downside, he might wind up with much less in exchange for larger headaches. When he viewed the project in such dispassionate terms, the entrepreneur finally agreed and gave it up.

Investors' primary considerations are:

**Cashing out.** Entrepreneurs frequently do not understand why investors have a short attention span. Many who see their ventures in terms of a life-time commitment expect that anyone else who gets involved will feel the same. When investors evaluate a business plan, they consider not only whether to get in but also how and when to get out.

Because small, fast-growing companies have little cash available for dividends, the main way investors can profit is from the sale of their holdings, either when the company goes public or is sold to another business. (Large corporations that invest in new enterprises may not sell their holdings if they're committed to integrating the venture into their operations and realizing long-term gains from income.)

Venture capital firms usually wish to liquidate their investments in small companies in three to seven years so as to pay gains while they generate funds for investment in new ventures. The professional investor wants to cash out with a large capital appreciation.

Investors want to know that entrepreneurs have thought about how to comply with this desire. Do they expect to go public, sell the company, or buy the investors out in three to seven years? Will the proceeds provide investors with a return on invested capital commensurate with the investment risk—in the range of 35% to 60%, compounded and adjusted for inflation?

Business plans often do not show when and how investors may liquidate their holdings. For example, one entrepreneur's software company sought $1.5 million to expand. But a panelist calculated that, to satisfy their goals, the investors "would need to own the entire company and then some."

**Making sound projections.** Five-year forecasts of profitability help lay the groundwork for negotiating the amount investors will receive in return for their money. Investors see such financial forecasts as yardsticks against which to judge future performance.

Too often, entrepreneurs go to extremes with their numbers. In some cases, they don't do enough work on their financials and rely on figures that are so skimpy or overoptimistic that anyone who has read more than a dozen business plans quickly sees through them.

In one MIT Enterprise Forum presentation, a management team proposing to manufacture and market scientific instruments forecast a net income after taxes of 25% of sales during the fourth and fifth years following investment. While a few industries such as computer software average such high profits, the scientific instruments business is so competitive, panelists noted, that expecting such margins is unrealistic.

In fact, the managers had grossly—and carelessly—understated some important costs. The panelists advised them to take their financial estimates back to the drawing board and before approaching investors to consult financial professionals.

Some entrepreneurs think that the financials *are* the business plan. They may cover the plan with a smog of numbers. Such "spreadsheet merchants," with their pages of computer printouts covering every business variation possible and analyzing product sensitivity, completely turn off many investors.

Investors are wary even when financial projections are solidly based on realistic marketing data because fledgling companies nearly always fail to achieve their rosy profit forecasts. Officials of five major venture capital firms we surveyed said they are satisfied when new ventures reach 50% of their financial goals. They agreed that the negotiations that determine the percentage of the company purchased by the investment dollars are affected by this "projection discount factor."

**The development stage.** All investors wish to reduce their risk. In evaluating the risk of a new and growing venture, they assess the status of the product and the management team. The farther along an enterprise is in each area, the lower the risk.

At one extreme is a single entrepreneur with an unproven idea. Unless the founder has a magnificent track record, such a venture has little chance of obtaining investment funds.

At the more desirable extreme is a venture that has an accepted product in a proven market and a competent and fully staffed management team. This business is most likely to win investment funds at the lowest cost.

Entrepreneurs who become aware of their status with investors and think it inadequate can improve it. Take the case of a young MIT engineering graduate who appeared at an MIT Enterprise Forum session with written schematics for the improvement of semiconductor equipment production. He had documented interest by several producers and was looking for money to complete development and begin production.

The panelists advised him to concentrate first on making a prototype and assembling a management team with marketing and financial know-how to complement his product-development expertise. They explained that because he had never before started a company, he needed to show a great deal of visible progress in building his venture to allay investors' concern about his inexperience.

**The price.** Once investors understand a company qualitatively, they can begin to do some quantitative analysis. One customary way is to calculate the company's value on the basis of the results expected in the fifth year following investment. Because risk and reward are closely related, investors believe companies with fully developed products and proven management teams should yield between 35% and 40% on their investment, while those with incomplete products and management teams are expected to bring in 60% annual compounded returns.

Investors calculate the potential worth of a company after five years to determine what percentage they must own to realize their return. Take the hypothetical case of a well-developed company expected to yield 35% annually. Investors would want to earn 4.5 times their original investment, before inflation, over a five-year period.

After allowing for the projection discount factor, investors may postulate that a company will have $20 million annual revenues after five years and a net profit of $1.5 million. Based on a conventional multiple for acquisitions of ten times earnings, the company would be worth $15 million in five years.

If the company wants $1 million of financing, it should grow to $4.5 million after five years to satisfy investors. To realize that return from a company worth $15 million, the investors would need to own a bit less than one-third. If inflation is expected to average 7.5% a year during the five-year period, however, investors would look for a value of $6.46 million as a reasonable return over five years, or 43% of the company.

For a less mature venture—from which investors would be seeking 60% annually, net of inflation—a $1 million investment would have to bring in close to $15 million in five years, with inflation figured at 7.5% annually. But few businesses can make a convincing case for such a rich return if they don't already have a product in the hands of some representative customers.

The final percentage of the company acquired by the investors is, of course, subject to some negotiation, depending on projected earnings and expected inflation.

## Make It Happen

The only way to tend to your needs is to satisfy those of the market and the investors—unless you are wealthy enough to furnish your own capital to finance the venture and test out the pet product or service.

Of course, you must confront other issues before you can convince investors that the enterprise will succeed. For example, what proprietary aspects are there to the product or service? How will you provide quality control? Have you focused the venture toward a particular market segment, or are you trying to do too much? If this is answered in the context of the market and investors, the result will be more effective than if you deal with them in terms of your own wishes.

An example helps illustrate the potential conflicts. An entrepreneur at an MIT Enterprise Forum session projected R&D spending of about half of gross sales revenues for his specialty chemical venture. A panelist who had analyzed comparable organic chemical suppliers asked why the company's R&D spending was so much higher than the industry average of 5% of gross revenues.

The entrepreneur explained that he wanted to continually develop new products in his field. While admitting his purpose was admirable, the panel unanimously advised him to bring his spending into line with the industry's. The presenter ignored the advice; he failed to obtain the needed financing and eventually went out of business.

Once you accept the idea that you should satisfy the market and the investors, you face the challenge of organizing your data into a convincing document so that you can sell your venture to investors and customers. We have provided some presentation guidelines in the insert called "Packaging Is Important."

## Packaging Is Important

A business plan gives financiers their first impressions of a company and its principals.

Potential investors expect the plan to look good, but not too good; to be the right length; to clearly and concisely explain early on all aspects of the company's business; and not to contain bad grammar and typographical or spelling errors.

Investors are looking for evidence that the principals treat their own property with care—and will likewise treat the investment carefully. In other words, form as well as content is important, and investors know that good form reflects good content and vice versa.

Among the format issues we think most important are the following:

### Appearance

The binding and printing must not be sloppy; neither should the presentation be too lavish. A stapled compilation of photocopied pages usually looks amateurish, while bookbinding with typeset pages may arouse concern about excessive and inappropriate spending. A plastic spiral binding holding together a pair of cover sheets of a single color provides both a neat appearance and sufficient strength to withstand the handling of a number of people without damage.

## Length

A business plan should be no more than 40 pages long. The first draft will likely exceed that, but editing should produce a final version that fits within the 40-page ideal. Adherence to this length forces entrepreneurs to sharpen their ideas and results in a document likely to hold investors' attention.

Background details can be included in an additional volume. Entrepreneurs can make this material available to investors during the investigative period after the initial expression of interest.

## The Cover and Title Page

The cover should bear the name of the company, its address and phone number, and the month and year in which the plan is issued. Surprisingly, a large number of business plans are submitted to potential investors without return addresses or phone numbers. An interested investor wants to be able to request further information or express an interest, either in the company or in some aspect of the plan.

Inside the front cover should be a well-designed title page on which the cover information is repeated and, in an upper or a lower corner, the legend "Copy number _____" provided. Besides helping entrepreneurs keep track of plans in circulation, holding down the number of copies outstanding—usually to no more than 20—has a psychological advantage. After all, no investor likes to think that the prospective investment is shopworn.

## The Executive Summary

The two pages immediately following the title page should concisely explain the company's current status, its products or services, the benefits to customers, the financial forecasts, the venture's objectives in three to seven years, the amount of financing needed, and how investors will benefit.

This is a tall order for a two-page summary, but it will either sell investors on reading the rest of the plan or convince them to forget the whole thing.

## The Table of Contents

After the executive summary, include a well-designed table of contents. List each of the business plan's sections and mark the pages for each section.

Even though we might wish it weren't so, writing effective business plans is as much an art as it is a science. The idea of a master document whose blanks executives can merely fill in—much in the way lawyers use sample wills or real estate agreements—is appealing but unrealistic.

Businesses differ in key marketing, production, and financial issues. Their plans must reflect such differences and must emphasize appropriate areas and deemphasize minor issues. Remember that investors view a plan as a distillation of the objectives and character of the business and its executives. A cookie-cutter, fill-in-the-blanks plan or, worse yet, a computer-generated package, will turn them off.

Write your business plans by looking outward to your key constituencies rather than by looking inward at what suits you best. You will save valuable time and energy this way and improve your chances of winning investors and customers.

# PART

# V

# Uncovering the Messages in Hidden Channels

# 1
# Management Communication and the Grapevine

## Keith Davis

Communication is involved in all human relations. It is the "nervous system" of any organized group, providing the information and understanding necessary for high productivity and morale. For the individual company it is a continuous process, a way of life, rather than a one-shot campaign. Top management, therefore, recognizes the importance of communication and wants to do something about it. But what? Often, in its frustration, management has used standard communication "packages" instead of dealing situationally with its individual problems. Or it has emphasized the means (communication techniques) rather than the ends (objectives of communication).

One big factor which management has tended to overlook is communication *within its own group*. Communication to the worker and from the worker is dependent on effective management communication; and clearly this in turn requires informal as well as formal channels.

## The Grapevine

A particularly neglected aspect of management communication concerns that informal channel, the grapevine. There is no dodging the fact that, as a carrier of news and gossip among executives and supervisors, the grapevine often affects the affairs of management. The proof of this is the strong feelings that different executives have about it. Some regard the grapevine as an evil—a thorn in the side which regularly spreads rumor, destroys morale and reputations, leads to irresponsible actions, and challenges authority. Some regard it as a good thing because it acts as a safety valve and carries news fast. Others regard it as a very mixed blessing.

Whether the grapevine is considered an asset or a liability, it is important for executives to try to understand it. For one thing is sure: although no executive can absolutely control the grapevine, he can *influence* it. And since it is here to stay, he should learn to live with it.


**PERSPECTIVE**

Of course, the grapevine is only part of the picture of communication in management. There is also formal communication—via conferences, reports, memoranda, and so on; this provides the basic core of information, and many administrators rely on it almost exclusively because they think it makes their job simpler to have everything reduced to explicit terms—as if that were possible! Another important part of the picture is the expression of attitudes, as contrasted with the transmission of information (which is what we will be dealing with in this article). Needless to say, all these factors influence the way the grapevine works in a given company, just as the grapevine in turn influences them.

In this article I want to examine (a) the significance, character, and operation of management communication patterns, with particular emphasis on the grapevine; and (b) the influence that various factors, such as organization and the chain of procedure, have upon such patterns. From this analysis, then, it will be possible to point up (c) the practical implications for management.

As for the research basis of the analysis, the major points are these:

1. *Company studied*—The company upon which the research is based is a real one. I shall refer to it as the "Jason Company." A manufacturer of leather goods, it has 67 people in the management group (that is, all people who supervise the work of others, from top executives to foremen) and about 600 employees. It is located in a rural town of 10,000 persons, and its products are distributed nationally.

In my opinion, the pattern of management communication at the Jason Company is typical of that in many businesses; there were no special conditions likely to make the executives and supervisors act differently from their counterparts in other companies. But let me emphasize that this is a matter of judgment, and hence broader generalizations cannot be made until further research is undertaken.

As a matter of fact, one of the purposes of this article is to encourage businessmen to take a close look at management communication in their own companies and to decide for themselves whether it is the same or different. In many companies, men in the management group now follow the popular practice of examining and discussing their problems of communicating with workers, but rarely do they risk the embarrassment of appraising their communications with each other.

2. *Methodology*—The methods used to study management communication in the Jason Company are new ones. Briefly, the basic approach was to learn from each communication recipient how he first received a given piece of information and then to trace it back to its source. Suppose D and E said they received it from G; G said he received it from B; and B from A. All the chains or sequences were plotted in this way—A to B to G to D and E—and when the data from all recipients were assembled, the pattern of the flow of communication emerged. The findings could be verified and developed further with the help of other data secured from the communication recipients.

This research approach, which I have called "ecco analysis," is discussed in detail elsewhere.[1]

### SIGNIFICANT CHARACTERISTICS

In the Jason Company many of the usual grapevine characteristics were found along with others less well known. For purposes of this discussion, the four most significant characteristics are these:

1. *Speed of transmission*—Traditionally the grapevine is fast, and this showed up in the Jason Company.

For example, a certain manager had an addition to his family at the local hospital at 11 o'clock at night, and by 2:00 P.M. the next day 46% of the whole management group knew about the event. The news was transmitted only by grapevine and mostly face-to-face conversation, with an occasional interoffice telephone call. Most communications occurred immediately before work began, during "coffee hour," and during lunch hour. The five staff executives who knew of the event learned of it during "coffee hour," indicating that the morning rest period performed an important social function for the staff as well as providing relaxation.

2. *Degree of selectivity*—It is often said that the grapevine acts without conscious direction or thought—that it will carry anything, any time,

anywhere. This viewpoint has been epitomized in the statement that "the grapevine is without conscience or consciousness." But flagrant grapevine irresponsibility was not evident in the Jason Company. In fact, the grapevine here showed that it could be highly selective and discriminating.

For example, the local representative of the company which carried the employee group insurance contract planned a picnic for company executives. The Jason Company president decided to invite 36 executives, mostly from higher executive levels. The grapevine immediately went to work spreading this information, but it was carried to *only two of the 31 executives not invited.* The grapevine communicators thought the news was confidential, so they had told only those who they thought would be invited (they had to guess, since they did not have access to the invitation list). The two uninvited executives who knew the information were foremen who were told by their invited superintendent; he had a very close working relationship with them and generally kept them well informed.

Many illustrations like the above could be gathered to show that the grapevine can be discriminating. Whether it may be *counted on* in that respect, however, is another question. The answer would of course differ with each case and would depend on many variables, including other factors in the communication picture having to do with attitudes, executive relationships, and so forth.

3. *Locale of operation*—The grapevine of company news operates mostly at the place of work.

Jason managers were frequently in contact with each other after work because the town is small; yet grapevine communications about company activities predominantly took place at the plant, rather than away from it. It was at the plant that executives and supervisors learned, for instance, that the president was taking a two weeks' business trip, that the style designer had gone to Florida to study fashion trends, and that an executive had resigned to begin a local insurance business.

The significance of at-the-company grapevines is this: since management has some control over the work environment, it has an opportunity to influence the grapevine. By exerting such influence the manager can more closely integrate grapevine interests with those of the formal communication system, and he can use it for effectively spreading more significant items of information than those commonly carried.

4. *Relation to formal communication*—Formal and informal communi-

cation systems tend to be jointly active, or jointly inactive. Where formal communication was inactive at the Jason Company, the grapevine did not rush in to fill the void (as has often been suggested[2]); instead, there simply was lack of communication. Similarly, where there was effective formal communication, there was an active grapevine.

Informal and formal communication may supplement each other. Often formal communication is simply used to confirm or to expand what has already been communicated by grapevine. Thus in the case of the picnic, as just described, management issued formal invitations even to those who already knew they were invited. This necessary process of confirmation results partly because of the speed of the grapevine, which formal systems fail to match, partly because of its unofficial function, and partly because of its transient nature. Formal communication needs to come along to stamp "Official" on the news and to put it "on the record," which the grapevine cannot suitably do.

## Spreading Information

Now let us turn to the actual operation of the grapevine. How is information passed along? What is the relationship among the various people who are involved?

Human communication requires at least two persons, but each person acts independently. Person A may talk or write, but he has not *communicated* until person B receives. The individual is, therefore, a basic communication unit. That is, he is one "link" in the communication "chain" for any bit of information.

The formal communication chain is largely determined by the chain of command or by formal procedures, but the grapevine chain is more flexible. There are four different ways of visualizing it, as Exhibit I indicates:

1. *The single-strand chain*—A tells B, who tells C, who tells D, and so on; this makes for a tenuous chain to a distant receiver. Such a chain is usually in mind when one speaks of how the grapevine distorts and filters information until the original item is not recognizable.

2. *The gossip chain*—A seeks and tells everyone else.

3. *The probability chain*—A communicates randomly, say, to F and D, in accordance with the laws of probability; then F and D tell others in the same manner.

4. *The cluster chain*—A tells three selected others; perhaps one of

## Exhibit 1   Types of communication chains

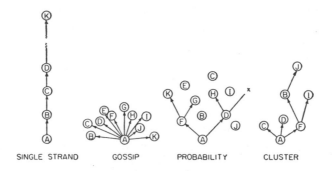

SINGLE STRAND        GOSSIP        PROBABILITY        CLUSTER

them tells two others; and then one of these two tells one other. This was virtually the only kind of chain found in the Jason Company, and may well be the normal one in industry generally.

### ACTIVE MINORITY

The predominance of the cluster chain at the Jason Company means that only a few of the persons who knew a unit of information ever transmitted it—what Jacobson and Seashore call the "liaison" individuals.[3] All others who received the information did not transmit it; they acted merely as passive receivers.

For example, when a quality-control problem occurred, 68% of the executives received the information, but only 20% transmitted it. Again, when an executive planned to resign to enter the insurance business, 81% of the executives knew about it, but only 11% passed the news on to others. Those liaison individuals who told the news to more than one other person amounted to fewer than 10% of the 67 executives in each case.

These active groups varied in membership. There was no evidence that any one group consistently acted as liaison persons; instead, different types of information passed through different liaison persons. However, as will be shown later, some individuals were invariably communication "isolates"; they received and transmitted information poorly or not at all.

The above findings indicate that if management wants more communication, it should increase the number and/or effectiveness of its liaison individuals. This appears to be a large order, but it is entirely possible. Liaison individuals tend to act in a predictable way. If an individual's unit of information concerns a job function in which he is interested, he is likely to tell others. If his information is about a person with whom he is associated socially, he also is likely to tell others. Furthermore, the sooner he knows of an event after it happened, the more likely he is to tell others. If he gets the information late, he does not want to advertise his late receipt of it by telling it to others.

In other words, three well-known communication principles which are so often mentioned in relation to attitudes also have a major influence on the spread of information by liaison individuals:

1. Tell people about what will affect them (job interest).
2. Tell people what they want to know, rather than simply what you want them to know (job and social interest).
3. Tell people soon (timing).

## Organizational Effects

The way an organization is divided horizontally into organizational levels and vertically into functions, such as production and sales, obviously has effects on management communication, for it cuts each company's over-all administrative function into small work assignments, or jobs, and sets each management person in certain relationships to others in his company.

### HORIZONTAL LEVELS

Organizational levels are perhaps the more dramatic in effect because they usually carry authority, pay increases, and status. From the communication point of view, they are especially important because of their number. In a typical firm there are usually several management levels, but only one or two worker levels; furthermore, as the firm grows, the management levels increase in number, while the worker levels remain stationary.

Communication problems are aggravated by these additional levels because the chain of communication is lengthened and complicated. Indeed, just because of this, some companies have been led to try to reduce the number of intermediate management levels. Our concern here is with the patterns of communication among individuals at the different levels.

At the Jason Company, executives at *higher* levels communicated more often and with more people than did executives at *lower* levels. In other words, the predominant communication flow was downward or horizontal. When an event happened at the bottom level, usually the news did reach a high level; but a single line of communication sufficed to carry it there, and from that point it went downward and outward in the same volume and manner (cluster chain) as if it had originated at the top.

Accordingly, the higher an executive was in the organizational hierarchy (with the exception of nonresident executives), the greater was his knowledge of company events. This was true of events which happened both above his level and below his level. Thus, if the president was out of town, a greater proportion at the fourth level knew of it than at the sixth level. Or—and this is less to be expected—if a foreman at the sixth level had an accident, a larger proportion of executives at the third level knew of it than at the fourth level, or even than at the sixth level where the accident happened. The more noteworthy the event, of course, the more likely it was to be known at upper levels—but, in a company of this size, it had to be quite trivial indeed before it failed to reach the ears of top executives.

The converse follows that in terms of communications transmitted and received the sixth and lowest level of supervision, the foreman level, was largely isolated from all other management. The average foreman was very hesitant to communicate with other members of management; and on the rare occasions when he did, he usually chose someone at his own level and preferably in his own department. Members of this group tended to be the last links in management communication, regardless of whether the chains were formal or informal.

A further significant fact concerns the eight departmental superintendents at the fourth level. Six of them supervised foremen directly; two others, with larger departments, each had a single line assistant between him and his foremen. The two who had line assistants were much more active in the communication chains than were the six others; indeed, all but one of the six appeared to have little to do with their foremen except in a formal way.

Perhaps the clue is that, with increased organizational levels, those at the higher (and hence further removed) levels both recognize a greater need for communication and have more time to practice it!

## FUNCTIONAL GROUPS

Functionalization, the second important way in which an organization is "cut up," also has a significant impact on communication in management. The functions which are delegated to a manager help to determine the people he contacts, his relationships with them, his status, and, as a result, the degree to which he receives and transmits information. More specifically, his role in communication is affected (a) by his position in the chain of command and (b) by his position in the chain of procedure, which involves the sequence of work performance and cuts across chains of command, as when a report goes from the superintendent in one chain of command to the chief engineer in another chain of command and to the controller in still another.

In the Jason Company the effects of functionalization showed up in three major ways:

1. *Staff men "in the know"*—More staff executives than line men usually knew about any company event. This was true at each level of management as well as for the management group as a whole. For example, when the president of the company made a trip to seek increased governmental allotments of hides to keep the line tannery operating at capacity, only 4% of the line executives knew the purpose of the trip, but 25% of the staff men did. In another case, when a popular line superintendent was awarded a hat as a prize in a training program for line superintendents, within six days a larger proportion of the staff executives than of the line executives knew about this event.

The explanation is not just that, with one staff executive to every three line executives, there were more line executives to be informed. More important is the fact that the *chain of procedure* usually involved more staff executives than line executives. Thus, when the superintendent was awarded his hat, a line executive had approved the award, but a staff personnel executive had processed it and a staff accounting executive had arranged for the special check.

Also the staff was more *mobile* than the line. Staff executives in such areas as personnel and control found that their duties both required and allowed them to get out of their offices, made it easy for them to walk through other departments without someone wondering whether they were "not working," to get away for coffee, and so on—all of which meant they heard more news from the other executives they talked with. (In a larger company staff members might be more fixed to their chairs, but the situation in the Jason Company doubtless applies to a great many other businesses.)

Because of its mobility and its role in the chain of procedure, the staff not only received but also transmitted communications more actively than did the line. Most of these communications were oral; at least in this respect, the staff was not the "paper mill" it is often said to be. It seems obvious that management would do well to make conscious use of staff men as communicators.

2. *Cross-communication*—A second significant effect of functionalization in the Jason Company was that the predominant flow of information for events of general interest was between the four large areas of production, sales, finance and office, and industrial relations, rather than within them. That is, if a production executive had a bit of news of general interest, he was more likely to tell a sales, finance, or personnel executive than another production executive.

Social relationships played a part in this, with executives in the various groups being lodge brothers, members of the same church, neighbors, parents of children in the same schools, and so on. In these relationships the desire to make an impression was a strong motivation for cross-communication, since imparting information to executives outside his own area served to make a man feel that the others would consider him "in the know." Procedural relationships, discussed earlier, also encouraged the executives to communicate across functional lines.

Since communications tended not to stay within an area, such as production, they tended even less to follow chains of command from boss to sub-boss to sub-sub-boss. Indeed, the chain of command was seldom used in this company except for very formal communications. Thus Exhibit II reproduces a communication chain concerning a quality control problem in production, first brought to the attention of a group sales manager in a letter from a customer. Although it was the type of problem that could have been communicated along the chain of command, the exhibit shows that, of 14 communications, only 3 were within the chain of command and only 6 remained within one functional area—sales—where the information was first received.

The fact that the chain of command may affect management com-

Exhibit 2    Communication chain for a quality control problem

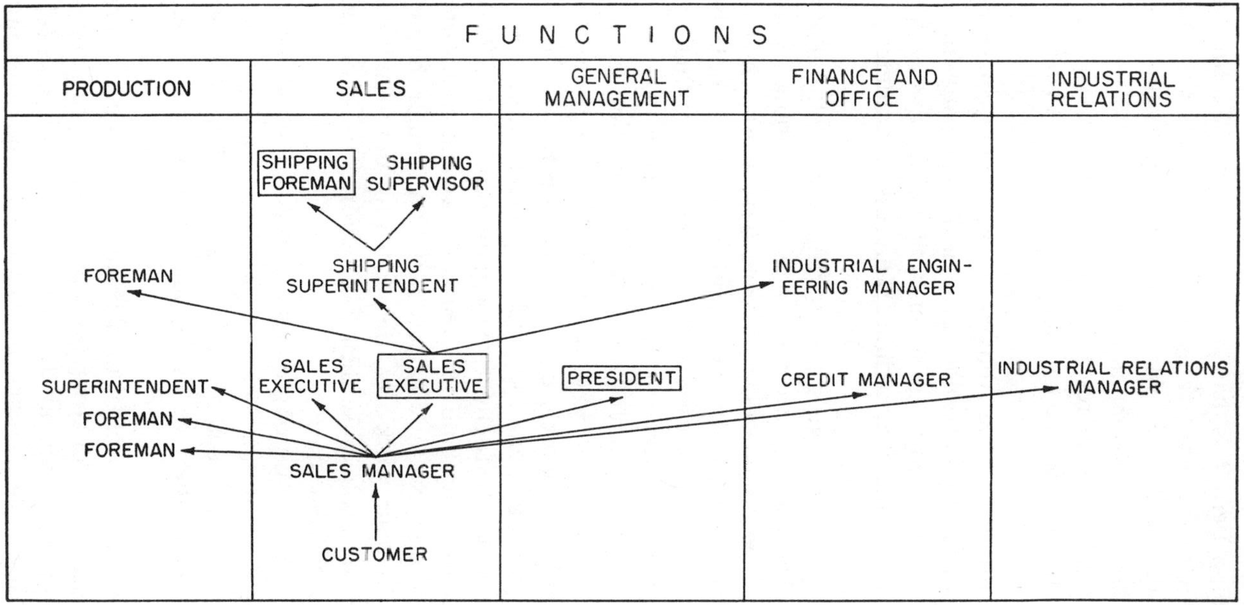

NOTE: Executives in boxes received chain-of-command communications.

munication patterns less than procedural and social influences—which has shown up in other companies too[4]—means that management needs to devote considerably more attention to the problems and opportunities of cross-communication.

3. *Group isolation*—The research in the Jason Company revealed that some functional groups were consistently isolated from communication chains. Also, there were other groups which received information but did not transmit it, and thus contributed to the same problem—the uneven spread of information through the company. Here are three examples at the foreman level illustrating different degrees of failure to participate in the communication process and different reasons for this failure:

(a) The foremen in one group were generally left out of communication chains. These men were of a different nationality from that of the rest of the employees, performed dirty work, and worked in a separate building. Also, their work fitted into the manufacturing process in such a way that it was seldom necessary for other executives to visit their work location.

(b) Another group often was in a communication chain but on the tail end of it. They were in a separate building some distance from the main manufacturing area, their function was not in the main manufacturing procedure, and they usually received information late. They had little chance or incentive to communicate to other executives.

(c) A third group both received and transmitted information, but transmitted only within a narrow radius. Although they were in the midst of the main work area, they failed to communicate with other functional groups because their jobs required constant attention and they felt socially isolated.

In sum, the reasons for group isolation at the Jason Company were: geographical separation; work association (being outside the main procedures or at the end of them); social isolation; and organizational level (the lower the level of a group, the greater its tendency to be isolated).

Obviously, it is not often feasible for management to undertake to remove such causes of group isolation as geographical or social separation. On the other hand, it may well be possible to compensate for them. For example, perhaps the volume of formal communication to men who happen to be in a separate building can be increased, or arrangements can be made for a coffee break that will bring men who are isolated because of the nature of their work or their nationality into greater contact with other supervisors. In each situation management should be able to work out measures that would be appropriate to the individual circumstances.

## Conclusion

The findings at the Jason Company have yet to be generalized by research in other industries, but they provide these starting points for action:

1. If management wants more communication among executives and supervisors, one way is to increase the number and effectiveness of the liaison individuals.

2. It should count on staff executives to be more active than line executives in spreading information.

3. It should devote more attention to cross-communication—that is, communication between men in different departments. It is erroneous to consider the chain of command as *the* communication system because it is only one of many influences. Indeed, procedural and social factors are even more important.

4. It should take steps to compensate for the fact that some groups are "isolated" from communication chains.

5. It should encourage further research about management grapevines in order to provide managers with a deeper understanding of them and to find new ways of integrating grapevine activities with the objectives of the firm.

6. "Ecco analysis," the recently developed research approach used at the Jason Company, should be useful for future studies.

If management wants to do a first-class communication job, at this stage it needs fewer medicines and more diagnoses. Communication analysis has now passed beyond "pure research" to a point where it is immediately useful to top management in the individual firm. The patterns of communication that show up should serve to indicate both the areas where communication is most deficient and the channels through which information can be made to flow most effectively.

In particular, no administrator in his right mind would try to abolish the management grapevine. It is as permanent as humanity is. Nevertheless, many administrators have abolished the grapevine from *their own minds*. They think and act without giving adequate weight to it or, worse, try to ignore it. This is a mistake. The grapevine is a factor to be reckoned with in the affairs of management. The administrator should analyze it and should consciously try to influence it.

## Notes

1. Keith Davis, "A Method of Studying Communication Patterns in Organizations," to be published in *Personnel Psychology*, Fall 1953.

2. For example, see National Industrial Conference Board, *Communicating with Employees*, Studies in Personnel Policy, No. 129 (New York, 1952), p. 34.

3. Eugene Jacobson and Stanley E. Seashore, "Communication Practices in Complex Organizations," *The Journal of Social Issues*, Vol. VII, No. 3, 1951, p. 37.

4. See Carroll L. Shartle, "Leadership and Executive Performance," *Personnel*, March 1949, pp. 377–378.

# 2
# The Hidden Messages Managers Send

Michael B. McCaskey

In the course of an ordinary day, the typical general manager spends an extraordinary amount of time meeting and talking with people. Part and parcel of a manager's communication are the imagery, the place, and the body movements that he or she uses. Images, setting, and body language are not just adjuncts to communication. They carry the messages; and indeed, in some cases, they *are* the messages. As such they are tremendously important to a manager. Yet managers often pay only haphazard attention to them or, worse, presume that they are not gifted in these areas. The truth is we all use these ways of communicating—whether we are aware of them or not. The gift is in knowing *what* is being communicated.

Like mathematics, French, and accounting, these are languages that can be learned. With intelligent practice, for example, a person can learn to read and to speak "place"—that is, to understand the symbolic, territorial, and behavior-influencing aspects of physical settings. Imagery, place, and body language rarely provide definitive information; but they do provide a manager with a way of knowing what is not available through other message channels. With skill in these languages, a manager can develop instincts and a good "feel" for a problem that makes additional appreciation of its subtleties possible.

If managers pay close attention to these features embedded in their everyday work life, they will enhance their awareness of communicating with others. In this article, I will present some ideas for understanding and practicing the languages and will indicate the right direction the reader can take to learn more on his or her own.

## Managers' Words and Their Images

A senior vice president in a large New York bank is talking about the group he formerly worked with: "You hit the bird cage and everyone is on a new perch. People are always moving there. People move so fast, and they—whew! I got out of there before it all came down."

The imagery is very graphic and tells a lot about this man and the world he lives in. If you could listen to him a little more, you would not be surprised to learn that he does not have a traditional banking background. He sees himself as an entrepreneur and feels that, while most of them are attractively dressed and schooled, the other executives in the bank don't have any fire in their guts. En masse (he doesn't see them as individuals) "they" are "birds," which suggests he thinks they are pretty, caged, and—quite likely—fragile. One can sense the relief this man felt when he moved to a part of the bank where he could be active, be himself, be entrepreneurial.

When you pay close attention to the words other people use, you notice that most people draw characteristic verbal pictures of themselves and the world around them. The imagery and metaphors that a person most frequently uses can be clues to understanding the world he or she inhabits. These vivid kernels of speech are drawn from the sports world, from literature, from religion, and from other fields of personal interest or background. The imagery shows what's valued, what's feared, and what the speaker's behavioral rules are.

Consider the following examples of imagery:

"It's like a fugue, everyone has a different part to play."
"What we do here is drop back five and punt."
"I am prepared to wait until hell freezes over."
"One more snide comment, and I would have exploded."

A recurring use of metaphors might suggest that a person sees life in the organization as a game or is fatalistic about outcomes. Metaphors can also reflect an optimistic, a pessimistic, or even a confused outlook. Think of your own metaphors. Can they be characterized as earthy, poetic, or violent? Taken in context, words in metaphor can be clues to how another is feeling, to what he or she views as important.

Another major point about the verbal environment of managers is that words are symbols, the meanings of which can vary greatly depending on who is using them. This point is troublesome, because it seems so obvious and at the same time contradicts an assumption we usually make in our everyday behavior. I have talked with managers who assume that words are entities and that communicating with another is essentially a process of logically ordering those entities. They direct all their efforts toward getting the words right and presenting a logically structured train of thought in order to persuade.

Much of the communication between two people, however, implicitly involves sentiments and feelings. These feelings are attached to the different experiences that words connote for an individual. A typical conversation bumps along without either party paying close attention to the different experiences and, therefore, the different meanings that lie behind the words. We tend to assume that we are all referring to the same thing when we say "the boss," "a good report," "a viable alternative," and "a workable solution," but most likely we are not.

As you examine misunderstandings between two managers, you will often find that what fouls the channels of communication is their mutual assumption that they are using the same words to mean the same things. A division vice president and general manager of a large consumer products company was in the early stages of trying to inculcate a team management style for his top group of managers. At one meeting his marketing vice president asked, "Who is driving the bus?"—implying that no one was. This was a clear metaphor based on familiar experience, probably made stronger by the active connotation of "driving" and the echo of "bus" in the word *business*. However, the seemingly clear question sparked off heated disagreement. The senior executive heard the marketing vice president saying he was uncomfortable that there would not be one person in charge. That was not at all what the division vice president had meant to convey by team management.

What makes communication problematic is that people fail to recognize the personally distinctive ways in which others use words. As Fritz Roethlisberger puts it, "As a result, we fail to notice the differences, and we read into our experiences similarities where differences exist."[1]

Keeping the differences in mind, try listening to conversations somewhat differently from usual. You might hear the following three features of the verbal environment:

Does the person use concrete or abstract words? Different people are comfortable with different levels of abstraction. Some people use vivid, concrete expressions; others favor "-ism" and "-ion" words that describe states and conditions. A "concrete" listener might simply reject out of hand—and not bother listening to—someone who talks at a more abstract level, and vice versa.

Does the person joke and kid a lot? Joking is one of the few ways some managers permit risky statements to be made. American managers especially allow each other greater leeway in delivering a hard truth if it is packaged as part of a joke.

Does the person say "I" or "we" more often? With whom does the person identify? For what groups is he or she willing to say, "We need to . . ."? In addition, a speaker who uses the royal or editorial "we" to refer to an action that he or she has obviously performed alone (royalty and editors excepted) can sound pompous.

The emotional baggage that words carry shows up in other ways as well. In an aerospace company, two managers disagreed about the best way to approach top management for renewed funding of a promising research project. On the one hand, the group research director wanted to "provide a menu of options." He wanted not only to give some choices but also to specify the range without dramatically posing the stakes. By using the word *menu* he was saying, in effect, "After all, everybody has to eat something—the question is what."

On the other hand, the project manager wanted the company to "bite the bullet." He wanted to challenge top management to do it right (that is, to put big funding behind the project) or not to do it at all. Complete with overtones of the American Wild West and palpable dangers, his phrasing depicts a situation in which a big step—even though painful or risky—was necessary for the long-run health of the project. In this case, both managers are using words as emotional flags; their phrasing expresses very different sets of assumptions, values, and readings of company mission and philosophy.

Emotional flag waving can, however, be a real impediment to discussion. When a manager assigns a pejorative word (such as a "Casanova," "brown nose," "Commie") to another's point of view, he is labeling that person. In labeling, a person is using a word to stop or impede thinking; it represents a quick put-down. Without making an effort to understand the other's meanings, a person using a label often cuts off any thoughtful response. If the label is couched in a witty jibe, the offended party may find it particularly difficult to continue the discussion in terms of the issues. A manager who is a third party to such an exchange can play a valuable role in identifying the labeling for what it is and in restating the matter for continued discussion.

Another important aspect of the verbal environment of managers is questions. Why are they so important? Questions often contain assumptions that not only frame the problem in a certain way but also tend to force its resolution to conform to the implicit assumption.

In the example used earlier, one executive asked, "Who is driving the bus?" As I indicated, the question as phrased contains the assumption that *one* person should be doing the driving. But it also contains the assumption that anyone else is a back-seat driver, which is bad enough in a passenger car, but frightening in a busload of back-seat drivers. Both assumptions are antithetical to a team management concept. From the division vice president's point of view, that was the wrong question to be asking, and he was savvy enough to make the assumption in the question explicit and to challenge it.

But aren't there other aspects of questions that a manager needs to attend to? Well, yes. Questions are not always what they appear to be. Some, like the one I just posed, are really disguised statements. Gestalt psychologist Fritz Perls would sometimes refuse to answer questions that patients put to him. He thought of them as traps, inviting him to be the power figure. He wanted people to acknowledge their own power and to face up to the statements they needed to make without hiding behind them as questions. In addition, Roethlisberger has noted that some (perhaps many) questions are so silly they don't deserve to be answered.[2]

Yet in the United States, people feel obliged to answer a question, even though answering should depend on whether the question is a good one, whether it is posed at the right time, and whether a person wants to answer. You might find it revealing to pay attention to the questions you and others ask in conversations. See how many of the questions are really statements. A question is *not* as simple as it seems.

Finally, in considering how people reveal themselves through the words they use, look out for "either/or" thinking. Some people habitually frame discussions in these terms: something is either right or wrong; you are either with me or against me; a job is either good or bad.

Studies of the development of the mind have found that either/or thinking characterizes the early stages of a young adult's development. In time, most people discover that life is multidimensional and does not fit into two neat categories. Under stress, however, one can return to dichotomized thinking; it becomes time to "throw the crooks out" without investigating either whether they really are crooks or whether throwing crooks out is the most appropriate response. It is much easier to stereotype the opposition—and let thinking and efforts to understand end there—than it is to search for a more complex truth.

When you hear yourself or another manager discuss a situation in either/or terms, you might examine whether a two-value framework is, in that situation, posing false choices. There may be ways to synthetically create a new solution that incorporates something of both sides. The discussion then moves from thinking in either/or terms to thinking in both/and terms.

Words and imagery provide clues to the meanings and the important values, assumptions, and experiences that lie behind a person's choice of words. Next I examine how the place and character of a physical setting can influence communication between two people.

## The Office and Place of Business

Depending on who they are and what kind of interactions they want with others, people use physical spaces in distinctive ways. Yet it often happens that both the receiver and the sender of messages about place are unaware of what is being communicated. A manager who becomes a little more thoughtful can better read what people are saying through their use of place. Managers can also examine their own physical settings to see if their arrangements influence behavior in ways that serve their ends.

The first thing to understand about place is that it represents territory. Animals mark off the range of their territory and defend it against intruders, and so does the human animal. Fences, doors, and boundary markers of all sorts separate what belongs to one person from what belongs to the rest of the world. Boundaries give security and privacy, protecting one from unwanted encroachments by others (at least boundaries make the statement that they are unwanted). For example, after a heavy snowfall in some Boston neighborhoods, people will claim as theirs the part of the street they have shovelled for parking. While the car is away, they will mark their claims with chairs or trash cans and strenuously object should anyone try to move in on "their spot."

For people to have a sense of "their own" and "home" seems quite important. Basketball teams like UCLA and Notre Dame are especially tough to beat when they have the home-court advantage. Home is familiar, predictable, and mine. The importance of having one's own territory shows up in a study of communal space in Coventry, England. Contrary to what one might expect, those families that had their own yards fraternized more than the families who shared a communal yard.

In analyzing this finding, one commentator suggests, "In suburbs and small towns, people are more likely to talk across their backyards if the property line is indicated by a fence. Because this boundary helps them maintain territoriality, it actually brings neighbors closer together."[3] This observation echoes Robert Frost's famous line, "Good fences make good neighbors."

The importance of place as territory shows up in the office as well. When a boss and a subordinate meet, whose office do they use? If the boss is sensitive to place as territory, the purpose of the meeting will decide the question. To conduct an adversary discussion, to emphasize hierarchy and authority, or to give directions, the boss should hold the meeting in his or her office. If, however, the boss wants to reach out to the subordinate—to have a conversation more on the other's terms—he or she might well consider traveling to the subordinate's office.

I know a manager who took the territoriality of office to heart. Just before beginning a tough negotiation session at another manager's office, he managed to sit in the other's big, ostentatious chair. He made light of his sitting in it by remarking on the feel of the chair as he swiveled from side to side. The second man was sufficiently discomfited by this unusual tactic that he lost the home-court advantage.

At the same time that place defines territoriality, other features of the setting also influence behavior, including the amount and type of interaction among people. Thomas Allen at MIT has studied communication patterns in R&D offices. He finds that beyond a distance of 25 or 30 yards personal interaction drops off markedly.[4] This suggests that a manager should physically locate together people in the organization who have the greatest need to talk to each other. If you are starting up a new team, locate core members close together, even if this means sacrificing status space for some members. When younger managers understand the dynamics of propinquity, they may try to locate their offices next to the boss's.

A manager can use the spaces in his or her office to influence the character of interactions there. For instance, many managers set up their offices with two different areas. In one, the manager talks across a desk to a person seated at the other side. Such an arrangement emphasizes the manager's authority and position. A subordinate is likely to feel that here the boss exercises a home-court advantage. In a second area, chairs are grouped around a coffee table or are placed at right angles to each other. Because this arrangement signals a willingness to downplay hierarchical differences, it encourages freer exchange and perhaps more sociable encounters.

Managers in a large financial services company I know are perfect examples of how people display instinctive reactions to physical settings. They have a marked preference for using one of four conference rooms, which are all alike except for the tables. Three of the rooms have rectangular tables that can be moved into squares or U-shapes; the fourth and most popular room has a round table. For reasons having to do with the culture and norms of this organization, the managers much prefer to work with each other around the round table.

Physical settings can be used in other ways to control interactions among people. A buyer for an electronics company housed in a building that lacked an elevator deliberately located his office on the third floor. A salesperson coming to the reception desk on the first floor would invariably be told that the buyer "could see you immediately." The salesperson would then trek the 40 steps to the buyer's office and, while still out of breath and somewhat disoriented, be greeted by the buyer.[5] In this case, physical setting was designed to control the interaction, beginning it on terms that put the salesperson at a disadvantage.

The impact these arrangements have on people is consistent with what cultural anthropologists have observed concerning people's sense of personal space. Edward T. Hall has studied how people in different cultures vary in what constitutes a comfortable distance for talking. His research shows that while the English and Germans stand farther apart than Americans when talking, the Arabs and Japanese stand closer together. Hall also identifies four basic distances for interaction: intimate space (touching to 18 inches), personal space (18 inches to 4 feet); social space (4 feet to 12 feet); and public space (12 feet and beyond).[6]

With chairs at right angles people can more easily move into each other's personal space. When a desk is placed between two people, the interaction shifts from a personal space to a social space. The content and nature of communication between two people change markedly when they move from one spatial zone to another. As a result of furniture arrangement, then, people often do become more distant— in both senses of the term.

The physical setting also influences behavior because it symbolizes the status of the occupants. Managers sense this, and one sometimes sees terrific battles fought over physical space in organizations as members vie for the visible manifestation of a more subtle and elusive phenomenon—power and influence. John Dean noticed this in his first days at the White House:

> As Bud and I went past the offices of White House staff members, I noticed furniture and files being moved. The White House, far more than any other government office, was in a state of perpetual internal flux. Offices were constantly exchanged and altered. . . .
> Everyone jockeyed for a position close to the President's ear, and even an unseasoned observer could sense minute changes in status. Success and failure could be seen in the size, decor, and location of offices. Anyone who moved to a smaller office was on the way down. If a carpenter or wallpaper hanger was busy in someone's office, this was a sure sign he was on the rise. Every day, workmen crawled over the White House complex like ants. Movers busied themselves with the continuous shuffling of furniture from one office to another as people moved in, up, down, or out. We learned to read office changes as an index of the internal bureaucratic power struggles.

By White House standards Dean's first office was shabby. When he complained, he was told it was only temporary, that Haldeman hadn't decided where to put him yet: "I did not have to be told what was happening. I was being tested and my performance would determine what I would get. I was at the bottom of the ladder, and instinctively, I began to climb."[7]

From the manager's point of view control over personal furnishings enhances power and authority. Or, depending on how he uses his office, the manager can emphasize other values that he considers essential to the high performance of the company.

Ken Olsen and the other top managers at Digital Equipment Corporation have built one of the most successful minicomputer companies in the world. Their offices in an old mill are far from grand. Sometimes separated by plywood partitions, the offices are faithful to the simple, Spartan beginnings of the company. These arrangements send very clear messages to the managers and to visitors—hard work and what is functional are important at DEC. Some may disagree with the DEC managers' choices now that they are so successful, but, regardless, they reveal the range possible in using physical space to support and convey the essential values of the organization.

Although it's easier to see when visiting another organization, you might tour your own and look at the messages you send by your use of physical space. Try touring it as if it were another company. How much of the space (and information) is locked up? Are files, phones, and offices fastened shut? How carefully do differences in the size, location, and furnishings of offices mark status?

Look at the bulletin boards. If they are extremely neat and if notices must be initialed, employees will feel less free to scrawl their own notes or to put up cartoons. Is there a coffee urn or somewhere else that serves as a "watering hole," or are people isolated from one another by the office layout? An informed reading of place can reveal a lot about how tight a company is, how hierarchical, how rules conscious, whether individual expression is encouraged, and what the company values.

Most individuals set up their office spaces to encourage certain types of interaction and, consciously or not, to send messages about themselves. When I enter a person's place for the first time, I often look at how much he or she has personalized it with pictures of family, mentors, friends, or favorite places. How much does that person declare about himself? Who are the special people, what kinds of things does he enjoy having around?

When you first walk into an office or a home, notice the textures. If the person had a choice, did he use tactile fabrics, long-haired rugs, coverings that invite a visitor to run a hand over them? This person may be signaling a desire to "be in touch," to interact at a closer distance. Or are the surfaces clean, polished, and smooth? Does the owner seem to prefer orderliness, to keep interactions at more of a distance? You might look at your own spaces in the same way and try to read the messages that others might find there about you and your preferred styles of interacting.

## Body Language and Paralinguistics

Like physical settings, body language and paralinguistics convey important messages that color, support, or contradict the words people use. They send nonverbal messages, although in the case of paralinguistics (which includes the tone of voice, pacing, and other extra-linguistic features that surround talking), they can involve sounds.

A project director in a huge aerospace company called a meeting of higher management people who supported his research project. Consonant with the oft-expressed company policy of commercially exploiting advanced research work, he wanted them to fund development of a new product internally. Early in the meeting, as he began to outline the sizable costs involved, he sensed their disapproval from facial expressions and body postures. His intuition told him that if they were asked to make an explicit decision on the project, it would be negative. So he changed his line of argument and began stressing the possibilities for external rather than internal funding of the project. And he assiduously avoided asking for a funding decision at that time.

This type of nonverbal communication and adjustment occurs every day in business, but frequently it goes unnoticed. Messages that are key to a situation—but that participants feel cannot be publicly or verbally acknowledged—are sent through these channels. Because nonverbal messages are ambiguous and subtle, one can readily reinterpret or deny them. Paradoxically, such messages can be safer and truer precisely because they are not precise. In the aerospace company, both the project director and higher management had their own reasons for keeping the communication ambiguous.

Several books have appeared lately in the popular press that claim to remove the ambiguity from body language. They offer a single translation for many facial expressions and body postures. For example, arms crossed against the chest "means" that the listener has closed his mind to what the speaker is saying. This kind of simplistic interpretation is an unfortunate misuse of the scholarly research on nonverbal communication. No gesture has a single, unvarying meaning. The researchers have stressed that the meaning of any gesture depends on cultural norms, personal style, the physical setting, what has gone before, and what both parties anticipate for the future.

Even when the person and the context are fairly well known, one should be cautious in interpreting body language. Recently I was walking down a company hallway with a staff person of a large manufacturer. We passed and exchanged greetings with a man named Jim who was just coming from a meeting where he had learned of his new assignment. His face was sagging, and his walk and carriage lacked their usual briskness.

Later at lunch we spent several minutes comparing our readings of Jim's nonverbal behavior, searching for alternative explanations, and wondering what each possibility might suggest for the department's future. Interpretations like this should be made cautiously and tentatively. We might find out, for example, that Jim was suffering from the flu—and that was the main source of his nonverbal behavior.

Keeping in mind that nonverbal languages are useful (because they are ambiguous) and the need for interpreting meanings within context, let us see how a manager could learn to read nonverbal languages with greater understanding. For many, the face is the most obvious conveyor of feelings—so obvious, in fact, that we have the expression, "It was written all over his face." Some research indicates that facial expression, along with tone of voice, accounts for more than 90% of the communication between two people. The dictionary meaning of words, then, accounts for only about 10% of the communication.[8]

The best way to improve one's reading of facial expressions is to watch soundless videotape or film of people's faces as they talk. Watch for raising or knitting of the eyebrows, widening of the pupils, flaring or wrinkling of the nose, tightening of the lips, baring or clenching of the teeth. To take one example, dilating pupils tend to mean that the listener is interested in what you are saying; contracting pupils suggest he or she does not like what you are saying.

But reading a facial expression is a complex process because a face often shows a mixture of several feelings at once, matching the mixture of feelings that the person may be experiencing inside.

Eye-to-eye contact is one of the most direct and powerful ways people communicate nonverbally. In U.S. culture, the social rules suggest that in most situations eye contact for a short period is appropriate. Prolonged eye contact is usually taken to be either threatening or, in another context, a sign of romantic interest. Most managers are aware that they look directly at individual members of an audience to enhance the impact of their presentation. Some, however, are not aware of how important eye contact is when they are listening. A good listener must be physically active to show good attention.

Among whites in the United States, the general rule is that the *speaker* in a conversation should find a way to break eye contact and look away. The *listener* shows attention by spending relatively more time looking at the speaker. Because it makes it harder for the speaker to continue, communication difficulties arise if the listener looks away too often. Knowing the impact looking away has can help a manager signal how much longer he or she wishes the other to continue speaking.

For example, in situations where the boss wishes to hear out the subordinate, he or she should be careful to provide the encouragement of eye attention, head nodding, and occasional "uh huhs" as the other is speaking. Even without saying words, a manager is sending nonverbal messages about the depth of his or her understanding and the degree of empathy.

The unspoken norms about patterns of eye contact do differ among racial groups. For blacks or Chicanos looking away does not necessarily mean the same lack of attention that it might mean among white speakers. A young white businessman learned this lesson in his first year of managing a subsidiary in a predominantly Chicano community. He was reprimanding a clerk named Carlos for a repeated error in record keeping. As he tried to discuss the matter, Carlos kept averting his eyes. The manager became angry and said, "Look at me when I'm talking to you." The young stock boy tried to establish eye contact but could not maintain it for long.

To the manager, this signaled disrespect and possibly defiance. For the stock boy (following his own cultural norms), it would have been a sign of disrespect to maintain eye contact with a boss who was reprimanding him. It was only after Carlos became extremely discomfited that the manager realized that Carlos's behavior was not meant to communicate disrespect. Thus patterns of nonverbal communication are highly variable among different cultures and groups, and one should be cautious in generalizing too broadly. Assuming that everyone follows the same rules can lead to misinterpretations.

The paralinguistic features of speech offer another powerful means of tuning in to another's feelings. How is something said? Paralanguage includes tone and quality of voice, pitch, pacing of speech, and sounds such as sighs or grunts. Managers can treat paralanguage as the music of communication—to observe how a person's voice tightens or catches at difficult passages or rushes and soars at moments of high emotion. Surprisingly, one can often hear the voice of another better without accompanying visual information. Because verbal messages can be distracting (an overload) or contradictory to the music of paralanguage, we do not attend as closely as we might to this valuable data source in face-to-face meetings.

Managers should notice pauses and silences as well as the pacing of speech. Silences can have a whole range of meanings. At one extreme, people use them as a weapon or tactic to close a sale or to seek agreement—waiting until the other is discomfited enough to make some concession toward their positions. Used another way, a pause in the conversation can be a valuable gift that allows the other person time to consider carefully his or her thoughts and feelings. The nonverbal behavior a person uses during the silence can help convey whether he or she intends one or the other effect.

One special type of pause is the *filled pause*, in which the speaker uses a sound such as "uhhh" to fill the spaces between words. Sociologist Erving Goffman notes that filled pauses are used to "provide continuity, showing that the speaker is still in the business of completing a reply even though he cannot immediately muster up the right words to effect this."[9] A filled pause is a signal that preserves the speaker's right to talk since it says, in effect, "Don't interrupt. I'm still talking."

The hidden messages of body language and paralanguage do not have to be the same as the verbal ones; and, in fact, a one-to-one correspondence is unlikely. But in situations where full and open communication is the aim, the nonverbal messages should add to the verbal ones in ways that are reasonable and trustworthy. When a person is communicating well, the body language moves in concert with the words. Smaller movements such as dropping the head, the hands, or the eye's gaze mark a pause, emphasize a point, or express some doubt or irony in one's speech. To mark larger transitions in thought, the speaker will change his body position altogether.[10] Nonverbal behavior, then, serves as punctuation for the verbal messages being sent.

In moments of great rapport, a remarkable pattern of nonverbal communication can develop. Two people will mirror each other's movements—dropping a hand, shifting their body at *exactly* the same time.[11] This happens so quickly that without videotape or film replay one is unlikely to notice the mirroring. But managers can learn to watch for disruptions in this mirroring because they are dramatically obvious when they occur. In the midst of talking, when a person feels that the other has violated his expectations or values, he or she will often signal distress. If norms or status differences make it unwise to express disagreement or doubt verbally, then the message will be conveyed through nonverbal "stumbles."

Instead of smooth mirroring, there will be a burst of movement, almost as if both are losing balance. Arms and legs may be thrust out and the whole body posture changed in order to regain balance.[12] Stumbles signal the need to renegotiate what's being discussed. The renegotiation occurs very rapidly and subtly and often through nonverbal channels. Managers who are aware of stumbles and what they mean have an option open to them that unaware managers do not. They can decide whether a given situation could be more effectively dealt with by verbally discussing it.

As with other languages, a manager can increase skill in sending nonverbal messages through intelligent practice. One helpful approach is to isolate and study one channel at a time. Because more information comes through several channels than one person can handle in a face-to-face encounter, for purposes of learning a person should try to latch on to one set of details at a time. Isolating a channel allows one to appreciate more fully the complexity and richness of each channel.

For example, one way managers can increase their listening skills and sharpen their appreciation of body language is by replaying video-tapes of their own and others' behavior or by watching television without the sound. Listening to audiotapes and hearing the music of paralanguage is also instructive.

The nonverbal channels often convey messages too sensitive for explicit verbal communication. Since the messages are subtle, ambiguous, and often tentative, they must be read with caution in order to realize their potential richness. These hidden messages reinforce or contradict what is proclaimed verbally and thus can aid an aware manager in making sense of a situation.

## Reading the Messages

One of the ways a manager can develop skill in all three languages is to work in a small group. It's often instructive for managers to try out proposed solutions to a managerial problem by playing roles while others watch. The observers will often be surprised at how quickly they can tell if one of the role players is feeling under attack or is trying to mislead the other. Even though a role player thinks he is hiding his discomfort or impatience, observers read the hidden messages quite clearly, although the role players themselves may not be aware of them.

Two lessons emerge. First, for those who are uncomfortable with the idea that they may be giving themselves away, it is very difficult to censor these messages. They "leak out" one way or another. Trying to censor them only increases the confusion of signals and diverts energy that could better be directed toward understanding what is going on. Second, body language, paralinguistics, and imagery are always part of an interaction. The messages are there to be read. With practice a manager can increase skill in reading and sending these messages, even to the point of being able to attend to them while in the middle of a specific situation.

In summary, none of these three languages alone gives a clear-cut message about the people using them. But cumulatively they can form the basis for impressions and hunches to be checked out through further inquiry. Our physical settings, like the clothes we wear, the words we utter, and the gestures we make, communicate to others about us and influence others with regard to us. Whether we are aware of it or not, our interactions with people will be affected by what they learn about us through our imagery, settings, and body language—and by what we learn about them through theirs.

## Notes

1. Fritz J. Roethlisberger, *Management and Morale* (Cambridge, Mass.: Harvard University Press, 1941), p. 98.

2. Ibid., p. 100.

3. David Dempsey, "Man's Hidden Environment," *Playboy*, May 1972, p. 108.

4. Thomas J. Allen, "Communication Networks in R&D Laboratories," *R&D Management*, Vol. 1, 1970, p. 14.

5. Luise Cahill Dittrich, "The Psychology of Place," ICCH 9-476-086, distributed by the Intercollegiate Case Clearing House, Soldiers Field, Boston, Mass. 02163.

6. Edward T. Hall, *The Hidden Dimension* (Garden City, N.Y.: Doubleday, 1966).

7. John W. Dean III, *Blind Ambition* (New York: Simon & Schuster, 1976), p. 29.

8. Albert Mehrabian, "Communications Without Words," *Psychology Today*, September 1968, p. 52.

9. Erving Goffman, *Frame Analysis: An Essay on the Organization of Experience* (New York: Harper & Row, 1974), p. 543.

10. W.S. Condon and W.D. Ogston, "A Segmentation of Behavior," *Journal of Psychiatric Research*, Vol. 5, 1967, p. 221; and Albert E. Scheflen, *How Behavior Means* (Garden City, N.Y.: Doubleday, 1974).

11. Ray L. Birdwhitsell, *Kinesics and Context* (Philadelphia: University of Pennsylvania Press, 1970).

12. Frederick Erickson, "Gatekeeping and the Melting Pot: Interaction in Counselling Encounters," *Harvard Educational Review*, Vol. 45, February 1975, p. 44.

# 3
# The Hidden Messages in Computer Networks

**Sara Kiesler**

Once computers were mostly the province of scientists and engineers. Today, as computers grow more powerful and versatile and less expensive, more people are using them. People usually perceive computers as special-purpose tools for calculations and data storage. But where we have studied computers—in companies and educational organizations—people tend to use them as a general-purpose tool to gather and distribute information and to talk with others. As computers become a shared technology, they influence the organization of work as well as work itself and enter the domain of management. Accordingly, managers are asking many questions about the impact computers have on the workplace:

> Does a computer network make managers more effective?
> When introducing computer mail into an organization, do managers spend less time in decision making?
> What kind of computer conference system is best suited to long-distance management?
> What are the changes technologies make that people care about the most?

New technology has three orders of effects. The first is the intended technical effects—the planned improvements in efficiency that justify investments in new technology. The second is the transient effects—the very important organizational adjustments made when a technology is introduced but that eventually disappear. The third is the unintended social effects—the permanent changes in the way social and work activities are organized. Smart executives try to make decisions about technology that win on the first level, minimize losses on the second, and retain flexibility and options on the third.

While the computer is today's most prominent new technology, it has much in common with past technical innovations, like the telephone and typewriter, that have had great social impact. We can and should learn from the histories of these other innovations.

The elevator is a technology whose intended effect was more efficient use of energy and space. If it had not been for the elevator we could not have built skyscrapers. The elevator also produced second-level outcomes—transient effects. When the elevator was introduced, people were afraid of stepping into a dangling cage. Eventually, regular elevator inspections, the posting of inspection forms in elevators, and, of course, their ubiquity and good safety record alleviated such fears.

The permanent third effect of elevators came about unintentionally and indirectly over a longer period. The elevator made it possible to build structures that increased the numbers of people who lived or worked in proximity but did not know one another. People became neighbors in the geographical but not in the personal sense; social contacts became more superficial. And now as more people live and work surrounded by strangers, they feel more alienated and distanced from each other than they did before the advent of the skyscraper.

When the telephone was introduced, it was supposed to improve business communication. A hundred years ago, the Pittsburgh telephone directory was 6 pages long and all but 6 of the 300 listings were business numbers. Even the 6 residential telephones were used for business purposes by their owners, who felt the need to keep in constant touch with their workplaces. The telephone did improve business: it made it possible for managers to leave the factory floor, for salespeople to change orders in quick response to client demands, for customers to order products directly, for companies to establish branch offices.

The telephone also had transient effects. Because of party lines and central operators, people using the telephone had no privacy. Another problem was "phonies" who used the telephone's anonymity to trick people into fake business deals. Understandably, people became concerned about whether to trust callers they didn't know.

In the end, though, the social effects of the telephone have been even more striking than the technical and transient outcomes. Today people use the telephone more for social and personal purposes than for business. In the early part of the century, farms and ranches were dismal, lonely, and even dangerous places. The telephone made it possible for people to sustain friendships and help each other quickly and easily. In urban and suburban areas, the telephone came to be used as a babysitter, and, like household appliances, it increased women's independence. Because it encouraged sustained interaction outside school, the telephone also made teenage peer groups socially important.

The workplace has also felt the social effects of the instrument. When it was introduced, many managers imagined they would use the telephone to enhance their control; they thought that when they were physically absent, they could use the telephone as a broadcast device for transmitting orders and information to their employees. But the telephone performed even better as a conversation medium than as a broadcast medium. Thus it gave employees a chance to talk back to their supervisors, to exchange information, and to send it up the hierarchy as well as receive it. The telephone did not militarize the workplace but democratized it.

In recounting this history, I have two general points in mind. First, the social effects of new technologies are hard to foresee. Hence we tend to exaggerate the technical changes and the significance of transient issues, and we underestimate the social effects. Second, the long-run social effects of a new technology are not the intended ones, but have more to do with the technology's indirect demands on our time and attention, and with the way it changes our work habits and our interpersonal relations.

## Changing the Social Arena Forever

Within this broad area of technology and social effects, I particularly want to discuss communication in organizations. Judging by current research, the effects of computers on communication are a critical new area for managers to understand and exploit. In organizations we have looked at, computer-mediated communication is changing the kind of information people receive and distribute. For one thing, people use the computer at their own discretion as a general-purpose tool for communication. They overcome temporal and geographical barriers to exchange information. But more important, computer-mediated communications can break down hierarchical and departmental barriers, standard operating procedures, and organizational norms.

## COMPUTERS CROSSING BOUNDARIES

All organizations control communication through structures and norms. Lightening the information burden on people contributes to organizational efficiency, but separating people from crucial information can be a barrier to effectiveness. Obviously, the costs of lacking important information are the costs of repairing the damage the lack causes. But having too much information can mean costly attention to things that don't need it. Because computer networks reach so many people so fast, the information effects are magnified. Changing the nature of information or its distribution in this environment can be very costly. Managers who introduce computers and computer networks are therefore in a position to make critical decisions.

One of the surprising properties of computing is that it is a social activity. Where I work, the most frequently run computer network program is the one called "Where" or "Finger" that finds other people who are logged onto the computer network. The most intensively used program is the text editor for preparing documents, memos, and letters. Other popular programs are electronic mail and bulletin boards—ways for people to communicate informally with each other.

On a typical day in one Pittsburgh company, the general electronic bulletin board announced where the lone company typewriter was located (on the floor in the back of one secretary's office) and reminded someone's friends about a Chinese dinner. On a management "board," professionals and managers argued about the technical directions of the company.

More than 15 years ago, the Department of Defense built a large computer network, the ARPANET, to allow research computers at many locations to share computing resources located at only a few sites. Soon most of the traffic over the ARPANET was not computer to computer but researcher to researcher. The ARPANET helped form entire communities of people who exchange reports, ideas, computer programs, gossip, and travel plans.

Now universities, government agencies, and corporations are installing networks. In 1983, the Manufacturers Hanover Trust mail network had more than 3,000 users, with 100 being added each month. The Digital Equipment network has more than 6,000 users. IBM has two networks; one links researchers in 65 cities in 12 countries, the other transmits 6,800 order-entry and other applications messages per minute during peak periods. These computer networks may be can-opener technologies, making life a little easier, or they may be something more than that—technologies that change organizations.

The most widely used computer-mediated communication technology is computer mail, often called electronic mail. An electronic mail system uses computer text editing and communications facilities to provide a high-speed information exchange service. Anyone with a computer account can use a terminal to compose a message or document and send it to any mailbox on that computer network or to any other computer linked into that network. Communicating computers may be in the same building and connected by a local area network or in different states, countries, or continents and connected by long-distance telecommunications.

A defining characteristic of the technology is its combination of text, speed, asynchrony, and potential audience reach. Computer mail is a writing medium, but it is more versatile than paper memoranda and postal mail. People can exchange any text—messages, documents, data files, even computer conferences consisting of the conversations of many people. Computer mail can be transmitted instantly, down the hall or across a continent. (Computer enthusiasts where I work will ask you if you want letters sent by computer mail or by "snail mail," by which they mean the postal service.)

Computer mail is sent at the convenience of the sender and read at the convenience of the recipient. The frustrations of scheduling telephone and face-to-face conversations vanish. Supervisors can send messages to a thousand people as easily as to one person, and automatically, within seconds, all specified recipients can get copies. Understandably, computer mail is attractive to organizations.

Three other features of electronic mail are also organizationally important:

Senders and receivers usually process their own electronic mail; computer messages do not have to go through an intermediary who processes them.

There are no tangible artifacts. Messages are composed on and read from video terminals (rather than teletype machines) with no hard copy left behind. It is possible to store messages on computer files and to create hard copies of them, but most messages are never put on paper; and if stored, they are stored electronically.

Senders can transmit their electronic messages in any format they choose: a corporate newsletter, an interoffice memo, a bulletin board notice, or a casual note. And it can be a two-word greeting or a two-thousand-word soliloquy.

People who design and sell computer technology assert that because electronic mail produces more timely and convenient information, managers and employees make better decisions. Everyone understands that information can be irrelevant, misinterpreted, or manipulated. But the first-order effect is presumed to be the addition of more timely and convenient information.

## THE HIDDEN EFFECTS

Unnoticed by technologists, however, is the third-order effect, that is, computer mail limits the information communicators get about the social context. Consider first the absence of dynamic personal information. Senders have no way to link the content or tone of messages to the receivers' responses so they can evaluate how their messages are being received. Similarly, without nonverbal tools, a sender cannot easily alter the mood of the message, communicate a sense of individuality, or exercise dominance or charisma.

When communication lacks dynamic personal information, people focus their attention on the message rather than on each other. Communicators feel a greater sense of anonymity and detect less individuality in others than they do talking on the phone or face-to-face. They feel less empathy, less guilt, less concern over how they compare with others, and are less influenced by norms.

Consider the absence of static personal information that relates to place, position, and person in computer mail. When a person sends a computer mail message, the transmission is instant. Because there is no hard copy and little delay between composing the message and sending it, the sender has little incentive to reflect on the message. Moreover, the large and easily accessible audience is a social hodge-podge. All computer mail looks pretty much the same. The only clue the sender has to the receiver's identity and situation may be his or her name and writing style; all indications of the receiver's job title, status, departmental affiliation, gender, race, appearance, and demeanor are missing. Missing also is information about the person's background, personality, style, and intention.

Similarly, a person receiving a message learns very little about the sender's social position, not even the information that a letterhead or a signature conveys. In addition, an electronic mail message contains scant information about a situation's norms. Reminders of the sender's setting are unavailable. Of course, people may possess relevant information from other sources, but the computer itself provides very few cues to evoke that knowledge.

Why is this effect important? When social definitions are weak or nonexistent, communication becomes unregulated. People are less bound by convention, less influenced by status, and unconcerned with making a good appearance. Their behavior becomes more extreme, impulsive, and self-centered. They become, in a sense, freer people.

To some degree all communication technologies weaken the controls over information distribution that people have in dealing with each other face-to-face. For instance, the telephone not only reduces distance constraints, it also eliminates direct access to visual cues. The telephone, therefore, reduces one's ability to clearly define the other person or grasp the situation. Over the telephone, though, one gets considerable information about the social context in nonvisual ways— from the secretary who answers or places calls, from variations on standard ways of greeting, and especially from the other person's pauses and tone of voice.

Because computer mail provides neither static nor dynamic cues, users have less social context information than with other communication devices, including paper. Paper communication still reminds people of the social context through such cues as hard copy, secretaries, letterheads, titles, handwriting variances, and the sending and receiving routines. True, a standard interoffice memorandum does not convey much social information, but interoffice memoranda are typically used as broadcast devices, not as conversation devices. Computer mail is unique because, like the telephone, it is used for personal interaction but, like the memo, it lacks social context information.

The new communication network advances—automatic file sending, electronic mail and distribution lists, computer conferencing and bulletin boards—allow people to do things faster. Executives now beginning to deploy these technologies can realize intended technical effects such as cost savings. But if we look beyond efficiency, at behavioral and organizational responses, we'll see where the real payoff is likely to be. These technologies overcome communication barriers and lessen social context information more than any other communication technology. The real payoffs, as well as the social issues, will come from the way the technologies loosen up communication.

## How the Arena Will Change

These technologies will have at least three important social effects. One effect is adding new information. In some organizations, computers automatically send production statistics, personnel data, or marketing analyses to managers regardless of whether they request them. In one large *Fortune 500* company that has used electronic mail for 15 years, administrators receive approximately 23 messages per day, most of them from distribution lists.. Of those messages, some 60% would not have been received any other way.

A second social effect is the creation of new groups. The distribution list is a list of people who will automatically receive messages sent to the electronic group. At the company just mentioned, there are distribution lists for people located in the same unit, as well as for people interested in particular technical projects: Chinese cooking, science fiction, or using a new computer. Many of these groups are composed of employees who are geographically or organizationally distant from one another and who have never had or might never have an opportunity to meet. Yet through these electronic groups they can explore common interests, exchange information, and sometimes get to know one another very well.

The third social effect is new forms of social interaction. In one company, a product developer sent a message asking for suggestions about how to add a feature to a product to distribution lists that reached hundreds of people. Within two weeks, he had received more than 150 messages cutting across geographical, departmental, divisional, and hierarchical boundaries. Some of these messages told the manager quite bluntly why it was a bad idea to add the feature.

Electronic group communication allows supervisors to build project groups around a topic, independent of other work they are doing. At both Digital Equipment and AT&T, bulletin boards and computer conferences form electronic project or decision-making groups whose members are chosen with more regard for their expertise or relevance to the decision than for their location, organizational unit, or place in the hierarchy. Most of these groups deal with routine organizational issues, but some use the electronic medium because they can respond to serious problems in a short time.

Electronic group dynamics are unlike the dynamics of face-to-face groups. In four decision-making experiments, the last one using university administrators and corporate managers as subjects, these differences became apparent. We asked the managers, both as individuals and as members of a three-person group, to make decisions about some investments. The executives made half the decisions face-to-face and half of them used a computer-mediated communication program that allows people to talk simultaneously, each using one "window" on the computer screen.

In this fourth experiment, the choice we gave the groups was one that has been of great interest to decision science researchers: suppose you have a choice between a safe investment that is guaranteed to return $20,000 over two years and an investment that has a 50% chance of returning $40,000 and a 50% chance of returning nothing. Which would you choose? Researchers have found that most people are risk averse and choose the safe alternative. When weighing one loss against another, however, and the choice is between a sure bet of *losing* $20,000 and a chance of losing nothing or $40,000, they are risk seeking and choose the latter option.

Groups that met face-to-face were risk averse for gain choices and risk seeking for loss choices. When the same groups met using the computer, however, they were slightly risk seeking no matter what the choice was. In other words, the face-to-face encounters produced conventional decisions whereas the computer-mediated discussions produced surprising decisions (at least they were surprising to us). We have learned that much of this effect came from risk-taking group members who initiated the move to break precedent. After that, the managers using the computer to communicate were just as influenced by majority rule as they were in the face-to-face situation. And they were every bit as confident of the decisions they made via computer as they were about those they made in person.

In that the experiment found unconventional decision making side by side with strong confidence in decisions, these findings are consistent with the notion that computer-mediated communication reduces social context information and increases self-centeredness.

In our experiments, we looked closely at other kinds of performance in the groups and asked, for instance, how much can you accomplish with the least wasted effort? While it took groups of managers longer to reach consensus on the computer, they also said less during that time. In conversing, people take more time to voice their concerns and to introduce discrete but important information, so redundancy may be an important contributor to effectiveness. Computer-mediated groups were efficient because participants told others what they preferred in few words and still made unconventional decisions.

In all our experiments, group members spoke uninhibitedly when they used the computer, engaging in name calling or making personal remarks to others (computer buffs call this "flaming"). On the ARPA-NET, a designated person regularly screens messages for some bulletin boards to prevent posting of inappropriate messages. When IBM's VNET was introduced, some managers used it to complain about company policy, causing the network to be renamed GRIPENET.

Flaming is a third-order effect of computer communication; it happens because senders and receivers flame when they are ignorant of the social context and feel free to express themselves.

Finally, members of computer-mediated groups tend to join in more readily than they do in face-to-face encounters. In a typical three-person group, one person may talk 45% of the time while another person may talk only 20% of the time. Usually, the person who talks the most is the person who has the highest social status or the most authority in the organization. It seems that in computer-mediated groups, where there are no salient reminders of status differences, communication is less closely regulated. Increasing the pool of information and at the same time mitigating the effects of status could contribute to organizational strength. It may also contribute to organizational instability.

## What Is an Effective Design?

What can executives do in managing the introduction of computer systems to assist organizational communication? First, let's consider effectiveness. How effective is a manager who dictates a memo that a secretary will type, give back for corrections, and send through the interoffice mail, compared with a manager who uses a computer keyboard to type a memo that will be sent immediately and informally? At a video teleconference at Westinghouse Electric, one person responsible for monitoring the use of technology in the company said to me, "I can measure how much this video teleconferencing equipment costs and guess about how much we save in travel expenses when we apply it, but I haven't the slightest idea how good the decisions are that our people reach when they use it."

Although we know that effective communication results in acceptable outcomes and actions that meet people's goals, we do not have a clear understanding of how to measure the communication's effectiveness.

Second, let's look at some design issues. Managers can do things now that 50 years ago they would have considered fantastical. Long-distance management, electronic project groups, and computer surveys of customer opinions are all the results of incremental system development. But how do you design a system to do things that have never been done? You can't possibly anticipate all of the things that might happen, so you design according to principles. You design according to levels of effects and hope you will meet your goals.

Participation is a principle that has become more popular. Many companies, some of them in imitation of Japanese practice, have formed quality circles and other employee participation plans. You can design computer-mediated communication systems and lay down open-access policies that will increase participation.

At a higher level, however, you should anticipate organizational effects. Because a computer network connects employees to the whole organization, attention tends to shift more toward the satisfaction of mutual interests. You have to decide, however, if you want this attention. More organizational participation could result both in more effective contributions and in more complaining, more junk mail.

A third issue is how computer-based communication technologies can be designed so they are compatible with the way people actually think about and relate to their associates. How, for instance, can computer-based communication systems provide social support or leadership in an organization? Research into group interaction gives us some hints on how people in groups relate to each other.

Suppose that I ask a random collection of people to read a criminal court case and declare the defendant guilty or innocent. Let's say that of ten individuals, six would acquit and four would convict. If you form them into a group or a jury and ask them to reach consensus on the same case, almost invariably they will unanimously agree to acquit. Groups generally follow the majority. During the discussion the majority exerts social pressure that magnifies its wishes and reduces the minority's impact.

The same thing seems to happen in complex organizational situations. People negotiate and follow procedures and norms to reach decisions. Technologists often speak of designing a system to prevent information underload or overload. I believe the real challenge is to build electronic communication facilities so that it is easy for people to negotiate and to implement procedures and norms—in other words, to design systems that somehow give back the social context that computer mediation wipes out. One suggestion: computer mail messages should be made easy to edit, store, retrieve, shorten, and lengthen so that people can use words to convey personal impact and social meaning. Another suggestion: make it easy to form and implement distribution-list electronic groups. Unlike computer bulletin boards, which are formed around topics and tend to attract marginal group attachment, distribution lists are formed around groups and receive more loyalty and greater attention to group norms and priorities.

## THE CONSEQUENCE OF DESIGN

Now I want to expand on design and discuss four issues—effectiveness, control, social life in the organization, and decision-making policy—and conclude with a discussion of how we should think about new technology in organizations.

First, again consider effectiveness. Recently, I talked with some people at AT&T, where a team deals with the implementation of internal communications. The issue of how far it should go in implementing electronic communication facilities depends, in part, on whether managers can be expected to work on special projects and committees using the computer and, if they can, how to design a computer conference system that will actually enhance the manager's effectiveness. If you just add technology to the office, you may wind up having more communications to monitor, more things to type, and more projects initiated that don't get completed; you may not improve performance. Because it is so expensive to implement a system and wait to see what happens, smart managers will consider the higher level effects.

Consider what you want management to accomplish. One of an executive's main jobs is to stand at the intersection of the organization and its environment, sensing external problems that his or her group should address. An organization may not adapt to change in the external environment because the managers are isolated from outside information or because the mechanisms filtering information to them are overly fine. The collected information determines what data managers use in making choices and also indicates what issues the organization thinks are important. Consider a company, such as Sears, that regularly collects information on employee morale and opinion. Inevitably, executives who receive this information are aware that top management thinks employee morale is important and are more likely than managers who don't receive such information to take employees into account when making decisions.

Communicating through computer-mediated networks can help executives span organizational boundaries. These networks gather new informants as well as genuinely new or previously uncirculated information. The question is whether the organization needs to be aware of all this information. The cost is that more people will spend their effort attending to external forces and coordinating responses to outside interests. The benefit is that the organization's problem-sensing capacity enlarges.

The second issue concerns managerial discretion and organizational control. The more information managers receive, the more they need the wherewithal to respond to that information. Computer-mediated networks move information from computer account to computer account, but management makes the policy decisions about who has access to that information and who can act on it. Will the systems allow group communication? Who will have access to group accounts? Who can create electronic distribution lists or bulletin boards? Who can send computer mail to whom? How closely will messages be monitored? And who passes on or responds to the information contained in these messages?

A light-handed policing policy that provides open access to the system will raise managerial initiative and the importance of local expertise. It might also require executives to coordinate and control these initiatives and to monitor their applications.

The social life of organizations is a third issue. How far does management want to go toward creating electronic communities? In one of our studies, people reported that they receive many work-related messages on the computer they would not have received any other way. Consequently, they feel dependent on the technology and connected with the other people on the network.

They also receive a great many messages that have nothing to do with work. People like to be sociable and will use a technology that makes it easy. Moreover, as we've seen, computer-mediated communication loosens cultural constraints (for instance, against "wasting time") by reducing the reminders a person gets of norms. Eliminating surveillance and social feedback, like laughter or a frown, reduces any embarrassment over being considered foolish and eliminates a feeling of obligation to respond in a certain way. Hence even busy, shy, or obnoxious people can communicate comfortably.

An important issue for managers to consider, then, is the extent to which the sociability that computer-mediated communication allows produces feelings of affiliation and commitment to the organization. By limiting access to the systems for control reasons, therefore, managers might also be limiting an important social benefit.

A fourth issue is the decision-making policy. Computer-mediated communication permits wide information searches. Because it promotes confrontation with minority views, it can be a bias buster: for instance, people from dispersed departments or locations can mobilize to get things changed. In implementing a computer network, a company needs to address certain questions. Do we want to make important decisions on the computer? What kinds of decision processes is it simply inappropriate to leave to computer messages? Conventionally, one would think that important collective decisions should be made face-to-face. But as we've seen in the case of the six-to-four jury that always votes to acquit, decisions arising from group action can be narrow-minded, inefficient, and prejudicial against minority views.

On the other hand, when decisions are important—as when employees' safety, lives of the public, large investments, or jobs are affected—one would want decision makers to be sensitive to all the social and organizational information available and personify this sensitivity in face-to-face discussion. Executives need to recognize that computer-mediated communication and information systems can never replace personal conversations.

## The Computer as Symbol

This contrast between computer-mediated decision making and traditional decision making brings me to a final observation. The choice to use computer-mediated communication to aid any organizational function may be as influenced by the symbolic meaning computers have for people as by the machines' other organizational consequences. In large part, computers' positive symbolic meaning dominates their introduction and use in organizations, and this may be true for some time to come. A group of students, concerned about their small college's heavy investment in computers, asked the president, "What about the new student union we need?" The president replied, "With a computer network, the whole campus will be your student union."

It makes sense to realize that computer technology design, acquisition, and implementation in organizations typically affect one another.

In one organization when it became apparent that the growing use of computers would increase the organization's legitimacy and market strength, executives decided to develop a new computer network. The technical network development team made a detailed plan of what the new one would look like.

It took several people more than a year to develop the plan, which required them to make a series of technical decisions and think about each very deeply. One team member asked a technical colleague, "How can I price this system?" The colleague answered, "You can't price workstations, but you can put a cost on delivering computer mail." The team made the decision without any intervention by management and without considering the higher level effects of pricing communication constraints.

Managers sometimes make decisions in this casual way without realizing that their actions are leading to a technology system that will have some management import. In making technology decisions, smart executives are aware of the three orders of technology effects and their whole array of organizational consequences.

New computer-mediated communication technologies are on the rise and will change the way information is distributed in organizations. In the computerized organization, more people will have information that always existed and some people will have new information. Computer networks will change existing groups and will create new, electronic groups. People will relate to one another in different ways, and the dynamics of decision making may change.

The effects can be potentially very interesting to technology designers and decision makers, but managers need to think more broadly. Today we can perform more and more technical miracles with computers, but real managerial leverage will come from asking what social miracles we perform with them.

# PART

# VI

# Articulating Your Company's Goals and Culture

# 1

# Speed, Simplicity, Self-Confidence: An Interview with Jack Welch

## Noel Tichy and Ram Charan

*John F. Welch, Jr., chairman and CEO of General Electric, leads one of the world's largest corporations. It is a very different corporation from the one he inherited in 1981. GE is now built around 14 distinct businesses—including aircraft engines, medical systems, engineering plastics, major appliances, NBC television, and financial services. They reflect the aggressive strategic redirection Welch unveiled soon after he became CEO.*

*By now the story of GE's business transformation is familiar. In 1981, Welch declared that the company would focus its operations on three "strategic circles"—core manufacturing units such as lighting and locomotives, technology-intensive businesses, and services—and that each of its businesses would rank first or second in its global market. GE has achieved world market-share leadership in nearly all of its 14 businesses. In 1988, its 300,000 employees generated revenues of more than $50 billion and net income of $3.4 billion.*

*GE's strategic redirection had essentially taken shape by the end of 1986. Since then, Welch has embarked on a more imposing challenge: building a revitalized "human engine" to animate GE's formidable "business engine."*

*His program has two central objectives. First, he is championing a company-wide drive to identify and eliminate unproductive work in order to energize GE's employees. It is neither realistic nor useful, Welch argues, to expect employees of a decidedly leaner corporation to complete all the reports, reviews, forecasts, and budgets that were standard operating procedure in more forgiving times. He is developing procedures to speed decision cycles, move information through the organization, provide quick and effective feedback, and evaluate and reward managers on qualities such as openness, candor, and self-confidence.*

*Second, and perhaps of even greater significance, Welch is leading a trans-*
*formation of attitudes at GE—struggling, in his words, to release "emotional*
*energy" at all levels of the organization and encourage creativity and feelings*
*of ownership and self-worth. His ultimate goal is to create an enterprise that*
*can tap the benefits of global scale and diversity without the stifling costs of*
*bureaucratic controls and hierarchical authority and without a managerial*
*focus on personal power and self-perpetuation. This requires a transformation*
*not only of systems and procedures, he argues, but also of people themselves.*

HBR: *What makes a good manager?*

Jack Welch: I prefer the term business leader. Good business leaders
create a vision, articulate the vision, passionately own the vision, and
relentlessly drive it to completion. Above all else, though, good leaders
are open. They go up, down, and around their organization to reach
people. They don't stick to the established channels. They're informal.
They're straight with people. They make a religion out of being accessible. They never get bored telling their story.

Real communication takes countless hours of eyeball to eyeball,
back and forth. It means more listening than talking. It's not pro-
nouncements on a videotape, it's not announcements in a newspaper.
It is human beings coming to see and accept things through a constant
interactive process aimed at consensus. And it must be absolutely
relentless. That's a real challenge for us. There's still not enough candor in this company.

*What do you mean by "candor"?*

I mean facing reality, seeing the world as it is rather than as you
wish it were. We've seen over and over again that businesses facing
market downturns, tougher competition, and more demanding customers inevitably make forecasts that are much too optimistic. This
means they don't take advantage of the opportunities change usually
offers. Change in the marketplace isn't something to fear; it's an enormous opportunity to shuffle the deck, to replay the game. Candid
managers—leaders—don't get paralyzed about the "fragility" of the
organization. They tell people the truth. That doesn't scare them because they realize their people know the truth anyway.

We've had managers at GE who couldn't change, who kept telling
us to leave them alone. They wanted to sit back, to keep things the
way they were. And that's just what they did—until they and most of
their staffs had to go. That's the lousy part of this job. What's worse is
that we still don't understand why so many people are incapable of
facing reality, of being candid with themselves and others.

But we are clearly making progress in facing reality, even if the progress is painfully slow. Take our locomotive business. That team was the only one we've ever had that took a business whose forecasts and plans were headed straight up, and whose market began to head straight down, a virtual collapse, and managed to change the tires while the car was moving. It's the team that forecast the great locomotive boom, convinced us to invest $300 million to renovate its plant in Erie, and then the market went boom all right—right into a crater. But when it did, that team turned on a dime. It reoriented the business.

Several of our other businesses in the same situation said, "Give it time, the market will come back." Locomotive didn't wait. And today, now that the market *is* coming back, the business looks great. The point is, what determines your destiny is not the hand you're dealt; it's how you play the hand. And the best way to play your hand is to face reality—see the world the way it is—and act accordingly.

*What makes an effective organization?*

For a large organization to be effective, it must be simple. For a large organization to be simple, its people must have self-confidence and intellectual self-assurance. Insecure managers create complexity. Frightened, nervous managers use thick, convoluted planning books and busy slides filled with everything they've known since childhood. Real leaders don't need clutter. People must have the self-confidence to be clear, precise, to be sure that every person in their organization—highest to lowest—understands what the business is trying to achieve. But it's not easy. You can't believe how hard it is for people to be simple, how much they fear being simple. They worry that if they're simple, people will think they're simpleminded. In reality, of course, it's just the reverse. Clear, tough-minded people are the most simple.

*Soon after you became CEO, you articulated GE's now-famous strategy of "number one or number two globally." Was that an exercise in the power of simplicity?*

Yes. In 1981, when we first defined our business strategy, the real focus was Japan. The entire organization had to understand that GE was in a tougher, more competitive world, with Japan as the cutting edge of the new competition. Nine years later, that competitive toughness has increased by a factor of five or ten. We face a revitalized Japan that's migrated around the world—to Thailand, Malaysia, Mexico, the United States—and responded successfully to a massive yen change. Europe is a different game today. There are great European businesspeople, dynamic leaders, people who are changing things. Plus you've got all the other Asian successes.

So being number one or number two globally is more important than ever. But scale alone is not enough. You have to combine financial strength, market position, and technology leadership with an organizational focus on speed, agility, and simplicity. The world moves so much faster today. You can be driving through Seoul, talking to France on the phone and making a deal, and have a fax waiting for you when you get back to the United States with the deal in good technical shape. Paolo Fresco, senior vice president of GE International, has been negotiating around-the-clock for the past two days on a deal in England. Last night I was talking with Larry Bossidy, one of our vice chairmen, who was in West Germany doing another deal. We never used to do business this way. So you can be the biggest, but if you're not flexible enough to handle rapid change and make quick decisions, you won't win.

*How have you implemented your commitment to simplicity at the highest levels of GE, where you can have the most direct impact on what happens?*

First, we took out management layers. Layers hide weaknesses. Layers mask mediocrity. I firmly believe that an overburdened, overstretched executive is the best executive because he or she doesn't have the time to meddle, to deal in trivia, to bother people. Remember the theory that a manager should have no more than 6 or 7 direct reports? I say the right number is closer to 10 or 15. This way you have no choice but to let people flex their muscles, let them grow and mature. With 10 or 15 reports, a leader can focus only on the big important issues, not on minutiae.

We also reduced the corporate staff. Headquarters can be the bane of corporate America. It can strangle, choke, delay, and create insecurity. If you're going to have simplicity in the field, you can't have a big staff at home. We don't need the questioners and the checkers, the nitpickers who bog down the process, people whose only role is to second-guess and kibitz, the people who clog communication inside the company. Today people at headquarters are experts in taxes, finance, or some other key area that can help people in the field. Our corporate staff no longer just challenges and questions; it assists. This is a mind-set change: staff essentially reports to the field rather than the other way around.

*So many CEOs disparage staff and middle management—you know, "If only those bureaucrats would buy into my vision." When you talk about "nitpickers" and "kibitzers," are you talking about lousy people or about good people forced into lousy jobs?*

People are not lousy, period. Leaders have to find a better fit between their organization's needs and their people's capabilities. Staff people, whom I prefer to call individual contributors, can be tremendous sources of added value in an organization. But each staff person has to ask, "How do I add value? How do I help make people on the line more effective and more competitive?" In the past, many staff functions were driven by control rather than adding value. Staffs with that focus have to be eliminated. They sap emotional energy in the organization. As for middle managers, they can be the stronghold of the organization. But their jobs have to be redefined. They have to see their roles as a combination of teacher, cheerleader, and liberator, not controller.

*You've dismantled GE's groups and sectors, the top levels of the corporate organization to which individual strategic business units once reported. That certainly makes the organization chart more simple—you now have 14 separate businesses reporting directly to you or your two vice chairmen. How does the new structure simplify how GE operates on a day-to-day basis?*

Cutting the groups and sectors eliminated communications filters. Today there is direct communication between the CEO and the leaders of the 14 businesses. We have very short cycle times for decisions and little interference by corporate staff. A major investment decision that used to take a year can now be made in a matter of days.

We also run a Corporate Executive Council, the CEC. For two days every quarter, we meet with the leaders of the 14 businesses and our top staff people. These aren't stuffy, formal strategic reviews. We share ideas and information candidly and openly, including programs that have failed. The important thing is that at the end of those two days everyone in the CEC has seen and discussed the same information. The CEC creates a sense of trust, a sense of personal familiarity and mutual obligation at the top of the company. We consider the CEC a piece of organizational technology that is very important for our future success.

*Still, how can it be "simple" to run a $50 billion enterprise? Doesn't a corporation as vast as GE need management layers, extensive review systems, and formal procedures—if for no other reason than to keep the business under control?*

People always overestimate how complex business is. This isn't rocket science; we've chosen one of the world's more simple professions. Most global businesses have three or four critical competitors, and you know who they are. And there aren't that many things you can do with a business. It's not as if you're choosing among 2,000 options.

You mentioned review systems. At our 1986 officers' meeting, which involves the top 100 or so executives at GE, we asked the 14 business leaders to present reports on the competitive dynamics in their businesses. How'd we do it? We had them each prepare one-page answers to five questions: What are your market dynamics globally today, and where are they going over the next several years? What actions have your competitors taken in the last three years to upset those global dynamics? What have you done in the last three years to affect those dynamics? What are the most dangerous things your competitor could do in the next three years to upset those dynamics? What are the most effective things you could do to bring your desired impact on those dynamics?

Five simple charts. After those initial reviews, which we update regularly, we could assume that everyone at the top knew the plays and had the same playbook. It doesn't take a genius. Fourteen businesses each with a playbook of five charts. So when Larry Bossidy is with a potential partner in Europe, or I'm with a company in the Far East, we're always there with a competitive understanding based on our playbooks. We know exactly what makes sense; we don't need a big staff to do endless analysis. That means we should be able to act with speed.

Probably the most important thing we promise our business leaders is fast action. Their job is to create and grow new global businesses. Our job in the executive office is to facilitate, to go out and negotiate a deal, to make the acquisition, or get our businesses the partners they need. When our business leaders call, they don't expect studies—they expect answers.

Take the deal with Thomson, where we swapped our consumer electronics business for their medical equipment business. We were presented with an opportunity, a great solution to a serious strategic problem, and we were able to act quickly. We didn't need to go back to headquarters for a strategic analysis and a bunch of reports. Conceptually, it took us about 30 minutes to decide that the deal made sense and then a meeting of maybe two hours with the Thomson people to work out the basic terms. We signed a letter of intent in five days. We had to close it with the usual legal details, of course, so from beginning to end it took five months. Thomson had the same clear view of where it wanted to go—so it worked perfectly for both sides.

Another of our jobs is to transfer best practices across all the businesses, with lightning speed. Staff often put people all over the place to do this. But they aren't effective lightning rods to transfer best practice; they don't have the stature in the organization. Business leaders do. That's why every CEC meeting deals in part with a generic business issue—a new pay plan, a drug-testing program, stock options. Every business is free to propose its own plan or program and present it at the CEC, and we put it through a central screen at corporate, strictly to make sure it's within the bounds of good sense. We don't approve the details. But we want to know what the details are so we can see which programs are working and immediately alert the other businesses to the successful ones.

*You make it sound so easy.*

Simple *doesn't* mean easy, especially as you try to move this approach down through the organization. When you take out layers, you change the exposure of the managers who remain. They sit right in the sun. Some of them blotch immediately; they can't stand the exposure of leadership.

We now have leaders in each of the businesses who *own* those businesses. Eight years ago, we had to sell the idea of ownership. Today the challenge is to move that sense of ownership, that commitment to relentless personal interaction and immediate sharing of information, down through the organization. We're very early in this, and it's going to be anything but easy. But it's something we have to do.

*From an organizational point of view, how are the 14 businesses changing? Are they going through a delayering process? Are their top people communicating as the CEC does?*

In addition to locomotives, which I've already discussed, we've had major delayering and streamlining in almost all of our businesses, and they have made significant improvements in total cost productivity.

The CEC concept is flowing down as well. For example, each of the businesses has created its own executive committee to meet on policy questions. These committees meet weekly or monthly and include the top staff and line people from the businesses. Everyone in the same room, everyone with the same information, everyone buying into the targets. Each business also has an operations committee. This is a bigger group of maybe 30 people for each business: 5 staffers, 7 people from manufacturing, 6 from engineering, 8 from marketing, and so on. They get together every quarter for a day and a half to thrash out problems, to get people talking across functions, to communicate with each other about their prospects and programs. That's 30 people in 14 businesses, more than 400 people all together, in a process of instant communication about their businesses and the company.

You see, I operate on a very simple belief about business. If there are six of us in a room, and we all get the same facts, in most cases, the six of us will reach roughly the same conclusion. And once we all accept that conclusion, we can force our energy into it and put it into action. The problem is, we don't get the same information. We each get different pieces. Business isn't complicated. The complications arise when people are cut off from information they need. That's what we're trying to change.

*That brings us to Work-Out, which you've been championing inside GE since early this year. Why are you pushing it so hard?*

Work-Out is absolutely fundamental to our becoming the kind of company we must become. That's why I'm so passionate about it. We're not going to succeed if people end up doing the same work they've always done, if they don't feel any psychic or financial impact from the way the organization is changing. The ultimate objective of Work-Out is so clear. We want 300,000 people with different career objectives, different family aspirations, different financial goals, to share directly in this company's vision, the information, the decision-making process, and the rewards. We want to build a more stimulating environment, a more creative environment, a freer work atmosphere, with incentives tied directly to what people do. (See "Work-Out: A Case Study.")

## Work-Out: A Case Study

GE Medical Systems (GEMS) is the world leader in medical diagnostic imaging equipment, including CT scanners, magnetic resonance equipment, and X-ray mammography. Its more than 15,000 employees face formidable international competition. Despite positive financial results, GEMS is working to transform its human organization. Work-Out is designed to identify sources of frustration and bureaucratic inefficiency, eliminate unnecessary and unproductive work, and overhaul how managers are evaluated and rewarded.

Work-Out began last fall when some 50 GEMS employees attended a five-day offsite session in Lake Lawn, Wisconsin. The participants included senior vice president and group executive John Trani, his staff, six employee relations managers, and informal leaders from technology, finance, sales, service, marketing, and manufacturing. Trani selected these informal leaders for their willingness to take business risks, challenge the status quo, and contribute in other key ways to GEMS. We participated as Work-Out faculty members and have participated in follow-up sessions that will run beyond 1989.

The Lake Lawn session took place after two important preliminary steps. First, we conducted in-depth interviews with managers at all levels of GEMS. Our interviews uncovered many objections to and criticisms of existing procedures, including measurement systems (too many, not focused enough on customers, cross-functional conflicts); pay and reward systems (lack of work goals, inconsistent signals); career development systems (ambiguous career paths, inadequate performance feedback); and an atmosphere in which blame, fear, and lack of trust overshadowed team commitments to solving problems. Here are some sample quotes from our interviews:

"I'm frustrated. I simply can't do the quality of work that I want to do and know how to do. I feel my hands are tied. I have no time. I need help on how to delegate and operate in this new culture."

"The goal of downsizing and delayering is correct. The execution stinks. The concept is to drop a lot of 'less important' work. This just didn't happen. We still have to know all the details, still have to follow all the old policies and systems."

"I'm overwhelmed. I can and want to do better work. The solution is not simply adding new people; I don't even want to. We need to team up on projects and work. Our leaders must stop piling on more and help us set priorities."

Second, just before the first Work-Out session, Jack Welch traveled to GEMS headquarters for a half-day roundtable with the Work-Out participants. Here are some sample quotes from middle managers:

To senior management: "Listen! Think carefully about what the middle managers say. Make them feel like they are the experts and that their opinions are respected. There appear to be too many preconceived beliefs on the part of Welch and Trani."

To senior management: "Listen to people, don't just pontificate. Trust people's judgment and don't continually second-guess. Treat other people like adults and not children."

About themselves: "I will recommend work to be discontinued. I will try to find 'blind spots' where I withhold power. Any person I send to speak for me will 'push' peers who resist change."

About themselves: "I will be more bold in making decisions. I will no longer accept the status quo. I will ask my boss for authority to make decisions. In fact, I will make more decisions on my own."

The five-day Work-Out session was an intense effort to unravel, evaluate, and reconsider the complex web of personal relationships, cross-functional interactions, and formal work procedures through which the business of GEMS gets done. Cross-functional teams cooperated to address actual business problems. Each functional group developed a vision of where its operations are headed.

John Trani participated in a roundtable where he listened and responded to the concerns and criticisms of middle managers. Senior members of the GEMS staff worked to build trust and more effective communication with the functional managers. All the participants focused on ways to reorganize work and maximize return on organization time, on team time, and on individual time.

The five-day session ended with individuals and functional teams signing close to 100 written contracts to implement the new procedures. There were contracts between functional teams, contracts between individuals, contracts between function heads and their staffs, and businesswide contracts with John Trani and his staff.

Work-Out has picked up steam since Lake Lawn. Managers from different product lines have participated in workshops to review and implement the attitudes, values, and new work procedures discussed at Lake Lawn. A Work-Out steering committee has held cross-functional information meetings for field employees around the world. Managers throughout GEMS are reviewing and modifying their reward and measurement systems. And Welch continues to receive regular briefings on Work-Out's progress.

No two GE businesses approach Work-Out in the same way; a process this intensive can't be "cloned" successfully among vastly different businesses. But Work-Out at GEMS offers a glimpse of the change process taking place throughout General Electric.

—Noel Tichy and Ram Charan

Now, the business leaders aren't particularly thrilled that we're so passionate about Work-Out. In 1989, the CEO is going to every business in this company to sit in on a Work-Out session. That's a little puzzling to them. "I own the business, what are you doing here?" they say. Well, I'm not there to tell them how to price products, what type of equipment they need, whom to hire; I have no comments on that.

But Work-Out is the next generation of what we're trying to do. We had to put in a process to focus on and change how work gets done in this company. We have to apply the same relentless passion to Work-Out that we did in selling the vision of number one and number two globally. That's why we're pushing it so hard, getting so involved.

*What is the essence of Work-Out, the basic goal?*

Work-Out has a practical and an intellectual goal. The practical objective is to get rid of thousands of bad habits accumulated since the creation of General Electric. How would you like to move from a house after 112 years? Think of what would be in the closets and the attic—those shoes that you'll wear to paint next spring, even though you know you'll never paint again. We've got 112 years of closets and attics in this company. We want to flush them out, to start with a brand new house with empty closets, to begin the whole game again.

The second thing we want to achieve, the intellectual part, begins by putting the leaders of each business in front of 100 or so of their people, eight to ten times a year, to let them hear what their people think about the company, what they like and don't like about their work, about how they're evaluated, about how they spend their time. Work-Out will expose the leaders to the vibrations of their business—opinions, feelings, emotions, resentments, not abstract theories of organization and management.

Ultimately, we're talking about redefining the relationship between boss and subordinate. I want to get to a point where people challenge their bosses every day: "Why do you require me to do these wasteful things? Why don't you let me do the things you shouldn't be doing so you can move on and create? That's the job of a leader—to create, not to control. Trust me to do my job, and don't make me waste all my time trying to deal with you on the control issue."

Now, how do you get people communicating with each other with that much candor? You put them together in a room and make them thrash it out.

These Work-Out sessions, and I've already done several of them, create all kinds of personal dynamics. Some people go and hide. Some don't like the dinner in the evening because they can't get along with the other people. Some emerge as forceful advocates. As people meet over and over, though, more of them will develop the courage to speak out. The norm will become the person who says, "Dammit, we're not doing it. Let's get on with doing it." Today the norm in most companies, not just GE, is not to bring up critical issues with a boss, certainly not in a public setting, and certainly not in an atmosphere where self-confidence has not been developed. This process will create more fulfilling and rewarding jobs. The quality of work life will improve dramatically.

*It's one thing to insist that the people who report directly to you, or who work one or two layers below you, become forceful advocates and criticize the status quo. They've got your support. But what about people lower in the organization, people who have to worry how their bosses will react?*

You're right on the hottest issue—when a boss reacts to criticism by saying, "I'll get that guy." Now, hopefully, that guy is so good he quits that same week and shows the boss where that attitude gets him. That's not the best result for GE, of course, but that's what it may take to shake people up.

It's not going to be easy to get the spirit and intent of Work-Out clear throughout the company. I had a technician at my house to install some appliances recently. He said, "I saw your videotape on Work-Out. The guys at my level understand what you're talking about: we'll be free to enjoy our work more, not just do more work, and to do more work on our own. But do you know how our supervisors interpreted it? They pointed to the screen and said, 'You see what he's saying, you guys better start busting your butts.'" We have a long way to go!

The potential for meanness in an organization, for a variety of reasons, is often in inverse proportion to level. People at the top have more time and resources to be fair. I wasn't trained to be a judge, but I spend a lot of time worrying about fairness. The data I get generally favor the manager over the employee. But we have two people at headquarters, fairness arbitrators so to speak, who sift the situation. So when I get a problem, I can smell it and feel it and try to figure out what's really happening. Managers down in the organization don't have the time or help for that. They too often say, "This is how we do it here, go do it." Work-Out is going to break down those attitudes. Managers will be in front of their people, challenged in a thousand different ways, held to account.

*To change behavior, you must also change how people are compensated and rewarded. Are those systems being changed at GE?*

We let every business come up with its own pay plan. It can create bonus plans in any way that makes sense. We're also doing all kinds of exciting things to reward people for their contributions, things we've never done before. For example, we now give out $20 to $30 million in management awards every year—cash payments to individuals for outstanding performance. We're trying desperately to push rewards down to levels where they never used to be. Stock options now go to 3,000 people, up from 400 ten years ago, and that's probably still not enough.

*Another way to influence behavior is to promote people based on the characteristics you want to encourage. How can you evaluate executives on qualities as subjective as candor and speed?*

Not only can we do it, we *are* doing it. Again, we're starting at the top of the company and, as the new systems prove themselves, we'll drive them down. We took three years to develop a statement on corporate values, what we as a company believe in. It was a brutal process. We talked to 5,000 people at our management development center in Crotonville. We sweated over every word. This will be the first year that our Session C meetings, the intensive process we use to evaluate the officers of the company, revolve around that value statement. We've told the business leaders that they must rank each of their officers on a scale of one to five against the business and individual characteristics in that statement [see the GE Value Statement]. Then I, Larry Bossidy, and Ed Hood, our other vice chairman, will rate the officers and see where we agree or disagree with the business leaders.

We had a long discussion about this in the CEC. People said just what you said: "How can you put a number on how open people are, on how directly they face reality?" Well, they're going to have to—the best numbers they can come up with, and then we'll argue about them. We have to know if our people are open and self-confident, if they believe in honest communication and quick action, if the people we hired years ago have changed. The only way to test our progress is through regular evaluations at the top and by listening to every audience we appear before in the company.

*All corporations, but especially giant corporations like GE, have implicit social and psychological contracts with their employees—mutual responsibilities and loyalties by which each side abides. What is GE's psychological contract with its people?*

Like many other large companies in the United States, Europe, and Japan, GE has had an implicit psychological contract based on perceived lifetime employment. People were rarely dismissed except for cause or severe business downturns, like in Aerospace after Vietnam. This produced a paternal, feudal, fuzzy kind of loyalty. You put in your time, worked hard, and the company took care of you for life.

# GE Value Statement

## BUSINESS CHARACTERISTICS

**Lean**

    What – Reduce tasks and the people required to do them.

    Why – Critical to developing world cost leadership.

**Agile**

    What – Delayering.

    Why – Create fast decision making in rapidly changing world through improved communication and increased individual response.

**Creative**

    What – Development of new ideas – innovation.

    Why – Increase customer satisfaction and operating margins through higher value products and services.

**Ownership**

    What – Self-confidence to trust others. Self-confidence to delegate to others the freedom to act while, at the same time, self-confidence to involve higher levels in issues critical to the business and the corporation.

    Why – Supports concept of more individual responsibility, capability to act quickly and independently. Should increase job satisfaction and improve understanding of risks and rewards. While delegation is critical, there is a small percentage of high-impact issues that need or require involvement of higher levels within the business and within the corporation.

**Reward**

    What – Recognition and compensation commensurate with risk and performance – highly differentiated by individual, with recognition of total team achievement.

    Why – Necessary to attract and motivate the type of individuals required to accomplish GE's objectives. A #1 business should provide #1 people with #1 opportunity.

# INDIVIDUAL CHARACTERISTICS

**Reality**
- What – Describe the environment as it is – not as we hope it to be.
- Why – Critical to developing a vision and a winning strategy, and to gaining universal acceptance for their implementation.

**Leadership**
- What – Sustained passion for and commitment to a proactive, shared vision and its implementation.
- Why – To rally teams toward achieving a common objective.

**Candor/Openness**
- What – Complete and frequent sharing of information with individuals (appraisals, etc.) and organization (everything).
- Why – Critical to employees knowing where they, their efforts, and their business stand.

**Simplicity**
- What – Strive for brevity, clarity, the "elegant, simple solution"– less is better.
- Why – Less complexity improves everything, from reduced bureaucracy to better product designs to lower costs.

**Integrity**
- What – Never bend or wink at the truth, and live within both the spirit and letter of the laws of every global business arena.
- Why – Critical to gaining the global arenas' acceptance of our right to grow and prosper. Every constituency; shareowners who invest; customers who purchase; community that supports; and employees who depend, expect, and deserve our unequivocal commitment to integrity in every facet of our behavior.

**Individual Dignity**
- What – Respect and leverage the talent and contribution of every individual in both good and bad times.
- Why – Teamwork depends on trust, mutual understanding, and the shared belief that the individual will be treated fairly in any environment.

That kind of loyalty tends to focus people inward. But given today's environment, people's emotional energy must be focused outward on a competitive world where no business is a safe haven for employment unless it is winning in the marketplace. The psychological contract has to change. People at all levels have to feel the risk-reward tension.

My concept of loyalty is not "giving time" to some corporate entity and, in turn, being shielded and protected from the outside world. Loyalty is an affinity among people who want to grapple with the outside world and win. Their personal values, dreams, and ambitions cause them to gravitate toward each other and toward a company like GE that gives them the resources and opportunities to flourish.

The new psychological contract, if there is such a thing, is that jobs at GE are the best in the world for people who are willing to compete. We have the best training and development resources and an environment committed to providing opportunities for personal and professional growth.

*How deeply have these changes penetrated? How different does it feel to be a GE manager today versus five years ago?*

It depends how far down you go. In some old-line factories, they probably feel it a lot less than we would like. They hear the words every now and then, but they don't feel a lot of difference. That's because the people above them haven't changed enough yet. Don't forget, we built much of this company in the 1950s around the blue books and POIM: plan, organize, integrate, measure. We brought people in buses over to Crotonville and drilled it into them. Now we're saying, "liberate, trust," and people look up and say, "What?" We're trying to make a massive cultural break. This is at least a five-year process, probably closer to ten.

*What troubles you about what's happened to date?*

First, there's a real danger of the expectation level getting ahead of reality. I was at Crotonville recently, talking about Work-Out, and someone said, "I don't feel it yet." Well, we're only a few months into it, it's much too early.

No matter how many exciting programs you implement, there seems to be a need for people to spend emotional energy criticizing the administration of the programs rather than focusing on the substance. I can sit in the Crotonville pit and ask, "How many of you are part of a new pay plan?" More than half the hands go up. "How many of you have received a management award in the last year?" More than 90% of the hands go up. "How many of you are aware of stock options?" All the hands go up. And yet many of these people don't see what we're trying to do with the programs, why we've put them in place. The emotional energy doesn't focus often enough on the objectives of the bonus plan or the excitement of the management award; it focuses on the details. The same is true of Work-Out. We'll have too much discussion on the Work-Out "process" and not enough on the "objective" to instill speed, simplicity, and self-confidence in every person in the organization.

*When will we know whether these changes have worked? What's your report card?*

A business magazine recently printed an article about GE that listed our businesses and the fact that we were number one or number two in virtually all of them. That magazine didn't get one complaint from our competitors. Those are the facts. That's what we said we wanted to do, and we've done it.

Ten years from now, we want magazines to write about GE as a place where people have the freedom to be creative, a place that brings out the best in everybody. An open, fair place where people have a sense that what they do matters, and where that sense of accomplishment is rewarded in both the pocketbook and the soul. That will be our report card.

# 2

# The Vision Trap

**Gerard H. Langeler**

Mentor Graphics Corporation is a slowly recovering witness to the power of vision to weaken a company. I was one of the company's founders, and I became the author of more and more ambitious visions that seemed for years to strengthen us, to sweep us to the heights like Cinderella. More recently, I discovered that these same visions nursed an illness that was turning us into a pumpkin.

Mentor Graphics's progress through the last ten years has been ballistic. We helped invent and then came to dominate an industry—design automation—that did not exist when the decade began. With more than $400 million in worldwide sales in 1990, we were the fifth most profitable and the eighteenth largest U.S. company founded in the 1980s. Then in the first quarter of 1991, we reported our first loss as a public company, which was followed by a more severe loss in the second quarter. Third-quarter results were even worse. In August, we got headlines as we laid off 15% of our work force.

While a lot of factors have contributed to our current problems—product transitions and a global recession head the list—I have come to believe that the sense of vision that initially drove Mentor Graphics forward came finally to lead us down a primrose path of self-infatuation that carried us away from our own best business interests.

## Inventing What People Will Buy

In January 1981, I was working at Tektronix, Oregon's largest electronics manufacturing company, along with several other young engineers and computer executives who would eventually make up the backbone of Mentor Graphics. Most of us were thirtyish MBAs with several years of work experience, a lot of self-confidence, and an impatient sense that we ought to have our own company. After work, we would get together to try and figure out what our company ought to make. On the basis of our talents and backgrounds, we knew the product should have something to do with computer graphics, and it didn't take us long to determine that the most promising application area was computer-aided engineering or CAE—the automation of schematic capture and simulation for engineers designing complex integrated circuits and printed circuit boards.

While certainly a leading-edge technology, we also figured CAE was an achievable goal. We were sure we could develop the necessary software; a company called Apollo Computer (another startup) was building a new kind of computer called a workstation that could handle the complex software CAE would necessarily entail; there seemed to be a need for CAE software in the electronics industry; and there was, as far as we knew, no clear competition.

But in one sense, at least, the product was secondary. Our real motive for founding Mentor Graphics was that it promised to be fun. We were all eager to create what we vaguely described as a "major enterprise." To do that, we needed to build something people would buy, and it seemed to us that CAE workstations were that something.

In those days, no one talked about a vision for the company. That would have seemed pompous. But, in fact, Build Something People Will Buy was precisely that: a vision driven by the need to build a successful company, a statement of purpose based on that most pragmatic of all business considerations, survival.

## Starting Up

Mentor Graphics became a corporation in April 1981, and I became its first vice president for marketing and sales. For the next several months, I traveled constantly with the vice president for engineering, visiting large and not-so-large electronics manufacturing companies from coast to coast. Despite our titles, we had nothing to market, sell, or engineer. We were traveling with blank overheads, marking pens, and a number of ideas for the product that would put Mentor Graphics on the map.

We captured the specifications for this product on blank transparencies, and they changed daily, often several times a day. As we visited with potential customers, we described the characteristics and capabilities of our tentative and fragile product—a computer-aided engineering workstation—and then listened intently and took notes furiously as they explained all the things the product really needed to do and how it might do them, and how, if it *did* do them, they might just buy it.

After each meeting, we took out our overheads and marking pens, and, working on a motel bed or a coffee-shop counter or an airplane tray, we would change the overheads to reflect the advice of our potential customers. The constant changes were not discouraging, they were exhilarating. We were creating a product—or, rather, the notion of a product, since our engineers still had to figure out if anyone could build it—based on expressed customer needs.

And then one day in August at the conclusion of a meeting with RCA engineering management in Moorestown, New Jersey, something unprecedented happened. There were no changes. There was consensus. The RCA engineers said we had defined a product that would quickly become indispensable to electronics manufacturing companies. They told us that if we could build it, we could certainly sell it. They also told us it wasn't very likely we *could* build it, given our admittedly limited engineering and financial resources.

But on the flight back to Oregon that evening, we didn't worry about whether we could build it. For a few hours, we savored the fact that actual customers had endorsed our concept of the Mentor Graphics product.

## Success!

By the fall of 1981, we had a business plan, financing, a full complement of employees, and final product specifications. Despite the RCA engineers' warning, we believed we could build the product. The question was, could we build it in time. It was critical that we be in Las Vegas in June for the 1982 Design Automation Conference, which is not only a technical conference but also the premier showcase for products and applications such as ours.

Achieving a presence at the Design Automation Conference was critically important to Mentor Graphics for three reasons. First, it was time for us to get out and confront the market. Second, we needed to give our venture capitalists good reasons to continue funding us.

Third, in November of 1981, a company called Daisy Systems had introduced a computer-aided engineering product. Suddenly we had clear competition.

The immovable deadline of the conference and the emergence of a tough competitor were galvanizing. As a small group—there were perhaps 15 of us at the time—we could not only share information very quickly, we could also create a sense of urgency and purpose without the help of an articulated vision. But there was a vision, of course. It was obvious to all of us that building a product people would buy was necessary for our very survival. The engineers redoubled their efforts, and I went back on the road with a new set of overheads. Now I was promoting the need for CAE, nourishing customer desire, persuading prospects that Mentor Graphics was building something they wanted, and telling everyone that they would see it in Las Vegas in June.

Driven by fear, tension, and excitement, we succeeded just barely in creating the demonstration software in time for the conference, but we were so concerned about its reliability that we decided to demonstrate our product in a hotel suite at Caesar's Palace rather than on the floor of the main exhibition. We reasoned that if our product performed poorly, it would at least do so with as few witnesses as possible.

Perhaps 10 of our 15 employees were in the suite when the conference opened, and the strain of getting ready showed. Our tempers were short and our frustrations visible. The computers balked before reluctantly swallowing and digesting our software. There was a heart-stopping power hiccup during our first trial run. To top it all off, for a few anxious minutes it appeared that we had thrown a party to which no one would come.

And then suddenly, finally, we were face to face with the market—a roomful of prospective customers, talking, listening, watching. I made the presentation while one of our engineers worked the keyboard of the CAE workstation, and the demonstration software performed flawlessly. I watched faces go from casual interest to intense scrutiny and on to slackjawed disbelief and undisguised enthusiasm. I saw prospects turn into customers. Word spread. People crowded into the room. People stood in the hallway craning their necks to catch a glimpse of our demonstrations. Over the course of the conference, perhaps as many as half the delegates found their way to our suite. And then came the jackpot: a purchase order for one system was delivered to us in our suite. We were *bona fide*. People had bought the something we had built.

## Competition

I went to college at Cornell and played intramural hockey as a goalie. There's a funny thing about goalies. Our never-ending fantasy is to score a goal, but there is virtually no chance we ever will. This makes us mean, and we take our revenge on those who do score goals by playing shutout games. We like victory, but what we like even more is holding the opposition scoreless. We're absolutely determined to win, but it's winning absolutely that we love.

Following the 1982 Design Automation Conference, Mentor Graphics entered a period of intense competition with Daisy Systems. A third company, Valid Logic, was also making computer-aided engineering products, but it was clear from the outset that Daisy would be our most formidable and ruthless competitor.

Survival was still our bottom line—now more than ever, perhaps—but the unarticulated vision (Build Something People Will Buy) that had seen us through the design conference began imperceptibly to change. From the fall of 1982 through the end of 1984, our goal was, increasingly, Beat Daisy. And that, it turned out, was not something we could achieve quickly or easily.

Constantly benchmarking our products against Daisy's, the market at that time chose pretty consistently to buy Daisy's rather than ours. Daisy, it seemed, was quicker, cleverer, more nimble, more willing to throw the roundhouse punch. Daisy, not Mentor, was setting the rules and winning the orders. They were beating us on software speed and on product price. (Because they made their own computers, their profit margins and pricing flexibility were far greater than ours.) The man who ran Daisy was a former Israeli military hero who saw competition with us as a form of warfare. Daisy seemed to have a killer instinct that Mentor lacked.

In March 1984, our sales manager saw an order from Gould-AMI Semiconductor in Idaho slipping away to Daisy, and he unceremoniously dragged me from warm San Jose to snowy Pocatello. With no coats and no luggage, and not in the sunniest of moods, he and I checked into a hotel which, as it turned out, was hosting something called the Simplot Games, a high school track-and-field competition. I was kept awake all night by screams and applause as a large gang of sturdy youngsters conducted extramural athletic events in the corridor outside my room.

The next day was an endless bidding war against a nonpresent Daisy. Daisy will do this, we heard, and Daisy will do that. We did our best to be competitive on specifications, price, and delivery against our invisible opponent. The time for our departure came and went, and still the battle went on. At last, long after our return flight had left without us, AMI finally decided to award the business to Daisy.

Downcast and grubby after two days in the same clothes, but with no way to get home that evening, my sales manager and I checked into a different hotel to avoid the high school athletes, and all *that* night, without apparent cause or remedy, the hotel fire alarm triggered itself every 30 minutes. In the morning—unshaven, unshowered, exhausted, demoralized, and cold—we caught a flight home. Defeat tasted as bad as ever, and I felt myself starting to get mad.

Our initial vision had been Build Something People Will Buy. We'd done that, but Daisy still led our fledgling industry. Daisy was scoring and we weren't. All our troubles were Daisy's fault—the disappointment, the loss of business, the all-night track meet, the lunatic fire alarm. I could almost feel the padding and the mask as the goalie in me spoke loud and clear in my mind. "We will never lose to Daisy again. We'll keep them scoreless. We won't give up one more goal."

Beat Daisy became our corporate vision. We tracked Daisy's sales, revenues, and profits. We talked to industry and financial analysts. We went head to head with Daisy at Design Automation Conferences, on the exhibit floor, in seminars and symposiums, even at dinners and receptions. At our headquarters in Beaverton, Oregon, we posted comparisons with Daisy on the bulletin boards, and we broadcast their quarterly results—and ours—over our intercom.

Although more explicit, Beat Daisy was a natural extension of Build Something People Will Buy. There was nothing artificial about either vision; the need to survive drove both. Beat Daisy nurtured the company and gave it direction. Moreover, we didn't like Daisy Systems (and they didn't like us), so this vision satisfied not only our business instincts but our emotional and visceral instincts as well. As a mission, goal, and vision, it *felt* good.

It's clear to me now that the world was a simpler place for Mentor Graphics in those days. Our vision was black and white, so the parameters of our decision making were more tangible and more basic than they have been since. What was bad for Daisy was good for Mentor, and what was good for Mentor was bad for Daisy. We took a lot of risks early in our corporate life, guided by those black-and-white signposts. We adopted the Apollo workstation while Daisy was building its own proprietary and very profitable computers. We acquired a California company because it would give us an edge on Daisy in the field of computer-aided design. We established international subsidiaries while Daisy was using less expensive distributors. We put down roots in Oregon although Daisy and Valid Logic and most of our customers were all in Silicon Valley.

That early and successful boldness was the result of a clear vision clearly executed, based on and driven by business concerns and a willingness—in fact, a hunger—to master superior skating and checking before even thinking about the Stanley Cup.

## Seeking Solutions

In 1985, a severe recession in the U.S. electronics industry caused us to slow hiring and hunker down in general. Sales were up 50%, but earnings were declining. Yet that was not the big news for Mentor Graphics. The big news was that we had beaten Daisy. For the first time, our revenues surpassed theirs.

Never mind that Daisy's worst enemy was not Mentor but Daisy itself, with its proprietary workstations in an era of openness, its limited software that customers could not readily stretch to meet expanding requirements, its predatory pricing that played havoc with customer loyalty. The point was, we were now number one.

But with Daisy beaten, what was to become of Beat Daisy as the driving Mentor vision?

Despite the recession, Mentor Graphics was still growing—and showing many of the classic signs of rapid expansion. For the first time, product quality began to deteriorate rather than improve; internal systems of checks and balances seemed increasingly ineffective; the value of our stock fell; and, with stunning abruptness, we saw evidence throughout the company of employee burnout, frustration, and aimlessness. The people we had come to call our "influencers"—employees who held special status within the company because they were founders or because they were charismatic or because they were very smart or, at least, not very shy—began to come to management in ones and twos, casually and informally, and request, no, *insist* that we discover a new vision for the company.

Initially, I found these pleas annoying and childish. I was tempted to respond that the best vision might be one that sent employees back to their desks, to work and make money for Mentor Graphics. (In retrospect, that might not have been such a bad response, providing, of course, that I had expressed it as a positive value instead of an irritation.)

In any case, it wasn't long before management acquiesced to this demand for a vision. We had already devoted a great deal of energy to corporate culture—articulating values and printing brochures and posters to capture them visually. It seemed to us that these were appropriate management activities and that leading the search for a new vision was a natural extension. Then, too, we were flattered. After all, there are followers and there are leaders, and the followers were asking us to lead.

The mistake we made was in letting the followers define the terms of leadership. Followers want their leaders to take them on increasingly inspirational journeys. In fact, they judge leaders on the basis of this ability, and I was getting high marks.

I have always been adept at reducing complex ideas to relatively straightforward, understandable graphics. In this case, I derived a vision for the company from the business areas in which we wanted to excel. Based partly on customer comments but even more on our own ambitions, I drew a big box labeled Mentor Graphics and, nested comfortably beneath it, six smaller boxes representing the six businesses in which we aspired to leadership: computer-aided engineering (CAE), computer-aided design (CAD), computer-aided software engineering (CASE), computer-aided publishing (CAP), computer-aided electronic packaging (CAEP), and computer-aided circuit testing (CAT).

It was as tidy and unassailable as a corporate organization chart, which it very nearly was. Today I see it as a "transitional" vision, combining elements of the pragmatic visions that preceded it with elements of the more grandiose visions that would follow. Like its precursors, it was simple and practical. It reflected a business model and incorporated what we thought our customers wanted. But like its successors, it was beginning to be remarkable more for what it did not say than for what it did.

For one thing, it skirted fundamental questions such as how, exactly, we intended to become a leader in each of these six areas. Where would the technology, the people, the skills, and the talent come from? And where would we find the money? Mentor had the capital to invest in at least some of these businesses, but how much were we willing to take from the bottom line? How long could we milk our cash cows, CAE and CAD, before we'd have to insist that the other four boxes turn a profit?

Beat Daisy had been a bit vague on specifics too, but because Beat Daisy gave us a living target, it also provided a solid guide for business performance. For example, our competitive engineering goal was to do what Daisy did—better. And our marketing goal was to win Daisy's customers and hold onto our own. Moreover, Beat Daisy was a warning. The full, unspoken text was really Beat Daisy or Die. Six Boxes lacked that kind of urgency. The fact was, we were moving beyond survival into dreams of glory. We wanted to challenge IBM in CAD-CAM. We wanted to make the *Fortune 500*. We wanted a billion-dollar year. This grander part of the vision was not explicit either.

Still, on the surface, Six Boxes was attractively simple. It was a stick-figure version of reality, and people embraced it because it was so easy to understand. Its call for leadership in all six areas inspired us. Its graphics showed each of us where we fit in the grand scheme of Mentor Graphics. Best of all, we could repeat the words "Six Boxes" over and over like a mantra. We understood the vision—or we believed we did, which served the same purpose—and we shared it, admired it, passed it back and forth, until we had assimilated it into the very fabric of the company.

I was hugely pleased with myself. Six Boxes had energized and renewed the company, and I happily took much of the credit. I had no reason then to ponder or even notice the fact that our vision had become a thing apart from the company. It was no longer organic, evolving naturally from our business environment. It was now a laboratory creation built to satisfy the needs not of Mentor Graphics's customers but of Mentor Graphics itself.

## Getting Eaten

By 1987, I had serious doubts. For two years, Six Boxes had been driving our business strategy in ways that made me profoundly uneasy. Each box had an appetite that we had to satisfy, and we found ourselves making decisions in order to assuage these appetites rather than to satisfy our company's business requirements.

For example, our computer-aided publishing business was not succeeding, despite huge investments of money, time, and energy. Part of the reason was our refusal to offer our software on the Sun Microsystems workstation, which had passed Apollo's as the preferred computer platform. (In fact, all Mentor products would continue to run only on Apollo until 1990, when we finally expanded to Sun and gained access to a much broader engineering market.) Sun or no Sun, however, I had come to the reluctant conclusion some months earlier that CAP was simply not a sustainable business.

But CAP was one of our Six Boxes, so the other senior managers and I were painfully slow to make the necessary decision to shut that business down. After all, what did that do to our vision? Could we call it *Five* Boxes? No, we were locked into six, and it was affecting our business judgment.

We had similar problems with the box called CASE—computer-aided software engineering. To satisfy the six-box imperative, we had purchased the business from Tektronix, but we lacked the resources to turn it into a leader. For that matter, I don't think we understood what our customers needed in the way of CASE tools. We'd been more interested in filling in the empty CASE box than in doing the research necessary to determine if it could be a useful, not to mention profitable, enterprise. We had forgotten the value of blank overheads and marking pens.

It was also clear that our tentative entry into mechanical design—what we called computer-aided electronic packaging or CAEP—would require massive infusions of capital and talent if we were going to compete successfully with IBM and Intergraph, companies that every year spent more money on CAEP *by mistake* than we had any prospect of doing on purpose.

The Six Boxes vision was deteriorating. Worse, deterioration was proceeding from the bottom up, as middle managers came to understand that the resources needed to lift their various boxes into leadership status were not in place and never would be. But top management refused to put Six Boxes out of its misery. Six Boxes had been so successful in its ability to simplify and inspire, and it was so tied to senior management's desire to see Mentor Graphics become the "major enterprise" we had all envisioned years earlier, that we simply couldn't kill it. Instead, we let it die a lingering death from neglect and malnutrition.

It is worth noting here that we might not have fallen so short of our goals if we'd had our applications software running on the Sun platform earlier. Here we fell victim to our vision and our history. We were slow to move to Sun because early on we'd made an unconventional but very smart decision to use Apollo rather than DEC or IBM. That decision gave us an exaggerated faith in our own judgment and a great contempt for conventional wisdom—"always conventional and almost always wrong," as we were fond of saying. Besides, our Six Boxes vision did not address platform decisions *or even their significance*. Our vision promised that the customers would come if we built the right software, period. In fact, although the very suggestion would have made us indignant, we were succumbing to smugness and a kind of conventional thinking of our own.

## Lost in Abstraction

Middle management was most affected by the failure of Six Boxes, and it was middle managers who came to me and asked for a new direction, a new sense of purpose—a new vision. By now, vision at Mentor Graphics had most definitely become a thing apart. There was no suggestion that the new vision should rise organically from the company's particular competences, opportunities, or strategies. The process was to be external. I was expected to order a *vision du jour* from some talismanic menu. If correctly chosen and properly cared for, it would somehow cure the ills afflicting the company.

By this time, of course, I was beginning to be skeptical. I had begun to wonder if any vision had the power to make things altogether whole and right. But it was I who had conceived and helped promulgate Six Boxes, I was discouraged by its collapse, and I felt responsible. Mistakenly, I decided I could not refuse to help.

Previous visions had died when our business climate changed. Once we started selling our product, Build Something People Will Buy no longer seemed to apply. When Daisy failed, Beat Daisy became obsolete. Now Six Boxes was unwinding because not all six businesses were viable. Bearing this in mind, I now sought a vision based not on the current business environment but on broader, more abstract issues. By ratcheting up the vision one conceptual level, I could save it from the volatile dictates of the marketplace. This seemed an excellent idea.

It was not. In fact, it was completely the wrong approach. As I was to learn, the more abstract the vision, the less effective it is and the greater its potential for mischief. But I didn't know that in 1987.

In 1987, business was focused on quality and productivity. Hewlett-Packard was successfully concluding a ten-year program to increase product reliability by a factor of ten. Motorola was just launching its Six Sigma quality program. Congress enacted the Malcolm Baldrige National Quality Improvement Act that summer. I took all this in, thought it over, and launched the new Mentor Graphics vision—the 10X Imperative.

The 10X Imperative—or 10X, as it came to be called—required each operational and staff organization to explore the ways and means of making its particular constituency—in most cases, an external customer—more productive by a factor of ten within ten years. To this we added the explicit goal of winning the Baldrige Award within five years.

In putting 10X together, I thought I had figured out a way of combining a focus on quality with a focus on customers. I remembered that suite at the 1982 Design Automation Conference, full of Mentor employees face to face with customers—talking, sharing, understanding, even arguing—and I wanted to recapture that close contact. I believed 10X would compel all of us in the company to start listening to customers again.

As I saw it, 10X had what programs like Motorola's Six Sigma lacked: it focused on the external customer rather than on internal operations. Six Sigma looked primarily at product defects, an easy thing to measure in manufacturing, but it did not ask whether customers cared more about defects than about, say, flexibility, cost, or speed. Moreover, Six Sigma measured quality only internally and ignored the impact on Motorola's customers. Mentor Graphics itself had been working for some time to increase the reliability of our software, also without knowing for sure that this was the right place to spend our energies. I was sure 10X would overcome these weaknesses.

Once again I was wrong. Six Sigma did have an internal focus, but it was not a weakness. Motorola had understood that it could only measure what happened at Motorola. We were asking external customers to quantify their productivity—something few of them could do even subjectively—and to pass their expensive results back to us for the sake of benefits that were anything but clear. Then we were asking our own people to figure out how their work affected, or might potentially affect, these grudging and unreliable data.

When our customers balked, our people stopped trying. They had never understood 10X anyway, and they had certainly never embraced it. Most of them found it hard to see where they fit into the overall plan. The words "10X Imperative" were abstract without being inspirational, the objectives were elusive, the measurements of success were arbitrary at best and, at worst, impossible.

On top of everything else, our people didn't want a vision that looked ahead five or ten years. Give us something to do today, they told us. Though I still couldn't see it clearly, a vision not only needs to be simple, practical, and firmly attached to business realities, it needs to be accessible. The 10X Imperative was none of the above, and by the spring of 1989, it was gone.

## Wrong Again

By 1989, Mentor Graphics was deeply into the development of a new generation of software. We called this effort 8.0 because it would be the eighth major software release (and the first big overhaul) since the company was founded. It was highly innovative. It incorporated concepts, principles, and practices that put it at the forefront of what we liked to call "bleeding-edge technology." It would reassert our industry dominance. So of course our quest to define a new vision for the company quickly identified 8.0 as the source of inspiration.

A few years earlier, as Mentor Graphics began growing larger and more complex, we had established a special council of some 30 people from all areas of the company to deal with the problems resulting from growth, decentralization, and internal politics. At a memorable meeting of this council in 1989, the question of company "vision" was the principal item on the agenda.

We all agreed that Mentor Graphics now lacked a compelling vision, one that would rejuvenate the company and return it to its former glory. Ignoring history, the council decided that in order to attract broad ownership and widespread enthusiasm, we needed something abstract and inspirational. We sought examples of such visions in other companies, and we were hard pressed to come up with any. This fact in itself should have triggered an alarm—most successful companies have thoroughly pragmatic mission statements—but we labored on. Eventually, someone in the group mentioned Apple Computer and its "Computers for the Rest of Us." Excitement rippled through the room.

Here was a company that had struck out boldly on its own path and was leading a revolution in personal computing, a company that had taken on the establishment (in other words, IBM) and succeeded. Apple had or seemed to have—or professed to have—changed the way the world used computers. Might not Mentor Graphics—gulp—*change the way the world designed*?

The council's enthusiasm was immediate, unanimous, and overwhelming. This was vision! This was galvanizing! This was stupendous!

Of course there were some nitpickers, people who wondered if such a vision might not be too arrogant. But we silenced their objections. Did Alexander the Great worry about arrogance? Arrogance was inherent in greatness!

Eventually, we cooled off enough to put our new vision into words: Changing the Way the World Designs. Together.

Arrogant or not, there was no denying its impact. Not since Six Boxes had a rallying cry been so broadly embraced and understood. Soon it was not just a vision but a part of our corporate culture. It became the theme of our advertising. Internal conferences about 8.0 took on the atmosphere of revivalist tent meetings.

## Back to Basics

Changing the Way the World Designs was the final extension of the vision creep that began with Six Boxes. It was an otherworldly vision, almost religious, enormously inspiring. But it had very little to do with business.

At first, this shortcoming was not obvious. The council met regularly in April and May to identify issues standing in the way of progress toward closure on the 8.0 specifications and to redefine tasks and rejigger schedules. On the surface, we were going forward, but as spring passed into summer, a disturbing trend began to appear. Each time the council met, new problems arose faster than old problems were laid to rest. And our schedules were slipping, sometimes incrementally, sometimes in large bites. On one occasion, the schedule slipped two months in the two weeks between two council meetings. The reasons given were always rational and reasonable and usually went something like this: "On looking into this question further, we have uncovered additional complexity and unanticipated problems. In order to meet all our design goals and find a radically new but elegant solution that we'll be able to build on for years to come, we'll need more time."

As I sat in a council meeting during the first week of September and listened to presenter after presenter go down this path, it dawned on me that we were not converging on a product, we were circling endlessly around a dream. We no longer had a vision, the vision had us. We were no longer making product, we were making poetry. We were "changing the world." Our vision said so, and our people would allow no compromise.

On September 11, 1989, I distributed a memo that began the long climb down from lofty abstraction to the terra firma of business. As the senior executive in charge of the 8.0 project, I instituted processes and procedures that would bring 8.0 back on schedule. I set cutoff dates to freeze software development and prevent perpetual refinement. I eliminated elegance and perfection as the criteria for success. I proposed that we close our ears to the siren song of Changing the Way the World Designs and listen instead to our customers, our shareholders, and our instincts. I insisted that we get back into the business of building things people would buy.

The memo marked the beginning of a long march back to basics, but it didn't end the problem. So great was the momentum to create perfect products that managers continued to add enhancements to the 8.0 specifications long after my first attempt to bring the project under control. And the new schedules I set for product shipments were not met. In fact, it is only now, two years later, that we're back to what I'd call a pragmatic vision of who we are and what we are trying to do.

With regard to vision, we had simply fallen into a trap. Early visions fueled our meteoric rise, but then the visions began to outgrow the company. They no longer fed us, we had to feed them. While we've paid a terrible price for that mistake in layoffs, delays, and losses, we've been lucky enough to return successfully to the basics that nurtured us in the first place.

We have discarded the businesses demanded by our Six Boxes but not by our customers. We have stopped defining our dreams in terms of a billion dollars or the desire to look like IBM or Hewlett-Packard. We have given up the notion of growth for growth's sake. We are trying instead to recognize our limitations, to be a company that grows and prospers by offering our customers solutions built on cooperative interactions with related companies.

In mid-September 1991, not quite a month after the layoffs, I chaired a meeting of some 300 Mentor Graphics employees, managers as well as rank and file. We'd called the meeting to review the state of the company and to talk about what came next. During the question-and-answer period, someone asked me, "Gerry, we haven't heard a word about Mentor Graphics's long-term vision. Can you tell us what that is?"

I had to smile. For years, I would have fallen all over myself to satisfy this need for an inspiring image of future corporate grandeur. Now, instead, I quickly reviewed the sequence of visions that had led us down the garden path through much of the 1980s, and then I said,

"Our current short-, medium-, and long-term vision is to build things people will buy."

The applause was immediate and lengthy. It told me that people like getting back to basics and that we're rebounding from the late delivery of 8.0, from the layoffs, from the sense that we'd lost our way. It told me that pragmatic visions can be inspiring. It told me that what used to be fun—skating, checking, teamwork, scoring goals—is still fun. It told me that the most fun of all is building things people will buy.

# About the Contributors

**Chris Argyris** is the James B. Conant Professor Emeritus at the Harvard graduate schools of business and education. He is the author of *Overcoming Organizational Defenses* and several *Harvard Business Review* articles, including "Double Loop Learning in Organizations" and "Teaching Smart People How to Learn."

**Fernando Bartolomé** is professor of management at Bentley College, specializing in the dynamics of hierarchical relationships in organizations and the interaction between the professional and private lives of executives. He lectures widely in Europe, the United States, and Latin America, and consults to a variety of businesses worldwide. Before taking his current position, he taught organizational behavior at INSEAD and was visiting professor of business administration at the Harvard Business School.

**Chester Burger** was formerly the president of Chester Burger and Company, a New York management consulting firm, and national manager of CBS Television News. He is the author of *Survival in the Executive Jungle*, *Executives Under Fire*, and other management books.

**Ram Charan** is a Dallas-based management consultant who advises companies in North America, Europe, and Asia on implementing global strategies. In a previous issue of the *Harvard Business Review*, he interviewed Citicorp chairman John Reed.

At the time his article appeared in the *Harvard Business Review*, **Keith Davis** was associate professor of management at Indiana University.

**John S. Fielden** has been an associate editor at the *Harvard Business Review* and the dean of the business schools at Boston University and the University of Alabama. He has written several articles for the *Harvard Business Review*, including the very popular "What Do You Mean I Can't Write?"

**John J. Gabarro** is the UPS Foundation Professor of Human Resource Management at the Harvard Business School. He is the author or coauthor of five books, including *Interpersonal Behavior* with Anthony G. Athos and *The Dynamics of Taking Charge* (Harvard Business School Press, 1987), which won the 1988 New Directions in Leadership Award.

**David E. Gumpert** was an editor of the *Harvard Business Review* at the time of his article's publication. He is the author of several *Harvard Business Review* articles and coauthor of *Business Plans That Win $$$: Lessons from the MIT Enterprise Forum*. Along with Stanley Rich, he cofounded Venture Resource Associates of Grantham, New Hampshire, which provides planning and strategic services to growing enterprises.

At the time his article appeared in the *Harvard Business Review*, **Antony Jay** was chairman of Video Arts, Ltd., a British film production and distribution company. Formerly, he was a BBC Television producer and executive. He is the author of *Management and Machiavelli* and *Corporation Man*, and is responsible with John Cleese of "Monty Python" for a series of comedy training films for industry and management.

**James M. Jenks** is chairman of the Alexander Hamilton Institute, which has supplied employment relations information to organizations for 84 years. He is the coauthor of *Managers Caught in the Crunch, How to Prepare for a Financially Secure Retirement*, and *Employee Benefits Plain and Simple* (forthcoming).

**Sara Kiesler** has been a professor at Carnegie-Mellon University for 13 years. In the past decade she has studied group and organizational aspects of computing and computer-based communication technologies. She has written for both research and professional audiences in such publications as *Communications of the ICM* and *Scientific American* and is the coauthor of *Connections: New Ways of Working in the Networked Organization*.

**Gerard H. Langeler** is a general partner of Olympic Venture Partners, a venture capital firm in Lake Oswego, Oregon. In this role, he serves on the boards of several young technology-based companies.

**Paul D. Lovett**, president of P.D. Lovett & Company in Allentown, Pennsylvania, is a management consultant focusing on business planning. His 25 years' experience includes a variety of line-management and business-planning positions.

**Michael B. McCaskey** was associate professor of organizational behavior at the Harvard Business School when his article was first published. At that time he studied how managers cope with ill-defined situations, citing nonverbal communication and imagery as useful tools for dealing with ambiguity. He has served as president and chief executive officer of the Chicago Bears since 1983 and was named the Executive of the Year by *Sporting News* in 1985.

At the time his article appeared in the *Harvard Business Review*, **Ralph G. Nichols** was the head of a communications program at the University of Minnesota. Prior to that, he was president of the National Society for the Study of Communication. He also served on the editorial boards of two national publications and was president of the State Speech Teachers Associations in Minnesota and Iowa.

When his article appeared in the *Harvard Business Review*, **George M. Prince** was chairman of Synectics, Inc., a Cambridge, Massachusetts, consulting firm specializing in improving the creativity and problem-solving ability of client managements.

**Stanley R. Rich** has helped found several technologically based businesses. He is a cofounder and has been chairman of the MIT Enterprise Forum, which assists emerging growth companies. He is also coauthor of *Business Plans That Win $$$: Lessons from the MIT Enterprise Forum*.

The late **F.J. Roethlisberger** was the Wallace Brett Donham Professor of Human Relations at the Harvard Business School. He is the author of *Man-in-Organization* as well as other books and articles.

The late **Carl R. Rogers** was a professor of psychology at the University of Chicago when his article appeared in the *Harvard Business Review*. His many books include the groundbreaking *Client-Centered Therapy*.

At the time his article appeared in the *Harvard Business Review*, **Leonard A. Stevens** was a freelance writer and consultant on oral presentation to a number of leading companies and was affiliated with Management Development Associates of New York. He collaborated with Ralph G. Nichols on several articles and *Are You Listening?*

**Marvin H. Swift** was associate professor of communication at the General Motors Institute when his article was published in the *Harvard Business Review*.

**Noel Tichy** was manager of GE's Management Education Operation from 1985 through 1987. He is a professor at the University of Michigan's School of Business Administration and director of its Global Leadership Program. His most recent book is *Control Your Destiny or Someone Else Will: How Jack Welch is Making General Electric the World's Most Competitive Company*, which he coauthored with Stratford Sherman.

**Brian L.P. Zevnik** is editor-in-chief of the Alexander Hamilton Institute. Along with James Jenks, he is the coauthor of *Managers Caught in the Crunch, How to Prepare for a Financially Secure Retirement,* and *Employee Benefits Plain and Simple* (forthcoming).

# INDEX